LAND LAW

Cavendish
Publishing
Limited

TITLES IN THE Q&A SERIES

THE CAVENDISH Q & A SERIES

LAND LAW

Martin Dixon MA
Fellow of Robinson College
Cambridge University

Cavendish
Publishing
Limited

First published in Great Britain 1993 by Cavendish Publishing Limited,
The Glass House, Wharton Street, London WC1X 9PX.

Telephone: 071-278 8000   Facsimile: 071-278 8080

© Dixon, Martin 1993

First Edition   1993
  Reprinted   1993
  Second reprint 1993
  Third reprint   1993
  Fourth reprint 1994

British Library Cataloguing in Publication Data

Dixon, Martin
Land Law - (Q & A Series)
I Title II Series
344.20643

ISBN 1-874241-22-8

Printed and bound in Great Britain

Contents

Preface

Writing a book - any book - takes a lot of effort and even more time, much of it belonging to people other than the author. Writing a book for students, where the aim is to make even the deepest mysteries of your subject accessible to a wider audience, only compounds this. I can safely say that I would not have completed this work in the relatively sane state of mind that I currently enjoy without the support of Judith Clarke. Much of the time spent on this book was rightly hers and much of the typing of it was achieved only through her skill. For these, and other things, I would like to record my thanks and gratitude.

Martin Dixon

Introduction

Land Law is, at the best of times, a difficult subject. Students face both conceptual and practical difficulties, as well as what can be a bewildering array of statutory and common law provisions. Moreover, an examination in land law cannot be treated as a series of separate questions on compartmentalised topics. The subject can only be viewed as an integrated whole and whatever the student learns in their first week of study may well be relevant in a question seemingly set on the work they covered in their last week.

This book of questions and answers in land law is designed to address some of these difficulties. The questions and their solutions are presented in a logical order - the order that gives the student a slowly developing but clear picture of the subject as a whole. Of course, the answers can be taken on their own for what they are: an aid to revision and examination performance. However, this book can be used as a teaching aid in itself.

The law is stated as at January 1993.

Martin Dixon
Cambridge
January 1993

Table of Cases

Table of Statutes xiii

Chapter 1

Registered Land

Introduction

Land lawyers in England and Wales fall into two broad groups. First, there are those who believe that the 1925 property legislation, and specifically the 1925 Land Registration Act, established a new machinery for controlling the creation and transfer of land but did not radically alter the nature of property law. Thus, some textbooks will explain in detail the nature of, say, co-ownership or easements, and add a section at the end of each chapter on the implications of 'registered land'. Others take the view that the system of registered conveyancing has produced fundamental changes in the nature of the rights and interests falling within the concept of 'land law'. Thus, on this view, a detailed understanding of the *mechanics* of registered land is necessary before a student can fully appreciate substantive property concepts such as easements or mortgages. There is, of course, merit in both approaches but even without the powerful theoretical arguments that could be used, there are practical advantages for the student in following the second approach. Since 1st December 1990, all of England and Wales is designated as an area of compulsory registration of title. In the fullness of time, therefore, unregistered conveyancing will diminish to a mere fraction of total volume of land transactions. Moreover, and more importantly for students, examiners set problem questions which require the student to explain how easements or leases or whatever operate in registered land and no amount of pre-1925 property law will solve these puzzles. There is, for example, no point in discussing the doctrine of notice in registered land when it is entirely irrelevant.

If a plot of land is described as 'registered', this means that 'title' to it (ie ownership) is located at the Land Registry. In contrast, 'unregistered land' is land to which title is not registered centrally but is established by title deeds. Whether title is registered or not depends simply on whether the land was located in a compulsory registration area and whether there have been any dealings with the land such as to give rise to the opportunity to register. As such, then, there is no magic about land being registered: it is simply a way of saying that the title is centrally recorded and that dealings with the land fall within the procedures established by the Land Registration Acts. When answering questions in examination, one of the first things to establish is whether the land is registered and this you will be told. If you are not told, it is not important as there is no way that you can deduce whether title is registered from the facts of a problem. After all, whether there has been registration of title does not depend on the quality of the land but whether it lies in a registration area.

Checklist

Broadly speaking, the system of registered land falls in to four sections, the first three of which are more important for the purposes of an examination. The student should be familiar with these basic issues before tackling examination questions.

A) Registered Titles: what Gray (*Elements of Land Law*) calls 'major interests'. These are the leasehold or the freehold and they are substantively registered in their own right with a title number. Most questions in land law examinations require no more than a passing knowledge of the mechanics of registering or transferring titles. Of much more interest and complexity are the rules relating to the transfer and creation of interests *in* the land such as easements, covenants etc. and short term leases (ie those which cannot be registered as titles, being for 21 years or less).

B) Overriding Interests: these are interests in the land which will bind a new purchaser of the land automatically. They do not have to be registered anywhere to take effect against a third party. They are exhaustively defined in s 70(1)(a to l) of the Land Registration Act 1925. All are inherently proprietary (that is, *capable* of binding third parties) but some are legal and some are equitable. No student should attempt a land law paper without a thorough understanding of overriding interests.

C) Minor Interests: these are those interests, nearly all of which are equitable, that have to be registered in order to bind a purchaser of registered land. If they are not registered they are generally not binding against a purchaser irrespective of the question of notice. In essence, this class comprises all rights and interests in land not falling in the other categories.

D) Registrable charges: these are essentially mortgages. They too must be registered to take effect as legal mortgages and are considered in the chapter on mortgages.

Question 1

What were the objectives of the Land Registration Act 1925? Have they been achieved?

Answer plan

Pre-1925 problems

- the mechanics of land registration: titles
  - overriding interests
  - minor interests
- mirror principle
- insurance principle
- curtain principle
- some problems
  - undiscoverable but binding interests
  - protecting the purchaser or the occupier
  - certainty or justice

Answer

The 1925 property legislation, and the 1925 Land Registration Act in particular, inaugurated a fundamental change in the structure of land law in England and Wales. Prior to then, the mechanics of conveyancing were hindered by formalism and abounding with danger for all but the most conscientious purchasers. Likewise, the operation of the equitable doctrine of notice meant not only that holders of equitable rights could have their rights destroyed through chance or caprice - because a purchaser might have no 'notice' of them - but also that purchasers of property might find their land burdened by legal rights of which they had no knowledge and which they could not have discovered even by the most diligent of inquiries. Similarly, the reliance on title deeds to prove ownership of land was both cumbersome and, for the purchaser, an expensive way to prove title, especially given the multitude of legal and equitable estates that could exist. The net result was a choking of the property market and at a time when the free movement of capital was essential for economic development. In conjunction with the Law of Property Act 1925 and the Settled Land Act 1925, the Land Registration Act 1925 sought to simplify and codify. It aimed to bring certainty where there was obscurity and to bring equity where there was often inequality.

The basic tenet of the Land Registration Act was that title to land (ie effective ownership) should be recorded in a central register and guaranteed by the state. Registration of title would replace deeds of title and the register would reflect the totality of land ownership throughout the entire country. The original timetable called for full registration of all land within thirty years and it is a matter of some regret that only on 1st December 1990 did all of England and Wales become a compulsory registration area. It will be some years yet before near universal registration of title is achieved. However, in addition to establishing a mechanism for registering ownership, the 1925 Act also established three other mechanisms for protecting rights in the land (usually owned by some other person). If correctly used these procedures will ensure that rights in land are not destroyed by a transfer of a registered title to a third party. First, there are registrable charges, usually mortgages, which must be registered (as a 'disposition') before they can be regarded as legal mortgages - s 26(1) Land Registration Act 1925. Once registered, these bind subsequent purchasers of the mortgaged land unless, of course, the mortgage is paid off (as most will be on sale, by the proceeds of that sale). If not registered, such mortgages take effect as equitable interests only and will be void against a purchaser unless protected by the land registration system in some other way.

Secondly, there are overriding interests. These are interests, statutorily defined in s 70(1) Land Registration Act 1925, that take effect against a purchaser automatically; that is, they require no registration and the doctrine of notice is irrelevant - s 20(1)(a), Land Registration Act. It is immaterial whether such interests are legal or equitable, so long as they fall within one of the defined classes. The logic behind the automatic effect of such interests is that they comprise such rights as *should* be obvious to a purchaser on inspection of the property or the title documents (eg legal easements, 70(1)(a)) or are such that they benefit the community as a whole without seriously restricting a purchaser's enjoyment of the land (eg liability in respect of embankments, sea and river walls - s 70(1)(d)). Whether this logic is still persuasive remains to be seen.

Thirdly, there are minor interests. This category essentially comprises all other interests that may subsist in or over land - s 3(xv) Land Registration Act. In order to bind a purchaser, such interests, whether legal or equitable (in practice nearly all are equitable), must be protected by entry on the register, either by way of a notice, caution, inhibition or restriction. Actual notice of the right (or lack of it) is irrelevant - s 59(6) Land Registration Act: the minor interest is binding if registered, void against a purchaser for value if not (s 20(1) Land Registration Act).

This reclassification of land law rights (proprietary rights) obviously places much more emphasis on statutory definition than it does on the legal or equitable quality of a right. Likewise, in registered land, it is clear that the doctrine of notice - particularly whether the purchaser knows of the existence of a right or interest - is irrelevant. Such a radical shift was designed to relieve the conveyancing logjam as well as to bring certainty and stability for persons with interests in land belonging to another. In this connection, it is often said that the Land Registration Act was premised on three principles: the mirror principle, the curtain principle and the insurance principle. The mirror principle suggests that the register should be a mirror of all the proprietary rights - both estates and interests - that exist in any given piece of land. Thus, the register should amount to a comprehensive picture of the land for any prospective purchaser. Obviously, however, this is not the case with the 1925 Act. The inclusion of overriding interests denies the mirror principle. In itself, this is not a cause of serious criticism. Overriding interests were not an accident. They were intended by the legislature and given automatic effect precisely because they should be obvious to any prospective purchaser. The problem is, however, that social and judicial developments have enlarged the opportunity for the existence of overriding interests with the result that a purchaser cannot determine whether such interests exist by inspection of the land or title documents. The most obvious example is the right of equitable co-ownership, stemming from *Pettitt v Pettitt*, whose effect, under s 70(1)(g), on an unwary purchaser was first fully appreciated in *Williams & Glyn's Bank v Boland*. Another example is the equitable estoppel easement said to fall within s 70(1)(a) in *Celsteel v Alton*. It is for this reason that the Law Commission has proposed (in Report No.158) the redefinition of overriding interests so as to insulate further the purchaser from rights that are not reflected in the register's mirror.

The curtain principle is perhaps, the most ambitious motive behind the 1925 Act. The aim is to keep certain types of equitable interests off the register completely. Such equitable rights, being those taking effect behind a trust, will not bind a purchaser on sale of the land because of overreaching. In essence, a purchaser will not be concerned with such equitable rights - they are behind the curtain - so long as purchase money is paid to two trustees, s 2 Law of Property Act 1925. The equitable interests then take effect in that purchase money, so that instead of having a right (or share) in land, the equitable owner has a right in money. Such a system works well when the statutory requirement of two trustees exists. However, the direct result of *Pettitt* and *Bull v Bull* is that on many occasions there will be just one trustee for sale and so overreaching will not be possible. In such circumstances a purchaser must look behind the curtain to determine whether any equitable interests exist and then must negotiate with the equitable owners as required. If the curtain is not raised, the purchaser could easily be bound by such equitable interests as *Boland* shows. This problem clearly involves balancing the protection of the purchaser and protection for the occupier of land and it is largely due to social and judicial changes (viz the rise of the equitable co-owner through the *Pettitt* rules) that it has become more pressing in recent years. Cases such as *Abbey National BS v Cann* and *Equity & Home Loans v Prestidge* illustrate that the full implications of this delicate balancing act are still being worked out.

Finally, there is the insurance principle, or rather, the idea that once title is registered, the state guarantees the authenticity and effectiveness of that title against the world ss 19, 20, 69 Land Registration Act. Obviously such a system cannot be absolute in its effect and there are provisions for rectification of the register in cases where registration has produced hardship or inequity - s 82 Land Registration Act. The potential wide ranging discretion given to the court under this section has caused some concern in the Law Commission (see eg *Argyle BS v Hammond*) as it could be used to undermine significantly the sanctity of registered title. However, while the indemnity provisions (s 83 LRA) which accompany the power to rectify remain so limited (eg *Re Chowood's Registered Land*) this fear may prove unfounded.

On a general level then, the Land Registration Act has clearly been a success. It introduced certainty, fairness and relative simplicity to a system of conveyancing that was completely unsuited to the modern age. Of course, there were and still are problems of detail and the question of the undiscoverable overriding interests may require a radical amendment of the Act. The Law Commission's proposals, will however, go a long way to meet these concerns and, even without them, the system of land registration is, with sensible judicial application, well able to reach into the next century. There is, obviously, a tension between the purchaser of land and the occupier of it, but generally speaking the provisions on overreaching can deal with this if the statutory mechanisms are observed. It is no fault of the Land Registration Act that the incidence of single-trustee co-ownership (*Pettitt*) has increased. This does produce problems but the way to tackle this is to establish clear rules on when joint ownership of property can arise rather than to alter the machinery which merely regulates it. Fortunately, decisions such as *Lloyds Bank v Rosset* and *Cann* are proving that this is possible.

Notes

A standard question on the scheme of the 1925 Registration system. The basic answer to the question will be known to most students, but correspondingly, it can be quite difficult to score highly with such well worn material. Examiners will be looking for originality and criticism and to this end a thorough knowledge of Law Commission Report 158 will be invaluable.

Question 2

In 1991, Abigail sold her large farm, title to which is registered, to Bernadette. At the time of purchase, Bernadette's solicitor made an official search of the register and obtained a clear certificate. Unfortunately, the search was carried out by an inexperienced clerk and failed to reveal a restrictive covenant correctly registered against the land for the benefit of the adjoining farm owned by Roger. The covenant stipulated that no trade or business other than farming may be carried on the land. When walking over the farm on the day after she has been registered with title, Bernadette discovers that Zeus, a new age squatter, has established a home in a derelict farm cottage. Next door, Bernadette finds Lydia who claims to have been paying rent to Abigail for the last four years under an agreement that she could live in the cottage for ten years. Lydia produces a written record of the agreement typed on a plain piece of white paper.

Bernadette comes to you for advice as she wants to build a an out-of-town supermarket on part of the site and, in any event, wants possession of the cottages.

Answer plan

- effect of registration as owner: overriding interests
  - minor interests
- primacy of register over search certificate
- rectification and indemnity

Answer

When Bernadette is registered as proprietor of the farm, the estate in the land is transferred to her statutorily under s 19 Land Registration Act 1925. However, under s 20 Land Registration Act, a registered owner takes the land subject to any minor interests appearing on the register and any overriding interests. It is necessary, therefore, to establish whether Bernadette's registered title is subject to any adverse interests which may prohibit her proposed development. Secondly, if Bernadette's title is so encumbered, there arises the question of rectification or indemnity.

a) The restrictive covenant

Bernadette will be unable to build the proposed supermarket if she is bound by the restrictive covenant. Assuming that all the conditions required by the law of freehold covenants are established (see Chapter 8), the issue turns upon whether the restrictive covenant has been properly protected within the system of registered land: in other words, whether it has been protected as a minor interest, usually by way of notice, s 20(1) Land Registration Act.

When Bernadette requested a search from the Land Registry, she received a clear search certificate. However, it is clear from *Parkash v Irani Finance Ltd* that it is the Register itself that is conclusive, irrespective of any statements made on an official certificate or by an officer of the Registry. In our case, therefore, Bernadette is bound by the restrictive covenant because it has been properly registered and this is so even though she is entirely blameless. Of course, Bernadette can make an application to the Lands Tribunal under s 83 Law of Property Act 1925 to have the restrictive covenant discharged if she wishes to proceed with her proposed development, but as a matter of property law it is binding on her.

It is possible that Bernadette will be eligible for a statutory indemnity under s 83(2) Land Registration Act if it can be established that she suffered loss because 'an error or omission has occurred *in the register*'. If it is not certain that this is possible (eg because the error was not in the register itself), she should be advised to sue the Land Registry in negligence (*Minister of Housing and Local Government v Sharp*).

b) The squatter

Zeus appears to be in the process of trying to establish a right to the land under the law of adverse possession. Again, whether Bernadette is bound depends on the application of the relevant provisions of the Land Registration Act. In the case of adverse possessors, it is clear that they may have an overriding interest against a new proprietor under s 70(1)(f) Land Registration Act, being a person having 'rights acquired or in the course of being acquired under the Limitation Acts'. Thus, so long as Zeus was in the process of acquiring his rights on the day when Bernadette was registered with the title to the farm (*Abbey National BS v Cann*), he has an overriding interest binding on her. Of course, if Zeus has not been in adverse possession of the cottage for the full limitation period (12 years), Bernadette may take proceedings to have him removed: after all, if 12 years has not been completed, it is only the 'process' of acquiring rights that is binding and that process can be stopped under the normal rules of ousting adverse possessors. The problem occurs, however, if Zeus has completed 12 years adverse possession; in other words if Bernadette's title is statute barred. In such circumstances, the 'statute bar' is binding on Bernadette under s 70(1)(f) and Zeus can apply to the Land Registry to be registered as proprietor of the land under s 75(2) Land Registration Act.

Can the register be rectified in favour of Zeus? Normally, the register will not be rectified against a proprietor in possession, and this is clearly Bernadette. However, even a proprietor in possession may have the register rectified against them to give effect to an overriding interest - s 82(3). Thus, if Zeus has completed 12 years adverse possession he can have the register rectified in his favour and Bernadette will be deprived of title to the cottage. This apparently makes a mockery of the principle that the state guarantees a registered title, so is Bernadette entitled to an indemnity on the ground that she has suffered loss? Under s 83(1) Land Registration Act, any person suffering loss 'by reason of any rectification of the register' is entitled to an indemnity. Unfortunately, according to *Re Chowood's Registered Land*, where rectification is ordered to give effect to an overriding interest, the former proprietor does not suffer loss 'by reason of any rectification': rather, the loss arises from a pre-existing overriding interest which the register has merely acknowledged. This technical construction of the Land Registration Act has been criticised by the Law Commission but, at present, it would invalidate Bernadette's claim to an indemnity.

c) Lydia is in occupation of the second farm cottage under some form of lease given to her by Abigail. Is this lease binding on Bernadette? Clearly, the lease claimed by Lydia is of less than 21 years duration (in fact, it is ten), so there is no question that it should have been substantively registered in its own right - it is not within s 8(1)(a) Land Registration Act. So, the lease can only be binding on Bernadette if it is a protected minor interest or an overriding interest.

If this is a legal lease, then it constitutes an overriding interest under s 70(1)(k) of the Land Registration Act. The lease is not made by deed - it is *written* but not in a deed - so the only circumstance in which it could be legal lease is if it amounts to a legal periodic tenancy where the period is three years or less - see ss 52(1) and 54(2) Law of Property Act (and Chapter 5). The question makes no reference to the period for which Lydia pays rent, we are told only that she has been in occupation for four years and expects to be free to occupy for another six. In such circumstances, the implication is against a legal periodic tenancy. It is worth noting, however, that even if this were a legal periodic tenancy, binding as an overriding interest, there is nothing to prevent Bernadette from terminating it according to its own terms - ie the giving of one period notice.

It is more likely that the lease is equitable. There is written evidence of it and it is probably capable of specific performance - see s 2 Law of Property (Miscellaneous Provisions) Act 1989 and *Walsh v Lonsdale*. Equitable leases can be protected as minor interests, but Lydia has not done this. However, this lease - assuming it is equitable - is still binding on Bernadette for its intended duration (ten years from grant by Abigail) because Lydia falls within s 70(1)(g) Land Registration Act, being a person with a proprietary interest (the lease) in actual occupation at the time the property was transferred - *Abbey National BS v Cann*.

To conclude, then, there is every possibility that Bernadette must allow Lydia to occupy one cottage until her lease expires in six years time. Although Zeus's rights as an adverse possessor are binding on her, she can evict him under normal process if 12 years have not elapsed. Should 12 years have expired, Zeus can apply to have the register rectified in his favour and Bernadette has no indemnity. She is also bound by the restrictive covenant even though it was not disclosed on the search certificate.

Question 3

Oswald, a diplomat, owns a large detached house, divided into two self-contained flats, title to which is registered in his sole name. In anticipation of an overseas posting, Oswald advertised for a tenant of the upper flat and entered into negotiations with Terrance. Unfortunately, they could not agree terms but, on payment of a deposit, Terrance was allowed to occupy the flat while their solicitors negotiated an acceptable lease. Meanwhile, Oswald agreed in writing to sell the bottom flat to his daughter Connie should he be posted abroad. Hearing of Oswald's possible departure, Eric, his neighbour asked whether he could use Oswald's drive for easier access to his large double garage. Oswald readily agreed provided that Eric pay for re-surfacing of the drive. Eric employs contractors and the drive is completely re-surfaced. On hearing of his overseas posting, Oswald realises that he needs to raise some capital. Penny, his mistress, is willing to buy the property at much more than his daughter could ever afford. Realising that Connie has not registered her interest, he sells the entire property to Penny by registered disposition. Penny wishes to re-convert the house and asks Terrance to leave. She also erects a fence preventing Eric from using her drive. Connie hears of the sale and seeks to enforce her right to buy the bottom flat against Penny.

Advise the parties.

Answer plan

- effect of registration as owner: overriding interests
  - minor interests
- formalities of leases
- conditions for proprietary estoppel
- *Midland Bank Trust Co v Green*

Answer

As the new registered proprietor of the land, Penny will be bound only by those overriding interests subsisting at the date of registration of her new title (ie those in s 70(1) (a) to (f) and (h) to (l)) LRA and those subsisting at the date of transfer of the title (ie that in s 70(1)(g) LRA, *Abbey National BS v Cann*), as well as any registered minor interests - s 20(1) Land Registration Act. In addition, there is the possibility that she could be bound by proprietary interests that are not protected in the proper fashion if there has been some fraud or bad faith associated with her purchase, see eg *Lyus v Prowsa Developments* and *Peffer v Rigg*.

a) Terrance

The essential question here is whether Terrance has any estate or interest in the land and, if so, whether they have been protected against a third party purchaser under the appropriate mechanism of the Land Registration Act. In order for a right to be binding on a purchaser it must be *capable* of being binding; that is, it must be proprietary. In this case, there is the possibility that Terrance has a lease and, of course, this is a proprietary interest. For example, Terrance he has paid some money and he appears to have gone into occupation in pursuance of it. Indeed, his lease in these circumstances would be a legal periodic tenancy of three years or less and binding (until terminated by appropriate notice) as an overriding interest under s 70(1)(k). (There is no possibility of an equitable tenancy because there is no written document within the formality requirements of s 2 Law of Property (Miscellaneous Provisions) Act 1989). However, there is every possibility that Terrance does not have a lease at all. He has, in fact, gone into occupation pending the negotiation of a lease in the knowledge that no agreement has been concluded with the landlord. Following *Javid v Aqil*, there will be no lease if there was no intention to create legal relations, as seems likely when negotiations are still proceeding. Terrance will, therefore, be a 'tenant at will' which (contrary to its name) confers no estate or interest in the land. Thus, if this is the case, there is no proprietary right capable of being a minor or an overriding interest and so Terrance must depart the flat at Penny's will.

b) Eric

In the case of Eric, the position is not so clear. From his point of view, he will be claiming first, that the right to use the drive amounted to an easement (right of way), and secondly that this easement is binding on Penny. First, does the easement exist? It is axiomatic that a right of way can amount to an easement but in this case there is the question of whether it has been properly created. Clearly, there is no deed nor even a written record of the agreement between Oswald and Eric: the easement is not legal and cannot be equitable within the *Walsh v Lonsdale* principle. However, it may be that Eric can claim the creation of an easement in his favour under the law of proprietary estoppel, as explained generally in *Taylor Fashions Ltd v Liverpool Victoria Trustees* and in respect of easements in particular in *Ives v High*. In this case, there appears to have been an assurance - by Oswald to Eric that he could use the drive - which was relied upon by Eric to his detriment. How else is it possible to explain Eric's expenditure on the driveway? This may well mean that Eric has the benefit of an easement, albeit an easement that must be equitable because of the informal manner in which it was created. If this is true, Eric has a right which is capable of binding Penny and will do so if it is either registered as a minor interest or amounts to an overriding interest. Clearly there is no registration. However, following *Celsteel v Alton*, an equitable easement which is openly enjoyed with the land may well fall within s 70(1)(a) Land Registration Act. In other words, estoppel easements may be overriding interests because even though they are equitable and apparently excluded by the wording of sub-paragraph (a), they are not 'required to be protected by notice on the register'. Despite the fact that the clear purpose of the Land Registration Act was to make equitable easements subject to a requirement of registration, Eric can rely on *Celsteel* to enforce his easement against Penny as an overriding interest.

c) Connie

By his written agreement with his daughter, Oswald has granted Connie some right in connection with the flat. What is the nature of that right? At first sight, it appears that Connie's right could be a 'right of pre-emption' - a right of first refusal to the land should the owner decide to sell. If this were the case, Penny may be able to ignore Connie's claim because, following *Pritchard v Briggs*, rights of pre-emption are not proprietary rights in themselves even capable of binding third parties. (They appear to become proprietary when exercised.) That decision has, however, been subject to considerable criticism and it would be better for Penny to argue an alternative reason why she is able to ignore Connie's claim.

The better view is that Oswald has granted Connie an option to purchase the flat. The essence of an option is that the grantee (Connie) has an enforceable right to purchase the property at a moment of their choosing providing that any conditions in the option are fulfilled. Here, the fact that the option is conditional upon the overseas posting does not alter its character because, if Oswald is posted, Connie has an enforceable right to buy at her choosing. Oswald has no choice if the condition is fulfilled (if he is posted) and he has no control over whether the condition will be fulfilled (see *Haslemere Estates Ltd v Baker* in support of this view). Assuming this to be an option, it is clear that it is a proprietary right, capable of binding third parties. Yet, once again, in order to be actually binding, the proprietary right must be protected in the proper manner under the Land Registration Act. There is no prospect of the option being an overriding interest as it (and Connie) do not fall within any of the statutory definitions. Hence it can only be a minor interest. In this case, however, the option has not been protected by entry on the register and is therefore void against a purchaser for value, Penny - s 20(1) and 59(6) Land Registration Act.

In such circumstances, the only slender hope - and it is very slender - is for Connie to establish that her unregistered interest has been defeated by fraud. However, even if Penny knows that Oswald is selling the property partly to defeat his daughter's claim, the better view is that this is not fraud - see eg *Midland Bank Trust Co v Green*. In this respect, *Peffer v Rigg*, which seems to require the purchaser to act 'in good faith' if they are to be free of unregistered minor interests (where 'good faith' is defined almost synonymously with notice) is probably no longer good law. Only if Penny had promised Connie and/or Oswald that she would honour the option despite the lack of registration (and had thereby obtained the property more cheaply) could the purchaser said to have committed fraud - see *Lyus v Prowsa Developments*. If that were the case - and there is no evidence to support it - Penny would be a constructive trustee of the option for Connie and necessarily bound by it.

In conclusion, then, Penny is bound by the easement as it qualifies under *Celsteel* as an equitable easement binding as an overriding interest. She is not, however, bound by the option to allow Connie to purchase the ground floor flat and may ask Terrance to leave as he has no estate in the land capable of being binding on her.

Notes

Both questions 2 and 3 revolve around the precise wording of the Land Registration Act and, for that reason, are sometimes viewed with reluctance. However, they are relatively straightforward so long as the Act is read closely. Particular attention should be paid to the provisions on rectification and indemnity. It is also apparent that these questions require the student to have some knowledge of other areas of law: such as how leases are created and when certain rights will be equitable or legal. The doctrine of *Walsh v Lonsdale* is crucial here, as is the new s 2 Law of Property (Miscellaneous Provisions Act) 1989.

Question 4

Is the system of land registration inaugurated by the 1925 Land Registration Act in need of radical reform?

Answer plan

- problems of overriding interests: existence; extent; undiscoverability; rectification; timing of binding interests; indemnity
- problems of minor interests: method of protection; land certificates
- questions of fraud and good faith

Answer

The land registration system inaugurated by the Land Registration Act 1925, as amended, has been in operation in England and Wales for over sixty-five years. However, it was not until 1st December 1990 that all land became subject to compulsory first registration of title. Of course, this in itself is a cause for regret, but it reflects more the significant changes in the pattern of ownership of land that have taken place in the last half-century than inherent defects in the system of land registration itself. When the Act first came into force, ownership of land was concentrated in a relatively small section of the community. Nowadays, property ownership in the form of house ownership is a social goal as well as a political ideal. It is not surprising that such an expansion of 'the property owning democracy' has created problems for the complex machinery of the Land Registration Act.

The underlying rationale of the Land Registration Act was laudable and relatively straightforward: that title to land should be centrally recorded and guaranteed and that interests in land should either be obvious on physical inspection or noted in a clear and unambiguous fashion on the title record. The advantages are also plain to see: purchasers could buy in the certainty that they were purchasing land suitable to their requirements as the existence of 'hidden' rights would be minimalised and owners of interests in land, such as easements and covenants, would have a relatively easy and inexpensive method of ensuring that their rights survived a conveyance to a third party. On a general level, there is no doubt these policy goals have been achieved by the Land Registration Acts: titles to land are centrally recorded and since the Land Registration Act 1986 the register is open to public inspection; purchasers are greatly benefited by the assurance that the register provides and, in the great majority of cases, they can be sure that they are purchasing unencumbered property; likewise, equitable interest holders do not have to rely on the capricious doctrine of notice to protect their right as registration, as a minor interest will ensure protection of that right irrespective of the purchaser's state of mind, ss 20(1), 59(6) Land Registration Act. Of course, the land registration system has its problems and some of them can seriously undermine the principles and policies of this major reform. They are considered below. On the whole, however, it would be churlish not to recognise the significant improvement in the mechanisms for the transfer and creation of rights in land that was inaugurated by the Land Registration Act and which still endure today.

It is often said that one of the main defects in the land registration system is the way in which overriding interests seriously prejudice both the policy behind the system and, more importantly, a purchaser's ability to use and enjoy their newly acquired land. To some extent, however, this criticism is misplaced. First, overriding interests were intended to be part of the registration system and purchasers (through their advisors) should be aware of the possibility of their existence. Secondly, the great majority of overriding interests (see s 70(1) LRA) are discoverable from a reasonable inspection of the property. It is a common error to believe that the Land Registration Act intended to do away with inspection by potential purchasers. It did not: it was intended to make conveyancing safer and more certain for prudent purchasers. Thirdly, such problems as do exist largely are the result of changes in other areas of the law and not because of defects inherent in the land registration system itself. Thus, the great problem with overriding interests is the existence of the equitable co-ownership right that can exist behind a trust for sale. If there is only one trustee for sale (as in *Williams & Glyn's Bank v Boland*), such rights cannot be overreached and a potential purchaser might well find his new property virtually useless. However, why is this? On one view, the problem arises because the equitable co-ownership is 'undiscoverable' or at least the rights of the co-owner can be easily hidden by a dishonest legal owner, as in *Chhokar v Chhokar*. This is nothing to do with the Land Registration Act but with the expansion of the *Pettitt v Pettitt* doctrine and the imposition of the trust for sale in all forms of co-ownership by *Bull v Bull*. There is much to suggest that it was never intended that a trust for sale be imposed in the *Pettitt* scenario (see eg the precise words of s 34 LPA) that overreaching is impossible in the bare trust that would have resulted (see Harpum, 1990 CLJ). These are not problems caused by the existence of overriding interests as a category of right recognised by the Land Registration Act; rather they are the consequences of developments - albeit socially desirable ones - in other areas of the law. Moreover, even with this problems, the system can work. There is nothing to prevent potential purchasers (especially large institutional lenders) insisting that money be paid to two trustees for sale. Likewise, the rule in *Abbey National BS v Cann*, by moving the relevant date by which an interest under s 70(1)(g) must be established, has given purchasers every chance to actually discover by inspection any adverse interests: the registration gap has been closed.

Of course, it would be better if the problem of 'surprise' overriding interests did not exist at all and to this end the Law Commission's proposals to reduce the categories of such interests may help. For example, if the recommendation to exclude equitable easements form overriding interests is followed, the effect *Celsteel v Alton* would be reversed. Likewise, pruning the number of so called 'public rights' is only sensible. However, even under the proposals in Report 158, the rights of persons in actual occupation of land (though not any longer those in receipt of rent and profits) would still bind automatically as overriding interests.

Moving to much less pressing reforms of the land registration system, there must be considerable merit in the Law Commission's proposals to widen the indemnity provisions. There is no sense in having a system where the State is supposed to guarantee a registered title but where compensation for loss caused by this paramount policy is not widely available. In this respect, the proposal to reverse *Re Chowood's Registered Land*, and provide an indemnity where loss is caused due to the recognition of an overriding interest is to be welcomed warmly. This, of course, will provide balance to the very existence of overriding interests. Other reforms proposed in the context of minor interests are also to be welcomed. At present, the provisions concerning the various forms of protection for a minor interest (notice, caution, restriction, inhibition) are complicated and unsystematic. The Law Commission proposes the use of the restriction and inhibition in tightly defined circumstances and (save in very special cases) that a notice should be used for acknowledged rights and a caution for those not accepted by the registered proprietor. To this end, the land certificate (ie the registered owner's record of title) need not be produced for a caution. The Law Commission also recommend that an unprotected minor interest should be void against a purchaser for valuable consideration *in good faith*. By adding the requirement of good faith, the Law Commission brings the Land Registration Act into line with the Law of Property Act, although out of line with the Land Charges Act (see *Midland Bank v Green*). It is to be hoped, however, that the Law Commission's clear view that notice of an unregistered minor interest does not amount to bad faith is also accepted. Finally, the Law Commission makes it clear that a protected minor interest should always take priority over an earlier, but unprotected interest (thus reversing *Barclays Bank v Taylor*). This is the sensible way to apply the registration machinery and it is unfortunate that the present statute gives no clear guidance on the subject.

In conclusion then, there are some changes that could be sensibly made to the Land Registration Act, primarily to bring it up to date with changes in the social and economic uses of land. Whether these are *radical* changes as the title of this question suggests is, however, open to some doubt. Essentially, the Act needs a sharper focus but its central objectives and its operation in the vast majority of cases is satisfactory and a considerable achievement.

Notes

Do not answer a question about reform of the 1925 legislation unless you are fully conversant with Law Commission Report 158. This is not a question about 'mirror', 'insurance' and 'curtain'. Indeed, there is a temptation to treat all essays on registered land as if they are about these factors. Most are not.

Unregistered Land

Introduction

On 1st December 1990, all land in England and Wales became subject to compulsory first registration of title. In effect, this means that on the first conveyance of title of an estate in unregistered land, it will become subject to registration requirements and thereafter cease to be governed by unregistered land conveyancing rules. It is most unlikely, therefore, that a question in an examination will turn on the conveyance of an unregistered title unless it is made clear that the relevant transactions are all complete before 1990. That does not mean, however, that the rules concerning unregistered land are no longer important. There are many situations where questions concerning the enforceability of interests in unregistered land are still important and have to be answered.

Checklist

As noted in Chapter 1, when land is described as unregistered, this means that title is to be found in title deeds rather than on any central register. The law of unregistered land conveyancing is, then, related to the rules of property law as they stood prior to the 1925 reforms. However, it would be a mistake to think that the law of unregistered land was unaffected by the 1925 reforms. The Law of Property Act, for example, applies in full to unregistered land as it does to registered land. What is different is that the enforceability of rights and interests in unregistered land - being those rights and interests capable of existing under the provisions of the Law of Property Act - is governed by its own set of rules and procedures.

A) Legal estates, both freehold and leasehold, are to be found in title deeds, not in a register. (The exception to this is the periodic tenancy for three years or less which is legal without a deed or any written document. Again, however, it is not registered anywhere).

B) As was the case before 1925, in unregistered conveyancing it is still true that 'legal rights bind the whole world'. In other words, once it is established that a right is 'legal' in character, that estate or interest is binding on whomsoever comes into possession of the land. So, for example, a legal periodic tenancy or a legal easement will be binding on any purchaser of the land over which those rights exist. There is, by definition no question of registration and no question of notice.

C) With certain well defined *exceptions* (see below), the 'doctrine of notice' has no part to play in unregistered land. It is a common mistake to believe that it does. The reason is simple: by statute, unregistered land has its own system of registration for equitable interests. This is the Land Charges Act 1925, as amended in 1972. One of the most frequent errors is to forget that in unregistered land there is also a requirement of registration for certain - indeed most - equitable interests. These 'registrable' equitable interests are binding if registered correctly under the Land Charges Act but void if not, irrespective of the question of notice.

D) There is a small class of equitable rights which, either deliberately or by subsequent judicial development, are excluded from the operation of the Land Charges Act. In other words, they are 'non registrable'. For these rights, their enforceability against a purchaser still does depend on the doctrine of the 'bona fide purchaser of a legal estate for value without notice' (equity's darling). This is the only circumstance when notice should form part of the answer to a question in land law today.

Question 5

How did the Land Charges Act 1925, as amended, safeguard equitable interests in land? Was it successful?

Answer plan

- the need for reform in 1925
- the system in outline
- inherent defects

Answer

Prior to 1925, the conveyancing system in England and Wales was in something of a mess. On the one hand, purchasers of land were faced with considerable difficulties when trying to establish whether any other person had rights or interests in that land and, on the other, an owner of an equitable interest might find that an interest is destroyed by a simple sale to a purchaser who was unaware of its existence. To meet both of those problems, it was decided to move towards full title registration wherein all titles and all interests in land would be centrally recorded and guaranteed by the state. It was recognised, however, that this mammoth task had to proceed in stages and that a set of transitional provisions were needed. The result was the Land Charges Act 1925, intended to operate for only some thirty years. Unfortunately, it was not until 1st December 1990 that all land in England and Wales became subject to compulsory first registration. Undoubtedly, the introduction of compulsory first registration of title across the country will mean that unregistered conveyancing will become less prevalent but the fact that it has taken so long has only multiplied those defects that were inherent when the scheme was established.

The Land Charges Act 1925 (now LCA 1972) is something of a hybrid. On the one hand, it adopts some of the rules of the old common law: thus it is still true with unregistered conveyancing today that legal estates or interests bind the whole world. However, unlike most legal rights, most equitable rights would not be apparent to a purchaser on physical inspection of the property and their simple informality made them vulnerable in the event of a transfer of the land. To deal with these twin problems, the Land Charges Act substantially replaced the common law doctrine of the *bona fide* purchaser of a legal estate for value without notice. In its place, the Land Charges Act 1925 (now LCA 1972) established a system of registration of its own.

The scheme of the Act is relatively straightforward. Equitable interests are divided into various categories known as land charges. These classes - Class A to F - are statutorily defined and were intended to comprise most of the equitable interests that could exist or could be created in land. Bearing in mind that these equitable interests would affect the title of land belonging to another (that title not being registered), s 3 of the Land Charges Act provides that a land charge should be registered in its appropriate class against the name of the estate owner whose land is to be bound by the charge. The general purpose of this requirement for registration is clear enough. Under s 4 of the Act, if the owner of an equitable interest has not registered their interest as a land charge, it will be void against a purchaser of the land. To be more precise, an equitable interest that should have been registered as a Class C(iv) or Class D land charge will be void against a purchaser of a legal estate in the land for money or monies worth and an equitable interest that should have been registered in any one of the other Classes will be void against a purchaser of any estate in the land for valuable consideration. Of course, the corollary of this is that if an equitable interest is correctly registered, it will be binding on any purchaser of the land as stipulated in s 198 of the Law of Property Act 1925. It should be noted at this point that even an unregistered equitable interest is binding against someone who is not a purchaser, such as a squatter. In principle, therefore, the position is relatively straightforward. Title to unregistered land is not centrally recorded but lies in the title deeds as was the position before 1925. Similarly, it is still true that legal estates and interests are automatically binding on a purchaser. The crucial change has occurred with equitable interests, most of which have to be registered as land charges if they are to bind the purchaser. If they are not so registered, they are void even if the purchaser had actual knowledge of them, *Midland Bank Trust Co v Green*.

Unfortunately, this simplicity masks serious difficulties that have emerged in the application of the Land Charges Act in practice. These problems are both inherent in the machinery as it was established and have emerged because of changes made in the substance of property law since 1925. One of the most serious criticisms of the system of land charges is its reliance on a name-based system of registration. Thus, an owner of an equitable interest has to register it against the name of the estate owner and all depends on both the owner of the equitable interest and any prospective purchaser knowing the correct name of the current estate owner. This has caused problems in three respects. Firstly, there are some circumstances where a prospective purchaser has no way of ascertaining the name of the estate owner of the land he is purchasing and so no knowledge of against whom to search. So, for example, under the rule in *Patman v Harland*, an intending purchaser of a lease has no right to examine the title of the freeholder and so no way of obtaining the names of persons against whom he should make a Land Charges search. He is, nevertheless, bound by land charges registered against former estate owners because s 198 LPA overrides the lessee's apparent protection of s 44(5) LPA - *White v Bijou Mansions*. Likewise, now that root of title in unregistered land is only 15 years (s 23 LPA 1969), the purchaser may well have no way of ascertaining the names of persons who held the land previously: these names are behind the root of title. However, any charges registered against these names are binding on the purchaser (s 198 LPA again) irrespective of the fact that the purchaser could not have discovered those names. Although a partial remedy is provided by s 25 LPA 1969 (compensation) this is a problem that will only get worse the longer it takes to complete full registration of title under the Land Registration Act.

Secondly, there is the problem of incorrect searches. It is axiomatic that a name based system will work only if all parties both register and search under the correct names. This is by no means a forgone conclusion. In *Diligent Finance Co Ltd v Alleyene*, for example, a wife had registered a Class F against her husband, but not against the full name as shown on the title deeds. When the purchaser then searched against the correct name, they received a clear search certificate (which is conclusive, s 10 LCA) and the wife's rights lost their priority. An even more complicated set of circumstances arises where there is both a defective search and a defective registration. Thus in *Oak Cooperative Building Society v Blackburn* both the registration and the search were made in different, but incorrect versions, of the estate owners name. In the event, the registration was deemed less defective than the search and took priority, but it was a pragmatic solution made necessary by the deficiencies of the system as a whole.

Thirdly, there is a problem with sub-sales as the LCA requires interests - such as a contract to buy the land - to be registered against the actual estate owner, s 3. If, therefore, a person is buying land at the end of a chain and their own vendor has not yet completed their purchase, the sub-sale should be registered against the head vendor, ie the estate owner at the time the sub-sale was agreed. Obviously, this can happen only if the end purchaser is aware of the existence of the chain and, if not, they are likely to register their charge against the wrong person, as in *Barrett v Hilton Developments Ltd*. It will then be void if the property is sold elsewhere.

Apart from problems arising out of the use of names, there are other difficulties too. Thus, when a purchaser has exchanged contracts with the vendor, only then will he be in a position to search the Land Charges Register for that is when previous owners are revealed in the title documents. Of course, by that time he is bound to complete the contract and also bound by any registered land charges. Again, it is only because of later amendment, in the form of s 24 LPA 1969, that a remedy has been found which enables a purchaser to pull out of the contract if he had no actual knowledge of the charge. Again, in unregistered land, there is no equivalent of s 70(1)(g) of the Land Registration Act. Thus, even those owners of equitable interests who are in actual occupation of property at the time of sale to a purchaser are not protected. As *Hollington Brothers v Rhodes* shows, these interests must be positively protected. Whether or not this was deliberate - and there is some doubt - clearly it is a significant weakness in the system. Finally, there is one problem that is not so much inherent in the system as originally devised but which has emerged due to legal, social and economic changes in the use of land. As noted above, it is essential to the success of this legislation that virtually all equitable interests fall within its ambit. Unfortunately that is not the case. There is a category of equitable interests which case law and, indeed, the Act itself, establishes are not registerable. These unregisterable interests are, of course, still capable of binding a purchaser but their effect depends entirely on the capricious doctrine of notice. In this respect, one of the most important aims of the Land Charges Act, namely the abolition of the doctrine of notice has not been achieved. The equitable rights included in this residual category are wide ranging. On the one hand, there are estoppel easements (*Ives v High*) and, on the other such matters as the right of re-entry in an equitable lease (*Shiloh Spinners v Harding*) and the right of a tenant to recover fixtures at the end of a lease (*Poster v Slough Lane Estates*). However, the most important is the right of equitable ownership behind a trust for sale. Such rights are specifically excluded from the category of land charges by s 2(4) LCA 1972, mainly because they are overreachable on a sale by two trustees and so take effect in purchase money. As we now know however, it is not all cases of a trust for sale that there are two trustees (*Pettitt v Pettitt, Bull v Bull*) and in such cases the doctrine of notice plays a vital part in assessing whether the purchaser is bound - *Kingsnorth Finance v Tizzard*.

The simple fact that there is an entire class of right that cannot be land charges and whose viability still depends on the doctrine of notice is a serious criticism of the Land Charges Act. This criticism would have been tolerable had the Land Charges Act really been the temporary measure that it was intended to be. That however is not the case and combined with the defects that were inherent in the system, the Land Charges Act has proved to be a difficult and complicated statutory mechanism. Of course, if one has registered an equitable interest properly and in the correct name, the system of registration is much more reliable than the system of notice and in this respect the Land Charges Act must be seen as a partial success. That however is not saying a great deal and it will be something of a relief to conveyancers, purchasers and owners of equitable interests when the system of unregistered conveyancing is fully replaced by that of the Land Registration Act.

Notes

This is a standard 'bookwork' question on the Land Charges Act.

Question 6

In 1970, when he retired, Frank sold his large farm to William and produced a conveyance from his father dated 1935 as proof of title. William, through his solicitors, made an official search of the Land Charges Register against the name of Frank and his father. The certificate revealed a restrictive covenant, registered against his father in 1934, preventing the building of more than one domestic residence on the farm. In 1970 Frank wished to live in peace and quiet (in the house he had built on the edge of the farm on land he now retained), and so a restrictive covenant was inserted in the sale to William preventing any trade or business on the farm except agricultural works. This was correctly registered against William. In 1982, William granted his daughter (Vanessa), for one hundred pounds, 'the right to buy my farm when I retire from farming at half its current market value'. By 1984, William had fallen in love with a younger woman and wished to start a new life in Australia. Realising that his farm had quadrupled in value since 1982, he decided to sell the land to Derek, his friend who was also a property developer. Derek thought he might turn the farm into an industrial estate. Derek paid three quarters of the market value in order to agree a quick sale. Derek searched against the name of 'Bill' (always having known his friend by this name) and Frank. He received a clear certificate.

Vanessa has just heard of the sale and wishes to buy the farm at the cheap 1982 price. Derek has just received a letter telling him that he can't build the industrial estate. Derek wonders whether this is true and asks whether, in any event, he can build a housing estate instead.

Advise the parties.

Answer plan

- root of title
- hidden charges
- compensation
- classes of land charge
- effect of registration
- possible fraud

Answer

As indicated in the facts of this problem, all the relevant transactions and events are completed before registration of title became compulsory in England and Wales on 1st December 1990. Thus, this problem falls to be decided under the rules of unregistered conveyancing. These rules, it might be noted, are a mixture of common law and statute, the most important being the Land Charges Act 1972 (an amendment of the LCA 1925).

a) Vanessa's claim to purchase the property

Whether Vanessa can claim a right against Derek to purchase the property depends on whether her father, William, granted her a proprietary right over the land and, secondly, whether this right is enforceable against Derek. First, there may well be some dispute about the nature of the right granted to Vanessa, for it may be that it cannot be regarded as proprietary in nature. On the one hand, the right may be a right of pre-emption - that is, a right of first refusal in the event that the grantor (William) wishes to sell the property. If this is the case, *Pritchard v Briggs*, despite the wording of s 2 Land Charges Act 1972, suggests that a right of pre-emption cannot be regarded as proprietary until it is exercised (thus registration would be effective from this later date only). However, the better view is that this is an option to purchase. An option to purchase is clearly an interest in land from the moment of its creation, whether conditional or not, *London & South-Western Railway v Gomm*. Moreover, it is clear than an option to purchase is an 'estate contract' within s 2 Land Charges Act 1972 and, therefore, it must be registered against the name of the estate owner who created it (ie William) if it is to bind a subsequent purchaser of a legal estate for money or money's worth, ss 3 and 4(6) Land Charges Act 1972. In our case, there is no evidence to suggest that Vanessa has registered her option as a land charge and presumptively, therefore, it is void against Derek - he, clearly, is a purchaser of a legal estate for money's worth.

There is, however, one small hope for Vanessa. She may be able to claim that she was fraudulently deprived of her right because of dishonest collusion between William - the creator of the right - and Derek the purchaser who obviously benefits from the fact that it is not binding on him. As the problem tells us, William wished to sell to Derek in order to obtain a higher price and he must have known that he would thereby defeat his daughter's claim. However, there is no suggestion that the sale was solely to defeat the daughter's claim or that Derek ever knew that she had an option to purchase. Indeed, even if this was the case, the House of Lords decision in *Midland Bank Trust Co v Green* makes it clear that that would not be enough to uphold the viability of an unregistered land charge against a purchaser. To recognise the sale to Derek, even though it destroys Vanessa's right, is to uphold the policy of the Land Charges Act, not to subvert it.

b) The restrictive covenants

i) The covenant against industry

If Derek wishes to build an industrial estate, he must first establish that the covenant against non-agricultural trade is not binding on him. This will be difficult. Derek has obtained a clear search certificate and we know that under s 10(4) Land Charges Act 1972, an official search is conclusive. However, it is conclusive only 'according to its tenor' and, therefore, is conclusive only in respect of the names actually searched. Here, Derek searched against 'Bill'. 'Bill' is not the estate owner and so the clear certificate is of no avail. In fact, Derek will be bound by the correctly entered covenant under s 198(1) Law of Property Act.

ii) The restriction on building dwelling houses

In the original conveyance from Frank's father to Frank in 1935, there was a restrictive covenant against building more than one dwelling house. This had been registered against Frank's father and clearly was binding on Frank. The question arises whether it is also binding on Derek, the successor in title to the burdened land.

Assuming that there was originally some land that could benefit from this covenant and that the benefit of it has passed in orthodox fashion to the person now seeking to enforce the covenant, the question here involves consideration of the particular problems caused by the Land Charges Register being a names register. When Derek buys the land, he must investigate root of title. Under s 23 Law of Property Act 1969, root of title is 15 years and so Derek can rely for good title on the conveyance by Frank to William (his vendor) in 1970. This was the first conveyance which was at least 15 years old. Seeing this document, Derek will realise that he must search against William and Frank - both are revealed in the root of title. Of course, he would not have discovered the restrictive covenant because it was registered against Frank's father, of whom Derek knew nothing and, indeed about whom he could not have known. The covenant is hidden behind the root of title and was in effect 'undiscoverable'. However, because of s 198(1) Law of Property Act 1925, Derek is deemed to have notice of all covenants correctly registered 'for all purposes' and it is binding on him.

Derek is thus bound by a registered, but essentially undiscoverable, land charge. Fortunately, he may be entitled to compensation under s 25(1) Law of Property Act 1969 if he can fulfil the three conditions stipulated therein. First, it is clear that the transaction which caused him loss has occurred after the commencement of the Act (ie after 1st January 1970). Secondly, we can infer that Derek has no actual (ie real) knowledge of the charge, as he would not otherwise have purchased the property and, thirdly, the name of the estate owner against whom the charge was registered (Frank's father) was not comprised in any title document that Derek would have seen when purchasing the property. He would be aware of Frank and William only. Although, then, he cannot build, he can claim compensation.

Notes

See also the possibility that the covenant could be discharged by application to the Land Tribunal.

Question 7

Molly is the freeholder of a large house, title to which is unregistered. In 1988, Molly contracted to sell the land to Saul and even though he did not register his rights, Saul agreed in writing to sell the land to Oscar. Oscar has registered his rights against Saul but none of these sales have taken place. Molly also agreed to allow her son, Tony, to occupy the basement while he was working as her cook. Tony, being a clever law student, has registered his right against his mother's name. Molly's neighbour, Harold has just bought three horses and asks whether he can make a path for walking access across Molly' back garden to reach his field. Molly agrees but only after they have agreed by deed that Harold should pay 100 pounds a year for the next ten years for this right. The next day, Harold asks whether he can build a wider drive over part of Molly's garden in order to take his horse-trailer to the field. Molly agrees. Molly also grants a restrictive covenant in favour of Harold saying she will not build in her garden. Harold's solicitor registers this covenant against 'Moll'. In 1989, Molly sells the house to Peter who, using the same solicitors as Harold, search against 'Milly'.

Peter wants to build in his garden and to stop Harold's access. He asks Tony to leave and is faced with a claim by Oscar to purchase the land.

Discuss.

Answer plan

- legal interests
- classes of land charge and effect of registration
- name registration

Answer

This problem concerns the sale of unregistered land and the consequences for a purchaser of the existence of rights over that land belonging to third parties. In the normal course of events, the position is simple: Peter the purchaser will be bound by any legal rights over the land as 'legal rights bind the whole world' and will be bound by equitable rights if they have been correctly registered under the Land Charges Act 1972. He must also be aware that certain equitable rights may bind him apart from registration if they fall into the category of unregistrable equitable rights whose binding effect depends on the doctrine of notice.

a) **The contracts of sale entered into with Saul, and the sub-sale to Oscar**

Clearly, both these contracts of sale (Molly/Saul and Saul/Oscar) amount to 'estate contracts' within s 2 Land Charges Act. They are Class C(iv) Land Charges, being 'a contract by an estate owner (Molly) or by a person entitled at the date of the contract to have a legal estate conveyed to him to convey or create a legal estate'. As such, they must be correctly registered against the name of the estate owner if they are to bind a subsequent purchaser of a legal estate for money or money's worth - s 4(6) Land Charges Act 1972. On these facts, there is no doubt that Saul's contract with Molly is not binding on Peter. Peter is a purchaser of a legal estate for money and the charge is not registered. It is void, s 4(6). However, what of Oscar's estate contract, for he has registered his rights? Unfortunately for Oscar, he is a victim of one of the flaws in the system of unregistered conveyancing. Despite being registered, Oscar's estate contract is also not binding on Peter because, under s 3 Land Charges Act 1972, a land charge must be registered against 'the name of the estate owner whose estate is to be affected'. When Oscar entered into his contract for sale, he registered it against Saul, but Saul was not then (nor has he ever been) the 'estate owner' whose estate is to be affected. That was, and still is, Molly. So, as in *Barrett v Hilton Developments*, a sub-purchaser under an initial contract for sale which is not completed at the time of the sub-sale, loses their rights against a subsequent purchaser of the land (ie someone to whom, the land was sold in breach of the initial contract for sale) when they have registered against their vendor instead of the estate owner.

b) Tony

As were are told, Tony has registered his right to occupy his mother's flat and we know that correct registration of an equitable interest will bind a subsequent purchaser, s 198 Law of Property Act. However, it is axiomatic that only those rights capable of binding third parties (ie proprietary rights) can, if registered, bind third parties. Registration can never make binding something which is inherently incapable of being binding. On this ground, Peter may be able to force Tony to leave, as it appears that Tony has only a licence to occupy the basement.

We are told that the occupation of the flat is granted while Tony acts as his mother's cook. The strong presumption on these facts is that this is a service occupancy, where the occupation is for the better performance of the duties of the employee, as in *Norris v Checksfield*. If this is true, the arrangement amounts to a licence and a licence is not an interest in land, *Ashburn Anstalt v Arnold.* It cannot, therefore, be binding on anybody, whether 'registered' or not. Of course, if it transpires that Tony has a lease, the registration is effective to bind Peter to the terms of that lease.

c) Harold and the path

From the facts of the problem, we know that Molly allows Harold access by foot over her garden. This might be a right of way - an easement - that is well capable of binding subsequent purchasers of the land. We are told further, that the right is created by deed. In such circumstances, it is reasonably clear that Molly has granted Harold a legal easement to use the garden path: it is a right capable of being an easement (*Re Ellenborough Park*) and is created by deed. In such circumstances, there is no question that Harold may continue to use the path because, as is the rule in unregistered land, legal rights bind the whole world. Peter is bound by the terms of the deed to allow Harold access on foot for as long as the agreement stipulates.

d) Harold and the driveway

To some extent this issue may be resolved as a matter of construction. If the right to use the path (above) encompassed the right to drive to the field then the matter is as c) above. However, this is unlikely, not only because the issue of the driveway arises after the easement over the path is created, but also because of the general rule in the law of easements that a specifically granted right of way does not include a more general right, *London and Suburban Land and Building Co v Carey*. On this ground, Harold has no claim on Peter. He had no easement against Molly, so nothing can be transmitted to Peter.

However, it may be that Molly has otherwise created an easement in respect of the driveway in Harold's favour. Under the rules of proprietary estoppel, an assurance, relied upon to detriment can give rise to a proprietary right. In fact, in *Ives v High*, an equitable easement was created by just such a process. Here, it is arguable that Molly has encouraged Harold to believe that he may use the driveway and also that Harold had relied on that assurance to his detriment viz the construction costs. This may well be an equitable easement and, if it is, the question arises whether it is binding on Peter. In that respect, the general rule is that equitable interests must be registered as land charges to be binding in unregistered land, ss 3 and 4 Land Charges Act 1972. This is not registered. However, certain equitable rights - outside the statutory definition of land charges - are binding in registered land under the old doctrine of notice. According to Lord Denning in *Ives*, the equitable estoppel easement is just such a right. Although it is true that Class D (iii) land charges include 'equitable easements', Lord Denning suggests that this category refers to easements which would have been legal before 1925 but, because of the changes then made in the way rights could be created, can now be equitable only. Estoppel easements, by contrast, can never be legal, and so are outside Class D(iii). The consequence is that validity is determined by notice and this is a question of fact. If, for example, the drive is under construction when Peter inspected the land, or the existence of the easement is obvious, or if Peter did not inspect at all but would have had notice had he done so, Peter will be bound.

e) Harold and the restrictive covenant

This particular problem shows how difficult the system of land charge registration can be in practice given that it depends on name registration. Clearly, Harold has registered his charge against the wrong name and it would not, therefore, be binding against a purchaser who made a correct search - _Diligent Finance Ltd v Alleyene_. Likewise, Peter has searched against the wrong name and it is clear that he would have been bound had the charge been registered correctly, s 198 Law of Property Act. In this case, however, we have two errors - a defective registration and a defective search. This was exactly the situation in _Oak Cooperative Building Society v Blackburn_ and it is clear that the solution must be a pragmatic one. According to that case, it seems that precedence will be given to the registration or search according to which is in the most sensible version of the estate owner's correct name. In our case, this might well be the registration (M♦ll instead of Molly). If that is the position, then Harold's covenant is binding on Peter. If, however, we were to take the view that 'Milly' was a more sensible version of the true name, the search certificate would take priority and, having been clear, it would absolve Peter under s 10(4) Land Charges Act.

Notes

Problems in Land Charges can be difficult as they are meant to highlight the inherent defects of the system which, in many cases, arise only in special or convoluted factual situations. Particular attention should be paid to the provisions for compensation for 'hidden' charges as these are not so simple as would first appear:

for example, the name against whom the charge is registered must not appear on any relevant title deed. Likewise, the different rules of 'voidness' can be troublesome. Students must be aware of the difference between a purchaser of any estate for valuable consideration and a purchaser of a legal estate for money or money's worth. If the Land Charge is C(iv) or D, for example, a purchaser of an equitable lease will be bound even if the charge is not registered.

Question 8

Compare and contrast the provisions of the Land Registration and Land Charges Acts 1972 in respect of the protection they give to equitable interests.

Answer plan

- brief outline of each system
- the differences in registration procedures
- the certificate and priority periods
- protection of occupation
- loopholes in unregistered land: notice

Answer

The machinery instituted by the Land Charges Act 1972 and the Land Registration Act 1925 were intended to achieve the same objective, albeit that the latter was far more wide ranging than the former. In essence, both of these systems were intended to bring stability to the system of conveyancing in England and Wales by protecting purchasers of land and owners of rights over that land.

The Land Registration Act achieves this by ensuring that title to land and any interests over land are centrally recorded. In respect of equitable interests, the protection is two-fold. On the one hand, equitable interests can be protected by registration as minor interests (by notice, restriction, inhibition, or caution) and on the other, they may qualify as overriding interests under one of the categories defined in s 70(1) LRA. Indeed, it is the ability of an equitable interest to qualify as an overriding interest that gives registered land its advantages. Thus, under s 70(1)(g), an owner of such a right is protected so long as they are in occupation whether or not they knew they had a right (as may be the case with many *Pettitt v Pettitt* claims) and whether or not they knew that it should be registered. This is particularly attractive if the equitable rights are acquired informally, as with equitable estoppel easements under s 70(1)(a) (*Celsteel v Alton*).

Of course, problems with registered land do exist. The fact that an owner of an equitable right need not actually register their right as minor interest poses something of a problem to a prospective purchaser. It undercuts somewhat the policy that all rights should either be registered or obvious (and therefore overriding). Thus, the curative effect of s 70(1) not only causes overlap with the minor interest provisions but may even amount to a disincentive to register. In the case of *Pettitt* type family interests, there is no doubt that registration is a hostile act and, in any event, registration of a right may alert a purchaser and so encourage them to seek overreaching by the appointment of a second trustee for sale. Of course, the ability to overreach on the appointment of a second trustee is not peculiar to registered land, but this does highlight why a prudent equitable owner will actually subvert the purposes of the LRA and rely on s 70(1) instead of registering as a minor interest.

The protection of equitable interests in registered land also has problems in other respects. Thus, the provisions dealing with the choice of method of protection are complicated and unsatisfactory. For example, because a notice can be lodged only by production of the land certificate, the consent of the registered proprietor is required. Likewise, the Land Registration Act makes it clear that an equitable interest that does not qualify as an overriding interest or is not protected as a minor interest is void against a purchaser for value of the legal estate, s 20(1) LRA. This position of principle has, however, been compromised by the decision in *Peffer v Rigg* where Graham J suggested that an unregistered minor interest would be binding against a purchaser of the land who took the land in bad faith. While it is true that a purchaser will be bound by any equitable interests whether registered or not if there has been fraud ('fraud unravels all'), it is doubtful whether simply knowing of the equitable interest, which Graham J equates with bad faith, should be sufficient to bind the purchaser. This is clearly not the position in unregistered land (see *Midland Bank Trust Co v Green*) and it is to be hoped that the Law Commission's proposals to redefine purchaser so as to include 'good faith' (Law Comm. No 158) does not allow the reintroduction of the doctrine of notice by a sidewind.

Perhaps, however, these are but small problems compared to those found when considering the protection of equitable interests in unregistered land. It is often easy to forget that unregistered land also has a system of registration of equitable interests that is intended to give equitable interests the same degree of protection as is available in registered land. Unfortunately, this is clearly not the case and the Land Charges Act falls considerably short of this goal. In unregistered land, equitable interests can be divided into three broad categories. First there are those equitable interests that are registerable as land charges. Land Charges fall into six distinct categories. Class A to F, the most important of which are Class C and Class D. It is, for example, in class C(iv) that all equitable leases fall and in Class D that all restrictive covenants and most equitable easements are to be found. Following a similar principle as that applicable to minor interests, these registerable land charges must be protected by entry on the Land Charges Register in order to bind a purchaser, s 4 LCA 1972. In the case of Classes A, B, C, except C(iv), and F, an unregistered charge will be void against the purchaser of any interest in the land for valuable consideration while Class C(iv) and D will be void against the purchaser of a legal estate for money or money's worth. In short, as with registered land, registration means validity and non-registration means voidness, save only that the policy of voidness in the event of non-registration has been more rigorously enforced in unregistered land (*Midland Bank*).

However, in a similar respect, the system of land charges does suffer from one considerable defect: its lack of protection for persons with equitable interests who occupy premises. In unregistered land, the fact of actual occupation of property does not, of itself, protect any equitable interest of the occupier. There is no equivalent of s 70(1)(g) LRA as amply illustrated by

Hollington Brothers v Rhodes where an equitable lease was void against a purchaser for lack of registration as a Class C(iv) charge despite the occupation of the tenants. If this had been registered land, the purchaser would have been bound. It is unfortunate that equitable interests in unregistered land are not protected in this way and, indeed, on one view there was supposed to be such protection in the Land Charges Act but the section conferring such privileges was inadvertently omitted from the 1925 consolidating statute (see *Harpum* (1990) CLJ 277). Whether that be the case, the protection does not exist and the omission is unfortunate.

The second category of equitable interests in unregistered land are those 'family' interests which are overreachable as existing behind a trust for sale. As with registered land, if there are two trustees for sale there is nothing the equitable owners can do to prevent sale or to remain in occupation of the property against a purchaser (*City of London Building Society v Flegg*). However, if there is only one trustee, in registered land the equitable interest may be overriding (*Boland*) or even a protected minor interest, whereas in unregistered land these equitable interests are not registrable (protectable) as land charges (s 2 LCA 1972) but can bind a purchaser only under the old doctrine of notice - *Kingsnorth v Tizzard*. Although it will be rare that a purchaser does not have notice (eg occupation will equal constructive notice of the equitable interest), it is undesirable that the inherently uncertain concept of notice should play a part in such a vital area as co-ownership of domestic property.

Indeed, it is not only with these equitable interests that notice is still relevant, for there is a third category of equitable interest within the scheme of unregistered land. These are equitable interests that either by design or by accident are outside the operation of Land Charges Act and are not within any of the Classes. These are unregistrable equitable interests whose validity against a purchaser rests on the doctrine of notice. They have no equivalent in registered land as the categories of overriding or 'minor' interests are all embracing. Of course, some such rights such as leasehold covenants cause few problems and this is why they were deliberately omitted. Indeed, equitable co-ownership would not have been a problem had the two-trustee trust for sale been the norm. However, such matters as estoppel easements

(*Ives v High*), equitable rights of re-entry (*Shiloh Spinners v Harding*) and a tenant's right to remove fixtures at the end of an equitable lease (*Poster v Slough Lane Estates*) which have merged as unregistrable since 1925 can cause serious difficulties, as these cases show. The existence of these rights means that a purchaser cannot rely with total security on a search of the Land Charges Register. There is always the possibility that an unregistrable but potentially binding equitable interest will exist that will affect the purchaser's title through the medium of notice. Such matters would not have been so important in practice had the Land Charges Act been replaced swiftly by full title registration, but that was not the case.

Finally, there are some other differences in the application of the Land Registration Act and the Land Charges Act that can cause practical difficulties. An obvious one is the fact that the Land Charges Act depends on a system of name registration. The problems that this gives rise to are well known, as in *Barrett v Hilton* (sub-sales), *Oak v Blackburn* (defective registration and defective searches) and *White v Bijou Mansions* (hidden charges). These are difficulties that do not arise in the Land Registration Act because it is a system based on titles rather than names. Likewise, the fact that charging orders over equitable co-ownership interests can be registered, and therefore protected, in registered land but cannot in unregistered land (*Perry v Phoenix Assurance*) only causes confusion. Last of all, it should be noted that the priority periods are different under the Land Charges and the Land Registration Act (15 days and 30 days respectively) and that in unregistered land, it is the official search that is conclusive, s 10(4) LCA (even if a charge is actually registered) whereas in registered land it is the register that is conclusive, *Parkash v Irani Finance*, (even if the official search is clear).

The Land Charges Act and the Land Registration Act have both done much to introduce certainty into the whole area of the purchaser and the equitable interest. There is no doubt, however, that as far as protecting equitable interests is concerned, the Land Registration Act offers considerably more comfort than the Land Charges Act. Above all, the safety net provided by the concept of actual occupation is a considerable advantage over the unregistered land system. Indeed, even for the purchaser the registered land system has its attractions. Although the existence of overriding interests may seriously compromise a title, most of these interests are reasonably ascertainable on inspection of the property. Those that are not, particularly the right of equitable co-ownership, is a problem that arises because of *Pettitt v Pettitt* and not because of the rules of the Land Registration Act. Furthermore, at least the purchaser in registered land has the benefit of indemnity provisions in cases where defective title registration causes loss. There is no such safety net in unregistered land. Moreover, the purchaser in unregistered land must always fear the existence of an unregistrable equitable interest that will be binding on him through the mechanism of constructive notice. These problems and the name based registration system make the introduction of compulsory registration of title on 1st December 1990 a very welcome development.

Notes

This question can be answered in many ways, although the central point is the lack of protection for occupiers and the lack of a 'safety net' in unregistered land. We could go on to consider whether the LRA itself is now so flawed because of changes in the social pattern of land use that it is as bad as the Land Charges Act.

Co-ownership

Introduction

The law relating to concurrent interests in property has changed considerably in recent years. This is not so much because of changes in the legislative framework surrounding co-ownership, but rather because the increased incidence of co-ownership has revealed many practical problems for which the 1925 legislation does not clearly provide. Particular difficulties have been caused by social and economic changes in the pattern of property ownership, particularly of residential or domestic houses. The emergence of the *Pettitt v Pettitt* line of authority, whereby a partner or spouse can acquire an interest in a house that formally belongs to someone else, has done much to channel the law of co-ownership in new directions. Co-ownership is no longer confined to commercial or business situations but is virtually an expected attribute of domestic life. The Law of Property Act, and the machinery of co-ownership it establishes, has had to deal with this shift in emphasis. As we shall see, where property is deliberately co-owned or when the statutory machinery is deliberately invoked, few serious problems exist. However, where co-ownership arises informally, considerable practical problems can arise.

Checklist

In this chapter, the various issues relating to co-ownership will be considered in turn and the student needs to have an understanding of the following issues. First, there is the question of the statutory machinery and the reasons for the 1925 reforms. Without this background understanding, much of the law of co-ownership will make no sense. Secondly, there is the question of the actual share which each co-owner really has in co-owned land: problems of severance and the like. Thirdly, there are important issues as to how implied co-ownership can arise or, in other words, when does single ownership turn into co-ownership without any formal documentation. Fourthly, there are issues about the consequences for purchasers when buying land subject to co-ownership, especially if that co-ownership has been informally created. In an examination, it is quite common for at least two of these issues to be addressed in different questions and it is quite possible for one question to raise all four matters.

Question 9

Analyse the changes made by the Law of Property Act 1925 in the law relating to the creation and transfer of concurrent interests in land.

Answer plan

* explanation of the meaning of 'concurrent interests' and types of co-ownership
* position before 1926 and the problems this generated
* sections 34 to 38 Law of Property Act 1925 and the statutory code
* advantages
* disadvantages

Answer

The law of concurrent interests in land - or co-ownership - was radically transformed by the Law of Property Act 1925. Concurrent ownership of land describes the situation where two or more persons are entitled to the simultaneous enjoyment of property, whether that be land used for commercial or residential purposes. Prior to the 1925 legislative reforms, there were several forms of co-ownership: in other words, the legal relationship between the individual co-owners could take various forms. However, this caused numerous problems and one of the most important reforms of the Law of Property Act was to limit the types of co-ownership that could be ~~could be~~ created thereafter. From 1926, land may be co-owned only under a joint-tenancy or, alternately, under a tenancy in common.

In a joint-tenancy, as far as the rest of the world are concerned, the individual persons are as one owner (although, of course, as between themselves they do have separate rights). In other words, there is but one title to the land and the individuals own that title jointly. In order for a joint-tenancy to exist, it is clear that the 'four unities' must exist (*AG Securities v Vaughan*): first, unity of possession, whereby each co-owner is entitled to possession of the whole of the property all of the time, there is no partition of the land for each co-owner; secondly, unity of interest, in that each co-owner's interest in the property is of the same extent and of the same duration; thirdly, unity of title, in that each co-owner must derive their title from the same document; and fourthly, unity of time, in that each co-owner's interest takes effect (vests) at the same time. It is only if all the four unities are present that a joint-tenancy exists, for it is only if all are present that there can be a single title to own jointly. The most important characteristic of a joint tenancy is, however, the right of survivorship (or *jus accrescendi*). Under this rule, if any joint-tenant dies before severing (ie terminating) the joint-tenancy, their interest automatically passes to the other joint-tenants without the need for any formal transfer or conveyance. Indeed, even if the deceased joint-tenant attempts to leave their share by will, the device is of no effect because survivorship takes place automatically at death and takes precedence over testamentary dispositions (*Gould v Kemp*). A tenancy in common, on the other hand, needs only one of the four unities, being the unity of possession. Each tenant in common is in possession of the property in common with the others (ie there is no partition) but is regarded as having a distinct share in the land, say one third. A tenancy in common is sometimes known as 'an undivided share in land' and this makes clear its true nature. The tenant in common has a distinct share which is not yet divided. Importantly, there is no right of survivorship under a tenancy in common and each tenant is able to deal with their share by will according to their wishes.

Of course, cases of co-ownership arise most frequently when land is conveyed deliberately to two or more people (but note the *Pettitt* rules discussed below). In such cases, and subject to what will be said below about legal title to property, it is a matter of construction in each case whether a joint-tenancy or a tenancy in common exists. The matter can be expressly resolved in the conveyance (cf *Goodman v Gallant*), but failing that there is a presumption in favour of a joint-tenancy unless some 'words of severance' are used. In other words, a conveyance to two or more people presumptively will be as joint-tenants unless the parties have indicated an intention to have distinct shares, as where the interest of one party is limited to a distinct portion (eg one quarter) or the parties have paid the purchase price in unequal proportions.

The Law of Property Act did not, however, merely limit the types of co-ownership that could exist: crucial changes were also made in the machinery by which co-ownership could be created and the machinery by which land subject to co-ownership could be transferred. Before 1926, if a purchaser wished to buy land subject to a tenancy in common, they would have to identify and locate every individual tenant in common. Each of them would have to give their consent because each had a separate title to the land. Obviously, not only was this expensive, it meant that just one tenant in common could prevent the sale of co-owned land. These problems were solved in an ingenious way. Under the 1925 Act, a legal tenancy in common cannot exist - s 1(6). After 1926, all legal titles to co-owned land must take the form of a joint-tenancy even if the document of conveyance purports to create a tenancy in common. So, whenever land is conveyed to two or more persons for concurrent ownership, it is statutorily deemed to be conveyed to them as joint-tenants of the legal title - ss 34, 36 Law of Property Act. However, this is a very special form of joint-tenancy because these statutory joint-tenants are, in fact, joint-tenant trustees for sale of the legal title. In other words, at law, all land subject to concurrent ownership is held as a joint-tenancy, but only where the trustees hold that legal title on trust for the equitable owners. In equity, however, the co-owners may be either joint-tenants or tenants in common, according to the presumptions and rules of construction discussed briefly above.

To give two examples: if 26 Grange Road is conveyed to A and B as joint tenants, each paying half the purchase price, this will take effect as a conveyance to A and B as joint-tenant trustees of the legal title, holding on trust for themselves as joint-tenants in equity (because they paid the price equally). Likewise, if a house is conveyed to Y and Z 'as tenants in common, 50% each', this will take effect as a conveyance to Y and Z at law as joint-tenant trustees upon the statutory trusts for sale - because a tenancy in common cannot exist at law - but holding on trust for themselves in equity as tenants in common, half each (because this is expressed in the conveyance). The use of the trust is, therefore, a device to ensure that all legal title to co-owned land is held as a joint-tenancy whilst also ensuring that in equity (where, after all, the real interest lies), the co-owners can be either joint-tenants or tenants in common as before. Frequently, as in the two examples above, the 'trustees' will be the same people as the 'beneficiaries' and there is no real change in their rights to use and enjoy the land.

Obviously, however, the use of this device must have had a purpose and it is clear that the overriding policy aim was to make co-owned land more alienable while at the same time giving some degree of protection to the rights of all the co-owners, especially those not on the legal title. To this end, the statutory trust is a trust for sale, meaning that the trustees are under a duty to sell the property unless they all agree to postpone sale. In the normal course of events, at least with residential property, the two trustees (eg husband and wife) will obviously agree to postpone sale because they have purchased the property to live in it. However, when a sale does take place, this apparently complicated statutory mechanism does have considerable advantages, at least when compared to the position before 1926. First, because the legal title must be held by way of joint-tenancy, there is only one title deed or land certificate (as the case may be). The purchaser only has to investigate one title, irrespective of the number or type of co-owners that exist in equity. The conveyancing advantages of this are obvious. Secondly, s 34(2) Law of Property Act limits the number of potential legal co-owners (ie trustees) to four - the first four persons named in a conveyance if there are a greater number. Thus, the purchaser only ever has a maximum of four people to deal with and in most domestic situations it will only be two. Thirdly, because there must be a joint-tenancy of the legal title, the right of survivorship applies. So, if one legal owner dies, no formal documents are need to transfer title to the remaining legal owners. Fourthly, the purchaser, if there are two or more legal owners (trustees), will automatically receive the land free of the rights of all the equitable owners, be they equitable joint-tenants or equitable tenants in common. This is because, by statute, a payment to two or more trustees for sale overreaches the equitable interests existing behind the trust - s 2 Law of Property Act. The purchaser, by means of proper overreaching is unaffected by the claims of the equitable owners. This does not mean, of course, that the equitable owners' rights are destroyed. Rather, their equitable rights are converted into money and the equitable joint-tenancy or equitable tenancy in common takes effect in the purchase money paid by the purchaser (eg *City of London BS v Flegg*). This purchase money is then held on trust by the trustees for sale in the same way that they held the legal title to the property.

It should be apparent from this, that the changes made by the 1925 Act greatly assist the easy transfer of co-owned land, both by simplifying the conveyancing machinery and by protecting the purchaser through the device of overreaching. The equitable owners' interests are also protected in the sense that they cannot be destroyed but take effect in money form. Of course, the system is not without its problems. The most striking is the fact that the equitable owners automatically have their rights transformed from rights over land to rights in money. This is all very well if another home can be purchased, but there is a real social and economic difference between having a share in land - and therefore occupation of it - and having a share in the proceeds of sale of that land. Also, problems arise if any of the two or more trustees disagree as to whether to sell the land, as where the relationship of husband and wife (being trustees for sale for themselves) breaks down and one party wishes to realise their capital investment. As we know, this legal ownership is a trust for sale and there is a paramount duty to sell when retention of the property does not command unanimous trustee support. This is a difficulty that frequently comes before the courts, in the shape of an application under s 30 LPA whereby 'any person interested' in co-owned land may apply for an order of sale ie to carry out the trust. In fact, the courts have developed a complicated set of principles under *Jones v Challenger* whereby sale will not be ordered if the 'secondary purpose' of the trust (the first being sale) can still be achieved. So, in theory at least, postponement of sale is possible if say, the house was purchased for, and is still needed for, a home for any children of the relationship, as in *Re Evers*. At least this does recognise that in many domestic situations the 'trust for sale' really is only a conveyancing device.

Further problems arise because of the nature of co-ownership itself. What happens, for example, if one trustee forces his co-trustee to leave the property or a single trustee forces out a beneficial owner? After *Bull v Bull* we know that an equitable owner does have a right to possession (as must a legal owner by virtue of legal title), but do they have a right to the payment of rent from the occupying owners if they are excluded? This would be vital if the dispossessed owner needs to find alternative accommodation. Theoretically, the payment of rent by one co-owner to another cannot be ordered - because each owner is entitled to occupy the whole of the property under the unity of possession. Fortunately, this logical but harsh position has not been adhered to strictly and the court's have been able to order the payment of 'compensation' in such cases (eg *Dennis v Macdonald*). Finally, and most importantly of all, the mechanism for dealing with co-owned land assumes that there will be at least two trustees for sale in all situations of co-ownership - because two trustees are vital for overreaching and vital for purchaser protection. However, as a result of *Pettitt v Pettitt*, it is clear that in many domestic situations there will be but one legal owner, holding on trust for himself and his partner as tenants in common in equity. If this is the case, the purchaser cannot risk buying the property for there is every possibility that they will be bound by the non-legal owner's equitable interest. In registered land, this will be so if either the equitable interest had been registered as a minor interest or if it amounts to an overriding interest within s 70(1)(g) LRA (as in *Williams & Glyn's Bank v Boland*). In unregistered land, this type of equitable interest cannot be protected as a land charge (it is specifically excluded because two trustees was expected to be the norm) and so will take effect against a purchaser if they have notice of such rights, as in *Kingsnorth v Tizzard*. In such cases, the statutory trust for sale does not operate in the way envisaged by the Law of Property Act.

Obviously, then, the reforms of 1925 have dealt well with a serious commercial problem in that co-owned land is no much more easily and cheaply alienable than was previously the case. The emphasis on purchaser protection has, however, been undermined by the 'single-trustee' scenario and the social change in the use of co-ownership from a device for commercial property holding to a device for residential property holding. In this respect, the 1925 Act is somewhat out of date

Notes

This is a good question to answer, provided that the student understands the concept of the trust for sale. It is often to difficult to explain the idea of legal owners holding on trust for themselves, but that is the core of the matter. All becomes more evident if the conveyancing advantages of this are stressed. If more time is available, we could consider whether the rise of the 'one trustee' scenario has deleteriously affected these changes so as to make the overreaching provisions in many cases redundant.

Question 10

In 1987, Tony and Tracy decided to live together as an experiment before getting married. They purchased a semi-detached house, of registered land, in the centre of town with the aid of a 90% mortgage from the Safe Building Society. The rest of the purchase price was proved by Tony out of his savings. The house was conveyed to Tony alone as Tracy does not have a full time job. Tony had an excellent job in the construction industry and Tracy had no need to work. She stays at home from where she does occasional work as a dressmaker, the money from which she uses to pay for holidays. In 1989, with the construction industry in decline, Tracy's income was useful to help pay the mortgage and Tony often said that he did not know how they would meet their commitments if Tracy gave up dressmaking. Later that year, however, Tony inherited enough money from his uncle to pay off the mortgage and the couple decided to get married as Tracy is now pregnant. They have a tropical wedding costing several thousand pounds but, on their return, they find that Tony's employer has gone into liquidation and he is unemployed. Despite the birth of their child, Tracy takes on more dressmaking to meet the mounting bills. Unfortunately, Tony's attempt to start his own business has failed and he owes the bank several thousand pounds. He is now bankrupt and his trustee is pressing for the house to be sold.

Advise Tracy.

Answer plan

- a resume of the 1925 machinery of co-ownership
- the trust for sale - Law of Property Act 1925 ss 34, 35, 36
- acquisition of beneficial ownership - *Pettitt v Pettitt* et al
- sale of co-owned property s 30 Law of Property Act
- Insolvency Act 1986

Answer

Much depends in this case on whether Tracy owns the house or, in other words, whether she has any equitable interest in it. If Tracy can establish that she has an 'ownership interest' in the property she may, although it is not certain, be able to resist the application of her husband's trustee in bankruptcy for sale of the property. If Tracy has no interest in the property, her only hope would be to show that she had taken advantage of the Matrimonial Homes Act 1983 s 1. This gives non-owning spouses a right of occupation against their partner which, if registered, can bind subsequent purchasers of the property. Although Tracy clearly has such a right, there is no evidence that she has entered it (by way of notice) on the registered title. In any event, if such a right is registered, a trustee in bankruptcy can apply for an order for sale to defeat such right under s 336 Insolvency Act 1986 and the position would be very similar to that discussed below in respect of sale if she does have an equitable interest.

Does Tracy have an interest in the property? When the property is purchased, it is conveyed into the sole name of Tony. The purchase is by mortgage and by cash deposit. Tony pays the entire cash deposit and, because he is to be the sole legal owner of the property, the mortgage is made to him. Title is registered in his name alone and there is no express declaration of trust in writing in favour of Tracy. Clearly, therefore, at the time of purchase, Tony is owner of the property both at law and in equity. There is no co-ownership - express or implied - and there is no trust for sale. In such circumstances, if Tracy is to establish any interest at all, she must fall back on a line of authority stemming from the House of Lord's landmark decision in *Pettitt v Pettitt*.

The *Pettitt* case, and a whole range of decisions following it, have established that it is possible for a non-legal owner of property (ie Tracy) to claim an equitable ownership interest in someone else's property. The principles are not limited to situations where a couple are married and, indeed, there need be no personal relationship between the parties. These rules are the application of traditional property law concepts to new situations. The basic principle flowing from *Pettitt* and a similar House decision in *Gissing v Gissing* is that a person may claim an equitable interest in property belonging to another if they can establish a common intention that this was to be the case. This may either be by way of resulting trust - based on contributions to the purchase price, as in *Dyer v Dyer* - or by constructive trust based upon inequitable conduct and detrimental reliance, as in *Grant v Edwards*.

In the 1970s, under the influence of Lord Denning's Court of Appeal, this doctrine quickly expanded. It became apparent that the *Pettitt* decision could be used to justify any re-ordering of property rights that seemed appropriate to the judge. Cases such as *Falconer v Falconer*, *Hestletine v Hestletine* and *Eves v Eves* appeared to give the court power to grant an equitable interest whenever the court thought it just and equitable to do so. Now, however, this jurisdiction has been more clearly defined and the House of Lord's decision in *Lloyds Bank v Rosset* has returned the law to the spirit of *Pettitt* and established reasonably clear guidelines for the future. According to *Rosset*, if Tracy is to establish any interest in the property she must bring herself within one of the following categories. First, she must show that the legal owner has made an express promise to her that she should have an interest and that she has relied on that promise to her detriment, as in *Eves* or *Grant v Edwards*. Such an interest arises under a constructive trust but it seems that on the facts Tracy cannot establish such a claim. It is doubtful whether Tony's words of gratitude about the value of her dressmaking count for this purpose. There is no oral promise that she should have an interest and *Rosset* and *Burns v Burns* make it clear that such a promise cannot be inferred from the fact that a person shares some of the obligations of communal living, such as cleaning the house. As Lord Bridge makes clear, sharing the obligations of a relationship is not the same as sharing the obligations of property ownership. Secondly, however, if Tracy has contributed directly to the purchase price of the house, an interest can arise in her favour. This will be in proportion to her contributions. Moreover, it is clear that such contributions can be by way of mortgage repayments as Lord Bridge specifically mentions this in Rosset. If such an interest exists, it seems to be under a resulting trust, although Lord Bridge also classifies this as a constructive trust in his judgment. Unfortunately, the difference may be important, for if Tracy is the beneficiary under a resulting trust, her interest could be measured by the level of her actual payments; whereas if she is the beneficiary under a constructive trust, the court may have a much wider discretion to grant her a share of the property that is equitable in all the circumstances. Tracy's dressmaking does generate some income and while purchasing holidays is not relevant, paying the mortgage in times of difficulty clearly is, especially as her income appears to have been vital for this purpose. On this ground, it appears that Tracy has an equitable interest in the property.

If Tracy can establish her interest in the above fashion, it is clear that the property is now co-owned. According to *Bull v Bull* this means that an implied statutory trust for sale comes into existence: Tony, the legal owner, holds the property on trust for sale for himself and Tracy as tenants in common in the shares established by the resulting trust (or constructive trust). This gives Tracy some measure of protection. There is, of course, only one trustee for sale and therefore no possibility of overreaching. Any purchaser may well be bound by Tracy's interest under the normal rules of registered conveyancing. In this case, there is no registration of a minor interest but, if Tracy is in actual occupation of the property at the time of any sale (*Abbey National BS v Cann*) to the purchaser, she will have an overriding interest under s 70(1)(g) LRA in similar fashion to *William & Glyn's Bank v Boland*.

However, that is not the end of Tracy's difficulties. When Tony becomes bankrupt, the trustee in bankruptcy becomes vested with all his property, including the legal title to the house. As we have just established, the trustee cannot sell the property immediately as Tracy's interest would be binding on a purchaser. In such circumstances, the trustee will apply to the court for an order for sale under s 30 Law of Property Act 1925. Under this section, 'any person interested' (which includes a trustee in bankruptcy) may apply for an order for sale if a required consent (here that of Tracy) cannot be obtained. If such an application is made, the court will have to balance the claims of the creditors against the claims of the wife. This general approach was re-affirmed in *Re Citro* where it became clear that applications to the court under s 30 involving bankruptcy should be dealt with on broadly similar principles to those established by the Insolvency Act. (This case cannot be dealt with under the Insolvency Act as Tracy is not a trustee). In our case, the wife's interest is likely to be small - given that it is related to a few mortgage payments - and the court is unlikely to postpone sale. However, should they wish to do so, a postponement of one year (following the Insolvency Act 1986 s 336) is all that is likely. The only possibility for long term relief is that the court considers this to be an exceptional case where the secondary purpose of the trust is still subsisting (*Jones v Challenger*). Although such a route was taken in *Re Evers* where the purpose of providing a home for the children could still be achieved, this is unlikely to be the case in our problem, especially as the rights of creditors seem to weigh heavily against the rights of equitable co-owners. The policy of the law, as exemplified by the Insolvency Act and *Citro* is not to postpone sale unless extreme circumstances so dictate. In short, then, Tracy will have an interest, it will be binding on any purchaser, but a court is likely to order sale. Of course, Tracy's interest will have priority and be satisfied out of the proceeds of sale before those proceeds are distributed to creditors.

Question 11

Gloria, a rich widow, is the registered proprietor of a large house in London. Recently, at a friend's party she met Simon an eighteen year old student and after a passionate affair of a few weeks, she invited him to live with her. Simon accepted. Being a proud man, Simon insisted that he share the expenses of running the house and over the next few months he paid the occasional bill and even paid for the cost of having the house redecorated both inside and out. Simon was a little concerned that, because of the difference in age, Gloria would soon tire of his charms and he repeatedly asked her of the future. Last year, after one particularly splendid dinner together, Gloria told Simon that 'what's mine is yours'. Next day, realising that his future was secure, Simon spent his life savings on a sports car. Unfortunately, unknown to Simon, Gloria was paying school fees for her five children and two months ago she had to take out a mortgage with the Eton Building Society to cover next year's charges. The Building Society visited the property when Simon was on a field trip abroad and Gloria executed the mortgage that day. The Building Society registered their charge at the Land Registry the day after he returned.

Gloria has now met someone more her own age and has emigrated to Australia. The Building Society is seeking possession of the property in order to realise their security. Advise Simon.

How would your answer differ if title to the property had been unregistered.

Answer plan

- acquisition of beneficial interests
- implied trust for sale: *Bull v Bull*
- overreaching machinery: s 2 Law of Property Act 1925
- registered land: one trustee; overriding interests; meaning of actual occupation; time of occupation
- unregistered land: one trustee; doctrine of notice

Answer

This question concerns the acquisition of beneficial interests in property belonging to another and the effects of such ownership, if any, on a third party purchaser - here a mortgagee. In concrete terms, this problems revolves around a contest between the Building Society, who have an interest in the property and a power of sale under s 101 of the Law of Property Act by virtue of their duly registered mortgage, and Simon who must claim, if he is to have any prospect of remaining in the property, an equitable right of ownership to it. The crucial questions are, therefore, whether Simon has such an interest and, if so, whether the Building Society are bound by that interest. If the Building Society are bound, there is no prospect of a sale of the property with vacant possession unless an application is made to the court under s 30 Law of Property Act and, in any event, Simon would be entitled to the money equivalent of his interest before the Building society could be paid.

If Simon is to have an interest in the property, it is clear that this must be established under the principles elaborated in *Pettitt v Pettitt* and recently codified by the House of Lords in *Lloyds Bank v Rosset*. In our case, there is no express conveyance to Simon as owner and no express written declaration of trust by Gloria in his favour. His only hope is the law of constructive or resulting trusts. In this respect, *Rosset* makes it clear that a person claiming an equitable interest in property, legal title to which is vested in another, must be able to show either some contribution to the purchase price of the property - so as to raise a resulting trust in their favour - or must prove some oral assurance that they were to have an interest in the property which they then relied on to their detriment. On the facts as stated, it seems clear that when Simon met Gloria, Gloria was sole legal owner of the property and that it was not subject to any charge by way of 'purchase mortgage'. In other words, the property was hers, paid for and complete. It follows that Simon cannot pursue the resulting trust path to an equitable interest - there is no purchase price to which he can make a contribution, not even monthly mortgage payments. Moreover, even if there were an outstanding 'purchase mortgage', Simon's contributions to the cost of running the house cannot be considered, for they are part of the costs of sharing property, not of acquiring it - per Lord Bridge in *Rosset* and Court of Appeal in *Burns v Burns*. The payment of the decoration expenses might have been relevant if the couple had been married: there is every chance that Simon could have relied on s 37 of the Matrimonial Proceedings and Property Act 1970 to establish a beneficial interest by way of improvement expenditure. However, this is not the case, and it is doubtful whether contributing to the costs of improving a house that is already purchased can, without any agreement to the contrary, give rise to an equitable interest.

It would seem, then, that Simon should rely on the doctrine of constructive trusts: he must plead a promise plus detrimental reliance. Once again, are the costs of decorating the house relevant here? If Simon can show that he spent his money on improvements because there was a promise or agreement that he should part-own the property, then a case is clearly made out.

Once again, however, there is no evidence to support this and such statements that Gloria does make are made *after* Simon spends money. Such expenditure could not have been made as a result of those particular statements.

Eventually, Gloria does make a promise of sorts to Simon and it is a matter of construction whether this is sufficient for the *Rosset* principles. First, a problem exists with intention: does Gloria, after a romantic dinner, intend by her words 'what's mine is yours' that Simon should have an interest in the property. Although it is not entirely clear, dicta in *Gissing v Gissing* suggest that the oral promise (the 'common intention') must be real rather than imagined and it is questionable whether Gloria's statement meets this criterion. On the other hand, no case has denied that if a reasonable person would have believed that the property owner was making a statement about ownership of the property, the particular promisee is entitled to rely on it even if this was not the actual intention of the property owner. In our case, we do not know what Gloria actually meant, but a reasonable person in Simon's position might well conclude that this was an assurance about the ownership of the shared home. On this ground, Simon has a strong case that the relevant promise was made and it seems clear from the facts that he relied on that promise when he spent his life savings on the sports car. There is here, however, a further problem. Certain cases, such as *Gissing* and *Christian v Christian* suggest that the detriment suffered as a result of the promise must be related to that property; for example, spending money on improvements. However, another view is that so long as the detriment was referable to the promise ie was caused by it, it does not matter that the actual detriment suffered was not property related. If the reason why an interest arises under a constructive trust is that a promise has been made and relied on (not, that property has been paid for), it should make no difference what form that detriment takes: whether it is property related or not, the promisee has still spent money that they would not otherwise have done. On this view, Simon has an equitable interest in the property if he can show that his lavish expenditure was a direct result of Gloria's promise.

Assuming, then, that Simon does have an interest what is his position vis-a-vis the purchaser-mortgagee. Clearly, when Eton advanced the money, they did not pay it to two trustees for sale: Gloria is the single trustee and, therefore, there can be no overreaching. The statutory conditions of s 2 Law of Property Act are not met. This makes the Building Society potentially subject to Simon's interest on either of two grounds: either he had registered his interest as a minor interest, or he can claim an overriding interest. As for a minor interest, there is nothing to suggest that Simon has protected his equitable ownership in this way as there is no evidence of registration. This leaves us with the overriding interest that can arise under s 70(1)(g) Land Registration Act 1925, as applied in *Williams & Glyn's Bank v Boland*. First, Simon must have an interest in land and this we have just established. Secondly, he must be in actual occupation and, following *Chhokar v Chhokar*, this is perfectly possible even though Simon was away from the house temporarily. On the facts, given that the house is his regular home he would seem to be in actual occupation - see also the Court of Appeal analysis in *Rosset*. Thirdly, Simon must be in actual occupation at the relevant time and, following, *Abbey National BS v Cann* it is clear that for claims under s 70(1)(g), the crucial time is the moment of creation of the mortgage or time of purchase. Thus, in our case, it is irrelevant that Simon returns before the charge is registered, we must determine whether he was in actual occupation at the time the charge was created. On the above facts this seems to be established.

To conclude, then, Simon has an interest under a constructive trust (possibly of one half as this is what he seems to have been promised) and he was in actual occupation of the property at the time the mortgage was made. Thus, under s 70(1)(g) he has an overriding interest against the Building Society and takes priority over them. They cannot obtain vacant possession under their normal powers as mortgagees and must apply to the court under s 30 Law of Property Act for an order for sale. Even if this is granted, they are unlikely to recover their money in full as Simon's interest takes priority and he must first be paid out of any proceeds of sale.

Finally, if the land had been unregistered, Simon would still have acquired an equitable interest as the principles are identical, but whether that interest would have bound the Building Society would have depended on whether they had had notice of it at the time the mortgage was created. In unregistered land, these type of equitable interests cannot be registered as Land Charges (s 2 Land Charges Act 1972) and thus their enforceability depends on the doctrine of notice. Following *Kingsnorth v Tizzard*, it is highly likely that Simon's occupation of the property (ie his presence in a general sense even though he was temporarily absent) would have given the Building Society notice of his interest and therefore they would be bound accordingly.

Question 12

Hilda and Harold, brother and sister, have recently discovered that their seventeen year old nephew, William, has been orphaned in a road accident and that they are his legal guardians. In anticipation of William coming to live with them, they decide to buy a bigger house with their savings and with some of the money left to William by his parents over which they have lawful control until William is eighteen. The new house, title to which is unregistered, is expressly conveyed into their joint names as legal and equitable joint-tenants. There is no mention of the fact that William's money was also used. William arrives and Hilda and Harold employ a live-in personal tutor, Mary. Mary lives in a self-contained part of the house for which she pays Hilda and Harold thirty pounds a week. Unknown to Mary and William, Hilda and Harold sell the property to Percy. Percy is told, and believes, that William and Mary are the vendors' children.

Advise Mary and William, who is now eighteen, as to their right to stay in the property. Is the law in this area satisfactory?

Answer plan

- co-ownership and expressly declared trusts
- acquisition of beneficial interests
- overreaching and two trustees: *City of London BS v Flegg*
- purchasers and existing tenants: s 70(1) Land Registration Act 1925
- Law Commission Report 188

Answer

In this problem, we are once again faced with the difficulties that can arise from the operation of the trust for sale and the overreaching provisions of the Law of Property Act 1925 as the mechanism for regulating concurrent co-ownership of land. Under the Law of Property Act 1925, when land is conveyed to two or more persons, they take that property as legal joint-tenants upon the statutory trusts for sale - ss 34, 36, Law of Property Act. In our case, therefore, when the new house is conveyed to Hilda and Harold, it becomes subject to the rules governing these statutory trusts. Hilda and Harold become the joint-tenant trustees for sale, with all of the powers thereof (including sale, s 18 LRA). Moreover, as the conveyance is expressly conveyed to them as joint-tenants in equity, they hold the legal on trust for themselves as equitable joint-tenants - *Goodman v Gallant*.

However, what of William, for it appears that some of his money has been used to purchase the property? It is axiomatic that when a person contributes to the purchase price of property but does not acquire legal title to that property, a resulting trust will arise in their favour giving them an interest commensurate with their contribution. As much was established in the early case of *Dyer v Dyer* and has recently been confirmed by the House of Lords in *Lloyds Bank v Rosset*. In fact, only if Hilda and Harold can establish that William's money was used by way of loan or gift can this presumption of a resulting trust be rebutted. There is no evidence of that here and it may be that William's money was used without his knowledge or consent. In such circumstances, it is clear that a resulting trust is raised in his favour. The express declaration of the equitable ownership that is found in the conveyance (ie to Harold and Hilda) does not prevent William claiming an interest by way of resulting trust, for in *Goodman* it was made clear that an express declaration of beneficial interests only precludes a claim of resulting or constructive trust for the parties to that declaration. William was not a party to it and is not bound by it. In the end, therefore, Hilda and Harold are trustees of the legal estate on the statutory trusts for sale holding on trust in equity for themselves as joint-tenants in the portion purchased by their own money and for William as a tenant in common of the share purchased with his money.

The property is now sold to Percy. This would seem to place William and Mary in considerable difficulty. It is obvious that Percy will not wish to share the property with other occupiers. The question becomes, then, whether William's interest, and any interest that Mary may have, can bind Percy.

First, what is the position of William? As seen above, William has an equitable interest in the property when Percy purchases the unregistered title. Normally, in unregistered land, equitable interests have to be registered as Land Charges to be binding against purchasers. However, under s 2 Land Charges Act 1972, these equitable ownership rights cannot be registered. They are, in fact, unregistrable and their binding effect continues in principle to be governed by the doctrine of notice. In our case, however, there is another important factor. Percy has purchased the property from two trustees for sale - in other words, he has complied with the statutory requirements of s 2 Law of Property Act 1925 for overreaching. As in *City of London BS v Flegg*, a sale by two trustees for sale overreaches all 'family style' equitable interests (ie William's equitable ownership) so that the purchaser cannot be bound. It does not matter that William knew nothing of the sale or that Percy knew nothing (or everything!) of William: the statutory magic operates in favour of the purchaser and protects him. Of course, William's equitable interest is reflected in the purchase money and he is entitled to a share of the proceeds of sale in proportion to his share of the property - if he can locate the trustees. He has, however, no claim against Percy and must surrender possession.

Mary's position is less clear. On one view, the arrangement she made with Hilda and Harold amounted to nothing more than that of lodger and landlord. If this is the case, she would have a mere licence, which is not an interest in land and which cannot, therefore, bind any purchaser irrespective of all questions of notice or registration - *Ashburn Anstalt v Arnold*. She would have to leave. Indeed, this may well be the case, especially if Hilda or Harold provided 'board and services' within the definition of a lodger in *Street v Mountford*. Likewise, if Mary was given accommodation 'for the better performance of her duties' as a tutor she would have only a licence, as in *Norris v Checksfield*. Then, she would be a service occupant under a licence and could not stay on against Percy. In fact, Mary's only hope is to claim that she has a tenancy - for this is capable of binding Percy in the right circumstances and, of course, such 'commercial' rights are not overreachable. In this case, there is evidence of 'rent' and it is payable weekly. This could mean that Mary has a legal periodic tenancy and, as such, it would be binding on Percy under the normal rules of unregistered land: viz legal rights bind the whole world. Of course, even if there is a legal periodic tenancy binding on Percy, Percy could terminate the tenancy according to its terms which, in the case of periodic tenancies, is usually on giving one period's notice. Finally, Mary might consider claiming an equitable tenancy under *Walsh v Lonsdale*, but only if there is a written record of the original tenancy agreement - s 2 Law of Property (Miscellaneous Provisions) Act 1989. In any event, however, to bind Percy in unregistered conveyancing such an equitable tenancy would need to have been registered as a Class C (iv) Land Charge - *Hollington Brothers v Rhodes*. There is no evidence of this. In the end, it looks as if Mary also has to leave and the best she can hope for is for one further period under the legal periodic tenancy that might possibly exist.

This question clearly identifies one of the most striking problems of the use of the trust for sale as a co-ownership device. William, the equitable owner, was deprived of his own property while he was in occupation of it because of the magic of overreaching. It is not enough to say that his interest is now in money form because a share of the proceeds of a house sale by no means guarantees that other accommodation can be purchased, even if the trustees do distribute the money properly. To meet these problems and to safeguard the position of the equitable owner in William's position, the Law Commission (in Report No 188) have recommended three alternative solutions:

a) that if the equitable owner registers their interest, they cannot be overreached. Unfortunately, as this case shows, this solution would only help those equitable owners who both knew of the requirement of registration and, more fundamentally, knew that they actually had an interest. William did not;

b) that in order for overreaching to take place, one of the trustees must be a solicitor or licensed conveyancer. This presupposes that such professional persons would not consent to a sale that destroyed an equitable owner's property rights without proper consideration of all material circumstances. This might or might not be true but it would be expensive, as well as introducing strangers into family affairs. In practice, the protection is likely to be negligible and formal;

c) that no beneficiary, of full age and in occupation, could be overreached without their consent. This undoubtedly would work. It would prevent sales of co-owned property such as the Fleggs suffered in the *City of London case* and William in this. What it does, however, is to take the law virtually back to the pre-1925 position. Any unwilling resident co-owner could prevent a sale, subject perhaps to a court order under s 30 Law of Property Act. If this really is the solution, why not re-invent the legal tenancy in common and do away with the trust for sale altogether?

Finally, we can also note that Mary's position, if she had a tenancy, is not satisfactory. In registered land, her tenancy whether legal or equitable would have been an overriding interest (under ss 70(1)(k) and (g) respectively) and would have automatically bound Percy. In unregistered land, however, there is no protection for occupiers of property under an equitable tenancy unless they positively register - see *Hollington Brothers v Rhodes*. In registered land, their actual occupation would trigger sub-paragraph (g). This is an unfortunate disparity between the two systems of conveyancing.

Question 13

Martin and Judith live together in a small country cottage, title to which is registered in the name of Judith only. They are not married but plan to have children shortly. Judith has an excellent job and persuades Martin that he should give up work and stay at home and look after the now expected child. Martin is unsure, especially because he dislikes relying on Judith so much, Yet, she assures him that 'when the children are born, this will be your home for the rest of your life'. Martin finally agrees, gives up work even though he was about to be promoted. After giving up work, but before the child is born, Martin completely re-decorates one room as a nursery meeting the cost out of his savings. It comes as a great shock to discover that Judith in fact is expecting twins and the couple go to see the Building Society about a mortgage to extend their house. This is easily arranged and the Building Society duly register their charge. Two years later, Judith has met another man and unknown to Martin she takes out a bigger mortgage with a different Building Society, paying off the first and using the balance to go on a round the world cruise.

She never returns. The second Building Society seek possession of the cottage. Martin seeks your advice.

Answer plan

- acquisition of beneficial interests
- nature of interest: life interest or equitable ownership
- sale by one trustee: overriding interest or implied consent
- priority of replacement mortgages
- ways to protect beneficial interests

Answer

Once again, this problem poses difficult questions about the acquisition of equitable interests in property belonging to another and its effect on third parties. In this particular case, Martin must hope to establish that he has an interest in the property and that it is binding on the first mortgagee or, at least, on the second. If he can do so, he may well be able to stay in the property and, in any event, will be entitled to a share of the proceeds of sale in priority to the lender.

a) Martin's interest

There is clearly no conveyance of the property to Martin and so Martin has no legal title to it. In fact, before the first mortgage is taken out, it appears that Judith is the sole owner, both at law and in equity. Likewise, there is no evidence that Judith has made a written declaration of trust in Martin's favour and so no possibility of an equitable interest arises in this way. Once again, we are thrown back on the law of resulting and constructive trusts. This may enable Martin to claim an interest in the property, even though legal title belongs to Judith, provided he can bring himself within the principles of *Pettitt v Pettitt* and *Lloyds Bank v Rosset*. In this instance, it appears that Judith did not require a mortgage to purchase the property or, if she did, that mortgage has been repaid before Martin has any dealings with the property. Therefore, there is no scope for Martin to claim an equitable interest under the resulting trust approach - he cannot claim to have made a contribution to the purchase price under the first method identified in by Lord Bridge in *Rosset*. However, what of constructive trusts? At any time after the acquisition of the house, has Judith made a promise or assurance that Martin has relied upon to his detriment? As ever, this must be a matter of construction of the words and acts of the parties, with the proviso (as stated in *Gissing v Gissing*) that the agreement ('common intention') must be real and not supplied by the courts.

Clearly, Judith has made some kind of oral promise to Martin. She states openly, without duress, that 'this will be your home for the rest of your life'. As in *Ungarian v Lesnoff* and *Eves v Eves* this must amount to a promise of some kind of interest in the property. Of course, under *Rosset*, Martin must rely on this assurance to his detriment before equity will come to his assistance: 'equity will not assist a volunteer'. In this respect, two matters are relevant. First, is there detrimental reliance when Martin stays at home and redecorates the intended nursery. Clearly, there is detriment because he spends his own money but there are doubts over whether this detriment was in reliance on the promise made by Judith. It is more likely that the redecoration of the room was motivated by natural parental affection. Perhaps Martin may be able to rely on *Greasley v Cook*, where Lord Denning (albeit in the context of proprietary estoppel) stated that if a promisee changed their position to their detriment after a promise was made, it could be inferred that this was because of the promise. However, even if this wide ranging statement is correct, this does no more than shift the burden of proof to the person denying the existence of the interest - ie the defendant would have to show that the promise was not the cause of the detriment. In our case, there is a real possibility that this could occur and that Martin will be held not to have relied on the promise when spending his money on redecoration.

However, Martin also suffers detriment by giving up his job and staying at home in readiness for the baby's arrival. We are told that he was unsure about this and was directly reassured that his position was secure. There is, here, no problem that the detriment was in reliance on the promise. Yet, that is not the end of the matter. Some authorities suggest (eg *Gissing*) that the detriment suffered must be related to the property itself before any interest crystallises in the promisee. If this is the position, now we have the situation where Martin has acted in reliance, to his detriment, but where the detriment does not qualify. It is suggested, however, that this limit on the type of qualifying detriment is not appropriate for constructive trust cases where the essence of the matter is loss suffered as a result of a promise denied. If the essence is a promise denied, causing loss, then Martin clearly qualifies and should be able to establish an equitable interest under a constructive trust within the second limb of *Rosset*.

b) The nature of Martin's interest

In this case, Martin was promised that the property would be his home 'for the rest of your life'. According to *Ungarian* this means that Martin has a life interest in the property, rather than an absolute share of the ownership. In short, that he becomes the tenant for life and the property becomes subject to the Settled Land Act. In *Ungarian*, this result was a direct consequence of the particular promise made and it is difficult to see how the same conclusion can be avoided here, especially as the authorities suggest that a person's interest under a constructive trust which arises out of a promise bears a direct relation to that promise: viz if Martin is promised a home for life, he gets a life interest. However, if this conclusion is correct, there are unfortunate consequences. First, the existence of a life interest brings into play the cumbersome machinery of the Settled Land Act - Martin is, in fact, entitled to call for the legal estate to be vested in him and will have full powers over the property when this is done. Secondly, however, pending the vesting of the legal estate in Martin, his position is precarious. This is registered land and under s 86(2) LRA, the interest of a tenant for life can never be an overriding interest. Thus, if the property is sold to a purchaser or mortgagee, the equitable tenant for life cannot gain automatic protection. In fact, as in our case, the equitable tenant for life can protect himself only by registering his interest as a minor interest and this Martin has not done. In other words, pending the transfer to him of the legal estate, Martin is very vulnerable to a third party purchaser.

c) The first mortgage

Clearly, the first mortgage is made to only one trustee - Judith. Whatever interest Martin has, it is not as joint-tenant of the legal title. This means, then, that overreaching cannot take place and the Building Society may be bound by subsisting equitable interests. However, the Society will only be bound by subsisting interests if they have been protected in the appropriate way. If they have not, the Society takes free of those interests even though no overreaching occurs - this is the effect of s 20 LRA. As we have seen above, if Martin has a life interest, he is statute barred from claiming an overriding interest and must register as a minor interest. In fact, Martin has not registered and the Society will take free. Indeed, only if Martin can show that he has a full ownership interest is it even possible for him to claim priority against the mortgagee. If that were the case, Martin would be a person with an interest in actual occupation at the time the mortgage was made, and might have an overriding interest within s 70(1)(g) LRA, *Williams & Glyn's Bank v Boland* and *Abbey National BS v Cann*. Even then, however, Martin might not be able to claim priority. Following *Paddington BS v Mendelson*, the Society might well be able to prove that Martin had impliedly consented to the mortgage, thereby losing any priority which he may have had as a result of an overriding interest. On the facts, it is clear that Martin knew of the first mortgage, went to the Society to discuss it and, indeed, was aware that the mortgage was needed for family purposes. With such evidence, it is most likely that implied consent will be held to exist. In other words, Martin's interest will be subject to the Society either because it was a life interest not properly protected and/or because he impliedly consented to a postponement of his rights.

d) It is, however, the providers of the second mortgage that are seeking possession. The first mortgage has been discharged. Martin knows nothing of the second mortgage and cannot be said to have consented to it in any sense. However, it is very important that the second mortgage is used to pay off the first. Following *Equity & Home Loans v Prestidge*, it seems that when a second mortgage is used to pay off a first mortgagee, the second mortgagee steps into the shoes of the first mortgagee, at least up to the value of the first mortgage. In other words, the second lender acquires the first lender's priority to the extent of the first mortgage (assuming the second mortgage to be on no less favourable terms). Objectively, this is a reasonable conclusion given that any equitable owner (Martin) is in no worse position simply because the identity of the lender has changed: he is still subject to a mortgage. So then, if Martin did impliedly consent to the first mortgage, he will be taken to have impliedly consented to its replacement, up to the same amount.

In fact, in our case, if Martin has a life interest which he has not protected, he will be subject to the whole of the second mortgage, for the same reason that his life interest was subject to the first - viz the second society is a purchaser of a legal estate and takes free of all interests except overriding interests (which this cannot be) and registered minor interests (which this is not).

Unfortunately, then, it seems that Martin's position is precarious. He has an interest in the property, but that is subject to the rights of the first mortgagee either because he consented to it or, being a life interest, because he has not protected it correctly. If it is a question of consent, the priority is passed to the second mortgagee, but only to the extent of the first mortgage. If it is a life interest, Martin is subject to the second lender up to the whole amount. The property is likely to be sold, with the proceeds being used in the following way.

a) If Martin has an ownership interest: pay off the value of the first mortgage, but to the second mortgagee, pay the cash equivalent to Martin of his interest; pay off the balance of the second mortgage; surplus to Judith.

b) If Martin has an equitable life interest, he ranks after both mortgagees but before Judith. It will be interesting to see how far down this chain of claimants the proceeds of sale actually reach.

Notes

The previous four questions all deal with various aspects of the same problem: the creation of co-ownership rights informally and the consequences this has for third party purchasers. There is no substitute for a thorough knowledge of Rosset, Flegg, Cann and Prestidge. There are useful case notes on all these cases in the *Student Law Review*, the CLJ and the Conveyancer. One of the difficult problems is going to be to distinguish between rights arising by constructive trust, and those arising by estoppel. The House of Lords in Cann has already made one allusion to this and it may be the issue of the future.

Question 14

Arnold, Bill, Claudio and Dominic and Eric are all trainee solicitors in London and they decide to buy a house together. All contribute equally to the purchase price and the house is conveyed to 'Arnold and Bill as joint-tenants in law and in equity'. Several months later, Bill is made redundant and forges Arnold's signature to a mortgage made with the Easy Loan Bank. At the same time, Arnold agrees in writing to sell his interest in the property to Eric and the agreement is executed. Meanwhile, Claudio has plans to marry and asks Dominic whether he will buy his share in the house. Dominic is very keen but disputes the price. Before they can come to a agreement, Claudio is killed in a road accident leaving all his property to his fiancee, Wendy. Very soon after, Eric becomes entangled in a city deal that goes badly wrong and, owing many millions, commits an act of bankruptcy. Before Eric is formally adjudged bankrupt, Dominic commits suicide leaving all his property to the Battersea Dogs' Home.

Eric's trustee in bankruptcy, Wendy, the Dogs' Home, Bill and Dominic's next of kin all claim an interest in the property. What is your advice. Would it make any difference if, before his death, Dominic had written to Eric informing him that he wished to leave the house as soon as possible?

Answer plan

- construction of the conveyance: nature of parties interest
- purpose of the law of severance
- *Williams v Hensman* : Act operating on one's own share
  - mutual agreement
  - possible course of dealing
- right of survivorship
- effect of bankruptcy of co-owner — S 336 Insolvency 86.
- section 36(2) Law of Property Act 1925

Answer

This question concerns the law of severance. Severance is the process by which a joint-tenancy can be converted into a tenancy in common. There may be many reasons why a joint-tenant should wish to sever his interest in this way, but very often the motivation is to avoid the operation of the right of survivorship. In a joint-tenancy, when one joint-tenant dies, their interest automatically passes to the other joint tenants, irrespective of any disposition made in a will. If, therefore, a co-owner is a joint-tenant but wishes to deal with their interest separately, severance of that tenancy is crucial. Before we consider the problem in detail, however, one point must be borne in mind. Under the Law of Property Act 1925, the only form of co-ownership that can exist at law is the joint-tenancy. This legal joint-tenancy is unseverable - s 36(2) Law of Property Act - because if it were otherwise a legal tenancy in common would result and under the Law of Property Act that is not possible - s 1(6). In other words, when we talk of severing the joint-tenancy, we are talking about severing the joint-tenancy in equity. As is made clear in the LPA, the equitable co-ownership that exists behind the joint-tenancy at law can take either form and so the equitable joint-tenancy can be transformed into a tenancy in common under the law of severance.

The law relating to severance is to be found both in statute and at common law. Under s 36(2) of the Law of Property Act 1925, any equitable joint-tenant may give notice in writing to the other joint-tenants of their intention to sever and this actually results in a severance in equity - see eg *Burgess v Rawnsley*. Similarly, at common law, *Williams v Hensman* establishes that severance may occur by three methods: first, where one joint-tenant does 'an act operating on their own share' (such as a sale of his interest) this is enough to sever; secondly, where joint-tenants agree to sever by 'mutual agreement', this acts to sever the shares of all those agreeing, even if the agreement is never carried out or is actually unenforceable - *Burgess* ; thirdly, severance can occur by 'mutual conduct' where the parties conduct is of a kind sufficient to evince an intention no longer to be part of a joint-tenancy.

In our problem, some or all of these principles may be relevant but first it is necessary to identify the nature of the co-ownership between the parties. Clearly, Arnold and Bill are the legal owners and are, by statute (s 35 LPA), the joint-tenant trustees of the legal estate holding for the equitable owners on a trust for sale. Who are the equitable owners and are they joint-tenants or tenants in common? Although the conveyance expressly declares that Arnold and Bill are joint-tenants, this conveyance can be conclusive only between the parties to it - *Goodman v Gallant*. Therefore, the doctrine of resulting and constructive trusts is not excluded for Claudio, Dominic and Eric. Following *Dyer v Dyer*, *Pettitt v Pettitt* and *Lloyds Bank v Rosset*, there is no doubt that Claudio, Dominic and Eric will be able to claim a share of the equitable ownership by virtue of their contribution to the purchase price of the property. In fact, because all five people contributed to the purchase price equally, they are in equity joint-tenants. So, the picture of the ownership of the house is as follows: Arnold and Bill hold the property as trustees for sale for Arnold, Bill, Claudio, Dominic, and Eric as joint-tenants in equity.

As the problem makes clear, there are now several claimants to the property and, if as seems likely it is sold, there will be confusion as to how the proceeds of sale should be distributed. Of course, if there have been no acts of severance, the surviving joint-tenants will be entitled to the property or its proceeds by virtue of the right of survivorship. In addition, it is quite possible that only one or some of the original joint-tenants have severed their interest so that survivorship might operate between only some of the surviving parties.

a) Bill's attempted mortgage to the Easy Loan Bank

Bill is a trustee of the legal title, but jointly with Arnold. Thus, no action on his part alone can deal with the legal title and without Arnold's agreement there can be no mortgage to the Bank. In other words, both legal owners must genuinely agree to any conveyance of the legal title - this is at the very heart of the legal joint-tenant trusteeship. So, forging the signature of the other legal owner is not sufficient to create a mortgage of the legal title - *First National Securities v Heggarty*. However, following *Ahmed v Kendrick* and s 63 of the Law of Property Act 1925, the attempted mortgage by Bill will be sufficient to mortgage to the bank such interest as Bill does control - in other words, his equitable interest. Without doubt, this mortgage of his equitable interest is 'an act operating on his own share' within *Hensman* and means that Bill severs his share of the equitable interest. He is now a tenant in common of one fifth, albeit mortgaged to the Bank. The other owners are still within a joint-tenancy of the remaining four-fifths. Legal title remains in Arnold and Bill as before.

b) When Arnold agrees in writing to sell his interest in the property to Eric, this is an enforceable agreement to sell his equitable interest - see s 2 Law of Property (Miscellaneous Provisions) Act 1989. This is not an agreement to sell the legal title as Bill would have had to concur. As above, this is an act operating on his own share and will sever Arnold's interest from the joint-tenancy. Thus, when the agreement is executed Arnold's equitable share passes to Eric. The overall position is now that Arnold and Bill hold on trust for Eric as tenant in common of one fifth, Bill as tenant in common of one fifth (but mortgaged) and Claudio, Dominic and Eric as joint-tenants of the remainder.

c) It is unclear whether Claudio's discussions with Dominic lead to any severance of the joint-tenancy between them. It seems that there is no 'mutual agreement' within *Hensman* as although Dominic is keen to buy, no price has been agreed. This probably prevents severance by mutual agreement. There has to be an agreement. It should be noted, however, that if an agreement can be inferred from the circumstances, the fact that this agreement would be unenforceable (because it is not in writing) does not prevent severance occurring - *Burgess*. Under an unenforceable 'mutual agreement' the transfer would not take place but severance would occur for both parties. However, assuming that mutual agreement is inapplicable here, can the discussions between Claudio and Dominic amount to severance by 'mutual conduct', being a course of dealing between the parties that show an intention to hold as tenants in common. This is unclear, because as a matter of principle it is difficult to see why a failed attempt to agree (as here) should have the same effect as a successful attempt to agree. If that were possible, the difference between mutual agreement and mutual conduct would become virtually non-existent. However, if one reads Lord Denning's judgment in *Burgess*, it is clear that he does suggest that negotiations between joint-tenants can give rise to severance. Essentially, the answer will depend on the facts of each case and whether the court is prepared, as a matter of policy, to extend the circumstances in which severance is possible. The degree of hardship caused by the operation of the right of survivorship might well be relevant in that calculation. In our case, the tentative conclusion is that severance has not occurred because of the potential overlap with mutual agreement. Thus, the position remains as at b) above.

d) When Claudio dies, he dies as a joint-tenant of three fifths of the property with Dominic and Eric. He has not severed his interest and thus it accrues to Dominic and Eric under the right of survivorship. The fact that he left his property by will to Wendy is irrelevant as survivorship takes precedence over testamentary dispositions - *Gould v Kemp*. Thus, Arnold and Bill hold on trust for Eric as tenant in common of one fifth, Bill as tenant in common of one fifth (but mortgaged) and Dominic and Eric as joint-tenants of the remainder.

e) Eric's bankruptcy and the suicide
Under the Insolvency Act (as applied in very similar circumstances to these *Re Dennis*), it is clear that a bankrupt's property does not become vested in the trustee in bankruptcy until he or she is formally adjudicated bankrupt. At that moment, of course, there is alienation of the bankrupt's property such as to

cause a severance of any joint-tenancy of which he may be part - it is really an act operating on his own share, albeit an involuntary one. In our case, however, when Dominic dies and leaves his property to the Dogs' Home, Eric has not been adjudicated bankrupt and so there has been no severance between the remaining two joint-tenants. Unfortunately, therefore, Dominic's interest passes to Eric under the right of survivorship. In other words, when Eric is adjudicated bankrupt he is, in fact, the sole surviving joint-tenant and all the property subject to that joint-tenancy accrued to him and will fall to the trustee in bankruptcy for use to pay the creditors.

The final position is, therefore, that Arnold and Bill are legal owners of the property holding as joint-tenant trustees in equity in the following way:

- for Eric as tenant in common of one fifth. This will pass to the trustee in bankruptcy;

- for Bill as tenant in common of one fifth, but as mortgaged to the bank;

- for Eric as owner of the remainder, having succeeded to the shares of Claudio and Dominic under the right of survivorship. This also passes to the trustee in bankruptcy for distribution among his creditors.

f) Would it have made any difference if Dominic had written to Eric before his death informing him that he wished to leave the property?

The only possible difference this could make is if this written communication can be regarded as written notice of severance under s 36(2) LPA 1925. Under that section, written notice to the other joint-tenants (here Eric), may sever a joint-tenancy providing that it is a communication of an intention to sever. This will be a matter of construction but, following the liberal construction used in *Re Draper's Conveyance* (where a court summons seeking sale of the property was held to sever under the section), this letter probably suffices: after all, an intention to leave the property almost certainly implies dealing separately with one's own share. However, there is one small problem in that the words of s 36(2) say that this form of severance is available where 'a legal estate is vested in joint-tenants beneficially', ie where the legal and equitable owners are the same people. That is not the case here - because only Arnold and Bill are legal owners. However, this restrictive construction is generally regarded as being incorrect and the better view is that severance by written notice is available for all joint-tenants in equity, whether or not they are legal owners as well. Thus, if Dominic had severed by this method before his death, he could successfully leave his one fifth share to the Dogs' Home in his will.

Notes

This is a disguised essay on the law of severance. The answer is to this, and similar problems, are not difficult and require a knowledge of the law of severance found in most textbooks. Gray's book is particularly good in this respect.

Question 15

Is the trust for sale an adequate tool for dealing with the complexities of concurrent interests in land?

Answer plan

- outline of 1925 legislation relating to co-ownership
- purpose of trust for sale
- some difficulties in application
- proposals for reform: Law Commission Report 188
  - Law Commission Report 181

Answer

The use of the trust for sale as the mechanism for the regulation of co-ownership in England and Wales is deliberate and largely the result of the wide ranging legislative reforms of 1925. Under ss 34 to 36 of the Law of Property Act 1925, whenever land is conveyed to two or more persons for their simultaneous enjoyment (successive interests in land operate under the Settled Land Act 1925, but also by trust for sale), it takes effect as a conveyance to them as joint-tenant trustees upon the statutory trusts for sale, holding for the equitable owners - usually themselves - in equitable co-ownership.

The powers and duties of the trustees for sale are set out in the Law of Property Act and the Settled Land Act but, in essence, they are under a duty to sell the land and hold the proceeds of sale for the equitable owners. Of course, in the normal course of events, the equitable owners (being also the legal owners) will have no wish to sell. If the property is commercial, it may well have been purchased for investment purposes to generate a steady income and if the property is residential it is likely that it is intended to be the family home. The trust for sale does, of course, recognise this as it encompasses a power for the trustees to postpone sale. This is, however, a power to postpone sale and in order to exercise the power all the trustees must agree. This should be contrasted with the duty to sell - this is a trust for sale and hence mandatory which must be carried out if there is no agreement to postpone. Here, then, is something of an oddity, at least in cases of residential co-ownership. The property is purchased for occupation, but unless both trustees (usually husband and wife) agree to postpone sale, the paramount duty to sell comes into operation. Obviously, this could cause difficulties and indeed it has proven to be so. Typically, the issue arises when the relationship between the trustees breaks down, as in marital separation. The question then arises whether a reluctant trustee can be forced to agree to a sale of the former home, especially if one trustee requires a release of capital to purchase alternative accommodation but the other needs accommodation for any children of the relationship. As things currently stand, in an application under s 30 LPA for sale, the court must start with a presumption in favour of sale - because this is the nature of the statutory trust. Indeed, exceptional or special reasons must be found to justify overriding one trustee's objection and continuing to postpone sale. Although the courts have, in this respect, developed the doctrine of 'secondary purpose' (eg *Jones v Challenger, Re Evers, Re Williams*), it is clear that this is not a satisfactory solution. The recent case of *Re Citro* shows how powerful the trust for sale can be, especially when a creditor of a bankrupt trustee is pressing for sale.

In this respect, the Law Commission have proposed (in Report 181) that the statutory trust for sale be replaced by a statutory trust of land ie that the duty to sell be removed. Although express trusts for sale will be able to be created deliberately, it is clear that under this proposal the majority of domestic co-ownership would fall within this new trust. Accompanying this, it is proposed to widen the ambit of s 30 so that the court has a greater degree of discretion when 'any person interested' makes an application for an order for sale of the co-owned property. This may be one of the trustees, should the others oppose a sale, a creditor or even a beneficiary that desires to realise their share in the property. In essence, the removal of the duty to sell and the wide discretion under s 30 would mean that courts will be able to consider all circumstances and decide what is best for all parties interested in the co-ownership. This must be better than the paramount obligation to sell, although it is not clear how a new s 30 would gel with the power of the court under the Insolvency Act to order a sale of co-owned property in the case of bankruptcy of one of the spouse-trustees. In that situation, the Insolvency Act makes it clear that a postponement of sale can be justified only in the most extreme circumstances and in *Re Citro* this logic was applied to bankruptcy and co-ownership disputes under the common law (eg where the parties are not married). Whether there is any change in this respect remains to be seen

Another problem always raised in connection with the trust for sale is the doctrine of conversion. Under the doctrine of conversion, equitable owners' interests behind a trust for sale are treated as if they are interests in money, rather than interests in land. This is said to follow from the equitable principle that 'what ought to be done (ie sale of co-owned property under a trust for sale) should be done'. Thus, because the equitable owners' interests will eventually be in money, equity regards them as if they were already in money. This doctrine, which the Law Commission has proposed should be abolished (in Report No 158) has created substantial difficulties. Thus, prior to *Bull v Bull* it was possible to argue that as the equitable owners' interests were really in money, they had no right to possession of the property. Furthermore, it could be argued that as these interests were not theoretically interests in land, they could not be overriding interests within s 70(1)(g) LRA. Fortunately, as indicated, *Bull v Bull* makes it clear that the rights of equitable co-owners to possess property after 1925 should be identical to those existing before 1925: Lord Denning rightly regarding the trust for sale as a conveyancing, not a substantive reform. Likewise, *Williams & Glyn's Bank v Boland* and *City of London BS v Flegg* are premised on the assumption that an equitable co-owner's interest behind the trust for sale is really an interest in land: if it were not, the Law of Property Act would have radically altered the nature of proprietary rights by nothing more than a sidewind.

Fortunately, therefore, the potential problems associated with the trust for sale have not caused serious harm for occupiers, although Law Commission Report 181 does recommend that the equitable owner's right of occupation - recognised in *Bull v Bull* - be put on a statutory footing, just in case. This is a precautionary measure but at least it amounts to formal recognition that the trust for sale is there to assist purchasers in the conveyancing process and not to destroy the rights of equitable co-owners to occupy co-owned property. In one respect, however, the effect of the doctrine of conversion has lingered on. In *Perry v Phoenix Assurance*, the court decided that a charging order over an equitable tenancy in common (ie that existing behind a trust for sale) could not be registered as a land charge under the provisions of the Land Charges and Charging Orders Acts. It could not, therefore, be protected should a purchaser acquire the co-owned land. The reason was that such an equitable interest is, under conversion, an interest in money and, therefore, a charging order over it was not an order over an interest in land. Fortunately, the abolition of the doctrine of conversion will reverse this decision.

One of the great problems associated with the trust for sale is, however, something that it would have been very difficult to avoid. As a concomitant to the use of the trust for sale as the mechanism for co-ownership, the 1925 legislation established the principle of overreaching. In simple terms, if the proper conditions are satisfied, a purchaser will be able to obtain the co-owned land without any fear of being bound by the rights of the equitable owners. These rights are not destroyed but are transferred to the purchase money. However, two problems arise in this respect. First, the overreaching machinery - and indeed the Law of

Property Act itself - assumes that there will always be two trustees for sale, in other words that overreaching will always be possible. In this respect, the implied trust for sale explained in *Bull v Bull* might never have been intended (see *Harpum* (1992) CLJ 54). However, whether or not the single trustee situation was ever intended to give rise to a trust for sale at all, the practical effect of the principles established in *Pettitt v Pettitt* and *Lloyds Bank v Rosset* is that there are many domestic situations where property will be co-owned in equity but where there will only be one legal owner and, after *Bull*, one trustee for sale that cannot overreach. The consequence is, of course, that a purchaser can easily be bound by the equitable owner's rights and in circumstances where they would have had no opportunity of discovering the existence of the equitable owner let alone that they had an interest - see eg *Kingsnorth v Tizzard* and *Chhokar v Chhokar*. This is the *Boland* principle, and it was once viewed with such horror by the Law Commission that they recommended its legislative repeal. Now, of course, it is highly regarded by those (including the Law Commission) who realise that the trust for sale and the overreaching provisions should protect occupiers as well as purchasers of co-owned land. Indeed, the solution to the *Boland* 'problem' lies, in most cases, in the hands of the purchaser (ie his solicitors) and the mortgagee. Given the high probability that domestic property will be co-owned by husband and wife or man and woman (or, indeed, by whoever is co-occupying), even if this is not declared in the title deeds, a wise and prudent purchaser should insist on the appointment of another trustee whenever faced with a purchase or mortgage of domestic property seemingly owned by one person. This might be expensive, but it is less expensive than a useless purchase or a useless security.

The other considerable difficulty of the trust for sale - at the other end of the spectrum - is typified by *City of London BS v Flegg*. While it is true that the purchaser may well end up bound by equitable rights if he pays the purchase money to one trustee, *Flegg* shows us that there is nothing the equitable owner can do to remain in the property should there be a sale to two trustees. Overreaching, when it does occur, is powerful and compelling: the equitable rights are transferred to money and neither occupation, registration or notice can help. This side effect of the trust for sale is clearly out of place where co-owned property is used for domestic occupation. Of course, in 1925 the incidence of domestic co-ownership was considerably less than 1992 but this means only that reform must come. To this end, the Law Commission have now recommended that even where there are two trustees (they once recommended that *Boland* should be overturned and then there was just one trustee!), an adult beneficiary in occupation should not be overreached without their consent. This is, of course, to turn the wheel full circle and take us back to the pre-1925 days when the purchaser had to obtain the consent of any and every co-owner before a sale of land could take place. Undoubtedly, social and economic pressures are different now, but we must accept, if these proposals are pursued, that the Law Commission is suggesting that we drive a very large hole through the original scheme of the 1925 legislation. Perhaps a better way forward is to adopt the recommendation contained in Law Commission Report 181, whereby binding limits could be placed on trustees powers (at present only recommended for express trusts). At least then if a residential house was the subject of co-ownership some protection could be given while at the same time preserving the conveyancing advantages for other circumstances of co-ownership.

The use of the trust for sale to regulate concurrent ownership was, in 1925, a remarkable reform. It is still a considerable advancement on pre-1925 principles. However, changing social and economic needs - particularly the rise of residential co-ownership and the equal distribution between men and women of property owning rights - means that some changes in the operation of the machinery may well be necessary for the next century.

Notes

This is all about Law Commission Reports, especially 158, 181 and 188. Without having understood their proposals this question cannot be answered.

Successive Interests in Land

Introduction

Although it is becoming less frequent, it was once quite common
for property to be left to one person for their life, then to another,
then to another and so on. These are successive interests in land
and they arise when one person is entitled to the possession of
land in succession to another, a typical example being where land
is left to A for life, with remainder to B for life, remainder to C in
fee simple. In such a case, A has a life interest in possession (and
is known somewhat confusingly as the 'life tenant'), B has a life
interest in remainder (and will be the life tenant when A dies) and
C has a fee simple in remainder (and will become the absolute
owner on the death of A and B).

The reasons for creating successive interests can, of course, be
many and varied, although one very common reason was so that
land could be 'kept in the family' by limiting its ownership to
successive heirs (subject to the perpetuity rules). Nowadays, this
is less of a motivating factor, although successive interests may
still be created in family or commercial relationships where the
settlor desires to make provision for several persons out of his
land. Today, there are essentially two methods of creating
successive interests: first, under a settlement (or strict settlement
as it is sometimes called) or, secondly, under a trust for sale. The
first is now governed by the Settled Land Act 1925 which did
much to free 'settled land' from the confines of the settlement so
that it became more alienable and more useful to the persons
interested in it, particularly the tenant for life. It was used most
often for 'family' arrangements. The trust for sale, on the other
hand, is more attuned to business ventures, for it allows the
trustees to sell the land, converting it into money, and using the
income and capital to make provision for the persons entitled
under the trust deed. Trusts for sale are outside the scope of the
Settled Land Act and are dealt with separately under the
provisions of the Law of Property Act.

There is no doubt that the law of successive interests is
complicated, especially when there is a settlement and the Settled
Land Act is called into play. It is no accident that the courts seek

to avoid the invocation of the Settled Land Act if a plaintiff can be satisfied without being granted a life estate under the Settled Land Act (see eg Chapter 3 on constructive trusts and Chapter 6 on proprietary estoppel).

Checklist

Generally, however, a student needs to have a working knowledge of the Settled Land Act, of the scope of the powers of the tenant for life, of the controls placed on the tenant for life and of the differences between the settlement and the trust for sale as a means of regulating successive ownership. An awareness of the history of settled land is also helpful.

Question 16

Compare and contrast the strict settlement and the trust for sale as a means of creating and regulating successive interests in land.

Answer plan

- the nature of successive interests
- salient features of the settlement and trust for sale
- relative advantages and disadvantages
- suitability for particular situations
- proposals for reform

Answer

Land can be said to be held in successive ownership when two or more persons are entitled to enjoyment of that land (or the income from it) in succession to each other, as opposed to simultaneous enjoyment which is the hallmark of co ownership. Originally, the purpose of such arrangements was to ensure that family land remained as family land, although it is now clear that successive ownership can be used in a commercial context also. Before 1925, the two methods of creating successive ownership - the settlement and the trust for sale - were subject to the same statutory controls

(Settled Land Acts 1882 and 1884) although for various reasons this was not satisfactory. After 1925, however, settlements are governed by the Settled Land Act 1925 but land subject to 'an immediate binding trust for sale' is excluded from it (s 1(7) SLA) and is governed instead by the provisions of the Law of Property Act 1925.

In general terms, a settlement occurs where land is left on trust for someone for life, with remainder to another, perhaps also with provision for others (such as a widow) by way of rentcharges. The Settled Land Act does, indeed, define settled land, and generally this is land limited in trust for any persons by way of succession, or land limited in trust for an infant for an estate in fee simple or term of years absolute in possession or, where land is charged by way of a family arrangement with the payment of any sums for the benefit of any persons (eg *Re Austen*). As opposed to this, the trust for sale arises where land is held on an immediate trust by trustees with a duty to sell the land and apply the income and capital for the benefit of the persons entitled under the trust. This usually means the payment of income to someone for life, with the capital on death to another person, subject again to ancillary payments being made to other persons. It is quite likely, given the duty to sell in a trust for sale (and despite the existence of a power to postpone), that the original trust property (land) has long since been replaced by other assets, such as shares, general investments and the like. The differences between these two concepts are not, however, merely that they operate under different statutory codes, or even that one (the settlement) is likely to remain as land while the other is likely to have been turned into money. There are also crucial differences of aim, purpose and operation.

Perhaps the most fundamental point of distinction between the two concepts is the location of legal title to the land and effective control over it. In a settlement, it is axiomatic that in most cases legal title to the land will be vested in the tenant for life, not the trustees of the settlement. Likewise, it is the tenant for life that has the important powers granted by the SLA to deal with the land. This is no accident, because before 1925, legal title could be in the trustees or split up among several beneficiaries and this made dealing with settled land a painful experience. Now, the legal title is vested solely in the tenant for life, for they are the person in immediate possession of the land and they are the person who may best judge how to deal with the land. Of course, it is not surprising that the tenant for life is trustee of both the legal title and the powers for the other persons entitled under the settlement (s 107 SLA) but that does not diminish the fact that it is the tenant that is in effective control of the land. In a trust for sale, on the other hand, it is the trustees that have legal title and who have all of the powers to deal with the land. It is they who control the land or its capital value and they who decide whether the land should be sold or retained. Indeed, it is this difference in the location of control that makes the settlement and the trust for sale suitable for different purposes. The settlement is suited to family arrangements where the present occupier of the land can be expected to manage it for the good of the family with, of course, the ability to deal with the land (and sell it) if the need should arise. In contrast, the trust for sale is ideal for commercial arrangements where the land as such is unimportant when compared to the desire to provide an investment for successive persons. Likewise, a trust for sale is useful if the settlor believes the tenant for life to be incompetent or untrustworthy or where the settlor wishes to provide for persons equally. A settlement, in contrast, will be used where the settlor wishes to favour one person (eg an eldest son) and to make subsidiary gifts to others.

Secondly, while it is true that the tenant for life does have control of the settled land, the Act makes it clear that a number of restraints can be placed on their dealing with the land. Thus, the powers and legal estate are held on trust, the exercise of powers can be made subject to specific consents and the trustees of the settlement have certain residual rights and general supervisory functions in respect of the settlement, *Wheelwright v Walker*. In the trust for sale, however, the trustees for sale are largely unfettered in their control of the land. They can, indeed, exercise those powers for which the tenant for life would have needed consent. Of course, being trustees, the trustees for sale are subject to the normal rules controlling persons in a fiduciary position and their powers can be made subject to the consent of specific persons (s 28(1) LPA), but this is very different from the existence of automatic restrictions such as those binding the tenant for life. It is now a matter of some debate as to whether it is easier to control the more informal trust for sale or the much more complicated strict settlement.

Thirdly, because of the complicated workings of the Settled Land Act, there are circumstances when the tenant for life will not have legal title and then it becomes difficult to determine where that legal title lay. So, for example, where the life tenant is an infant or the settlement establishes no life tenant, the powers and the legal estate may variously be vested in the trustees, the settlor's personal representatives or any person on whom such powers are conferred expressly by the settlement. Likewise, on the death of the tenant for life, the legal estate can be transferred only by vesting deeds: an expensive process. However, in a trust for sale, the trustees always have the legal title, irrespective of the complicated nature of the beneficiaries interests or the circumstances surrounding the establishment of the trust. In addition, on the death of a trustee for sale, legal title passes automatically to the remaining trustees under the right of survivorship without the need for any documentation.

Moreover, there are further problems when the settlement or trust for sale arises informally. So, in *Ungarian v Lesnoff*, the informal rights created in the plaintiff's favour were held to be a life interest but, of course, she had no legal title to the land as it still remained in the unwitting settlor. This could have been disastrous for her, as a life interest cannot amount to an overriding interest under the Land Registration Act 1925 (s 86(2)) and can only bind a potential purchaser if registered as a minor interest. Such registration is, of course, completely unlikely when the interest arises informally. In such circumstances, the life tenant is in a very vulnerable position. In an informally created trust for sale, however, it is now trite law that a beneficiary's interest can be overriding (ie by virtue of actual occupation, s 70(1)(g), *Williams & Glyn's Bank v Boland*) and that they will almost certainly be protected for this reason against a purchaser.

Indeed, on the whole, the trust for sale is generally regarded as the better model for the creation of successive interests. It is easier to create, easier to operate and hence less expensive for all concerned. Of course, the settlement does have some advantages. Thus, on a sale of settled land, a purchaser who deals in good faith is protected against the claims of the beneficiaries and does not need to see the trust instrument (s 110 SLA). In a trust for sale, on the other hand, if overreaching cannot occur (usually because there is but one trustee for sale in an impliedly created trust, *Bull v Bull*), the purchaser would be wise to 'look behind the curtain' and search out the beneficial interests so as to avoid being bound by them through the doctrine of notice (unregistered land) or an overriding interest (registered land). Again, joint-tenant trustees for sale have a duty to sell and must do so in the event of disagreement, whereas joint-tenants for life have only a power of sale and must retain the land in the event of disagreement. This is an advantage for the settlement if it is desired to retain the land. Trustees for sale will often be compelled to sell under their paramount duty (*Jones v Challenger*), whereas joint-tenants for life will not be ordered to sell unless the refusal of one of them is made mala fides, *Re 90 Thornhill Road*. Yet, these are relatively small points that pale into insignificance beside the monolithic and complicated body of the Settled Land Act. The defects in the trust for sale have been addressed by the Law Commission and if acted upon will go a long way to meet the concerns just raised (Law Com. Reports Nos 181, 188). Likewise, it is no surprise that the Law Commission have proposed the abolition of the strict settlement as a means of creating successive interests in land (Report 181) on the ground that it is unnecessary, unwieldy and more of a hindrance than a help to a potential settlor.

Notes

Although a long question, the answer is not difficult providing that the student has a working understanding of the Settled Land Act and the Trust for Sale. An even fuller answer would consider the Law Commission's proposals in Report No 181 in more detail.

Question 17

Analyse the powers given to a tenant for life under a strict settlement by the Settled Land Act 1925. Can a wayward tenant be controlled in the exercise of those powers?

Answer plan

- the nature of a settlement
- the position of the tenant for life in relation to the trustees and other beneficiaries
- the powers of the tenant for life
- the controls of the trustees

Answer

It is in the nature of a settlement under the Settled Land Act 1925 that there may be many occasions for conflict between the persons intended to be benefited by the settlor. A settlement necessarily gives one person a life interest in the property (the tenant for life) and another (or others) interests in the land after that life estate has ended. In this sense, therefore, two often contradictory interests need to be reconciled: the interest of the life tenant in actual possession of the property who wishes to enjoy the land (or the income it generates) during their life, and the interest of the persons entitled in remainder in keeping as much value locked into the settlement until their interest falls in on the life tenant's death. Prior to 1925, it was the persons entitled in remainder that held the upper hand as it was relatively easy to restrict the life tenant's ability to deal with the land or diminish its value. Unfortunately, this meant that much settled land stagnated because the tenant for life had no means of raising the money necessary to use the land profitably. Indeed, given that the tenant for life's rights over the land were so limited, there was little incentive for them to manage the land effectively. Now, the position has changed, as it is a fundamental feature of the Settled Land Act 1925 that the tenant for life shall have both the legal estate in the land and extensive powers to deal with it, even to the point of selling it and converting all the beneficiaries' interests into money.

In the normal course of events, when the settlement is created, the settlor will appoint trustees of the settlement and in some exceptional circumstances they will have legal title and the powers conferred by the Act. In the normal case, however, these powers and the title will rest with the tenant for life. Of course, being trustees, the persons so appointed will have fiduciary responsibilities to all the beneficiaries, especially those entitled in remainder and, as *Wheelwright v Walker* makes clear, the trustees have a general supervisory function in relation to the settlement. This can result in an application to the court to control the tenant for life. However, the SLA makes it clear in no uncertain terms that the policy of behind the Act (encouraging the proper use of settled land) will be best served by giving considerable control to the tenant for life.

In brief terms, the Act gives the tenant for life a wide range of powers and then subjects them to varying degrees of control by the trustees. Thus, a life tenant has a power of sale over the land (which will overreach the beneficial interests), although he is obliged to obtain the best price that can reasonably be made, *Wheelwright v Walker (No 2)*. There is also the power to exchange the land, to grant and accept leases, to mortgage the land in order to raise funds for its benefit and to grant options over the land. All of these powers may be exercised without the consent of the trustees, providing that the tenant gives written notice to the trustees and their solicitor, although it is clear from *Wheelwright* that if there are no trustees these powers cannot be exercised. However, even if the trustees have been given notice in the appropriate manner, they are under no obligation to interfere (*England v Public Trustee*) and they may accept less than the required one months notice or waive it in writing altogether. Indeed, except for the power of mortgaging, the tenant for life may give general notice that he intends to exercise his powers at some point and this will suffice. In any event, under s 110 SLA, a purchaser from the tenant for life is protected against non-compliance by the life tenant. These are, of course, fairly limited and relaxed controls and it is unlikely that they give great comfort to the other beneficiaries under the settlement. In respect of other powers - such as the power to dispose of the main house, to cut and sell timber, to sell chattels and to compromise claims - there is more control as these depend variously on obtaining the consent of the trustees or of the court. As such this is not surprising, as these powers relate to those matters of a more personal nature (ie as opposed to the land itself) in which the other beneficiaries may well have a legitimate interest. Even so, the fact that the tenant for life can sell the land with only minimal intervention by the trustees speaks volumes for the policy operating behind this statute.

Indeed, the matter is even clearer when we realise that it is virtually impossible to restrict the tenant for life in the exercise of his powers, other than under the mild provisions of the statute. Thus, under s 106 SLA, any provision in the settlement which attempts or purports to forbid the exercise of a statutory power by the tenant for life or which attempts, tends or is intended to induce the tenant for life not to exercise a power is void. Thus, in *Re Patten*, certain gift overs of property which would de facto induce the tenant for life not to sell (and thereby not lose the property subject to the gifts over) were void. Likewise in *Re Orelebar*, a provision which forfeited the life tenant's interest if they quit the land was held void if their leaving was due to an exercise of a statutory power, although it would be upheld if the tenant for life left for any other reason. Some limitation on this very wide protection for the life tenant was provided by *Re Aberconway* which decided that if what might be lost to the life tenant by virtue of an exercise of a power was not a benefit nor ancillary to his enjoyment of the land, s 106 would not operate to invalidate that stipulation. In similar vein, the tenant for life cannot give up his powers, even if parting with all his interest, *Re Mundy*, although a surrender to the person next entitled (s 105 SLA), order of the court (SLA s 24) and cases of lunacy can lead to those powers being exercised by other persons.

Perhaps, indeed, the only real control over the tenant for life arises under the general equitable jurisdiction to restrain breach of trust and supervise the actions of fiduciaries. By virtue of s 107 SLA, the tenant for life is deemed to be trustee for the beneficiaries of both the legal estate and the statutory powers. This means, in effect, that he must have regard to the interests of others when exercising his powers. On sale, therefore, the life tenant must sell as fairly as any trustee would sell, for the best price and recognising the interest of the remainderman, *Wheelwright v Walker*. Likewise, the tenant cannot accept payment in order to exercise his powers (*Chandler v Bradley*) as he is under a trustee's duty not to profit from his trust. There can be no fraud on the power (*Middlemas v Stevens*), but the transaction will not be invalidated simply because the tenant had an uncharitable motive, such as lack of interest in the land or dislike for the remainderman, *Cardigan v Curzon-Howe*. Of course, the extent of this general equitable jurisdiction is as flexible as it needs to be and it is supported by the ability under s 24 SLA for an application to be made where a tenant for life has definitely refused (although not merely neglected) to exercise his powers under the Act, *Re 90 Thornhill Road*.

Finally, we must note that s 18 SLA gives a measure of protection to the other beneficiaries by providing that any transaction not authorised by the Act shall be invalidated (*Weston v Henshaw*), although it is not clear how this gels with the strong protection given to a purchaser who deals in good faith with the tenant for life under s 110 (*Re Morgan*).

All in all then, the tenant for life has a very wide measure of control over settled land and the trustees of the settlement can do little to restrain him save in clear cases of abuse. This is entirely consistent with the purposes behind the Settled Land Act: that use of land takes precedence over the motives of the settlor in trying to tie up land for his family.

Notes

A bookwork question needing much citation from the Settled Land Act. If more detail is required, the complicated arguments about how *Weston v Henshaw* and *Re Morgan* can be reconciled may be pursued.

Leases

Introduction

Leasehold interests are one of the two estates (along with freeholds) that are capable of existing at law or in equity - s 1 Law of Property Act 1925. All other estates, such as the fee tail and life estate, can exist in equity only. In fact, the leasehold estate, whether it be equitable or legal, is one of the most versatile concepts throughout the whole of the law of real property. Indeed, even the terminology of leases reflects the many purposes to which they may be put. The 'term of years', 'tenancies', 'sub-leases', and 'leasehold estate' are all synonymous and in terms of the legal rules governing their creation and operation the principles are the same, although one particular description may be more appropriate than another depending on the situation. So, for example, the term 'lease' is most often used for commercial or long term lettings whereas the term 'tenancy' is used for 'domestic' or shorter term lettings.

One of the most important feature of leaseholds is that they allow two or more estate owners to enjoy the benefits of the same piece of land and the same time: for example, the freeholder will receive the rent and profits and the leaseholder will enjoy physical possession and occupation of the property. Indeed, if a 'sub-tenancy' is involved, one lease will be carved out of another as where a freeholder, L, grants land to A for 30 years, who sublets to B for 25 years, who sublets to C for 10 years and so on. It is this ability of the leasehold estate to facilitate multiple enjoyment of land that gives it its special character. In addition, it is inherent in a lease that the rights and obligations undertaken by the original landlord and tenant concerning the land can be transmitted to persons who later step into the shoes of the original parties, as where a landlord assigns the reversion or the tenant assigns the lease. The ability to make duties and obligations 'run' with the land is a special feature of the 'privity of estate' that exists between landlord and tenant and their respective successors.

Checklist

Questions on leasehold interests are a favourite for examiners, not least because they offer such diversity. In order to tackle questions concerning leases, the student must have an understanding of several important issues:

A) The methods of creation of leasehold interests and the differences between equitable and legal leases

B) The difference in theory and practice between a 'lease' and a 'licence'

C) The place of leasehold interests, both equitable and legal, within the machinery of registered and unregistered land

D) The rules relating to covenants in leases: types of covenants and the enforceability of leasehold covenants between the original parties and their successors in title

E) The remedies for breach of leasehold covenants, with particular reference to the remedy of forfeiture

F) The determination of leases

Question 18

What is a lease?

Answer plan

- definition of a lease: *Street v Mountford*
- time certain: *Lace v Chandler, Prudential Assurance v London Residuary Body*
- exclusive possession
- rent
- sections 52 and 54 Law of Property Act 1925
- periodic tenancies
- section 2 Law of Property (Miscellaneous Provisions) Act 1989
- *Walsh v Lonsdale*

Answer

By virtue of s 1 Law of Property Act 1925, a term of years absolute in possession is one of the two estates in land that may exist either at law or in equity. The term of years (or lease) is consequently one of the major forms of land ownership in England and Wales. It is, in addition, a concept of considerable versatility that can provide both occupation in a domestic or commercial enterprise, as well as income for the freeholder and even the leaseholder if the premises are sublet. It is, indeed, a peculiar feature of the leasehold estate that it can give several different estate-owners the use or enjoyment of the land or its profits at the same time.

According to *Street v Mountford*, a lease can be defined as exclusive possession of property, for a term, at a rent. These three conditions are commonly regarded as the indicia of a leasehold, irrespective of the purpose for which the estate is created. It is clear, however, from *Ashburn Anstalt v Arnold* (relying on s 205 LPA) that rent is not essential to the existence of a lease although it will be a rare situation indeed where the parties to a transaction have intended to be legally bound by the relationship of landlord and tenant but have not specified the payment of rent. With this in mind, rent will be discussed below as if it were synonymous with the existence of a tenancy.

In addition to the principles established by *Street* which are, in fact, conditions required by the common law, the nature of leases is also governed by various statutory provisions. These provisions are largely to be found in the Law of Property Act 1925 and determine whether any particular lease is legal or equitable. Briefly, the position is that any lease for a period of more than three years must be by deed if it is to take effect as a legal estate (s 52 LPA). Leases for three years or less that give the tenant an immediate right to occupy without the payment of an initial premium may also be legal (s 54 LPA) and into this category come many short term periodic tenancies, mainly governing domestic occupancy. Equitable leases, on the other hand usually result from a binding contract between landlord and tenant that has not been put into effect by deed. If this contract is in writing (s 2 Law of Property (Miscellaneous Provisions) Act 1989) and can be specifically enforceable, equity will regard the relationship between the parties as one governed by an equitable lease on the same terms as the negotiated (but unexecuted) legal lease - *Walsh v Lonsdale*. The exception to this are equitable leases arising out of proprietary estoppel. These can be completely oral and arise out of the inequitable conduct of the landlord - see *Taylor Fashions v Liverpool Victoria Trustees*.

Turning, then, to the position at common law. These requirements define the inherent nature of a lease and set the parameters outside of which a lease simply cannot exist, irrespective of the statutory conditions. The most important, and over the last few years the most troublesome, is the requirement of time certain or, in other words, the requirement that the lease must exist for a clearly defined period of time. This means not only that the lease must start at a clearly defined moment, but also that the term granted must be certain. The lease must be of certain maximum duration at the commencement of the lease. Any lease, or rather any intended lease, that fails to satisfy this condition is necessarily void because it does not amount to a term. In *Lace v Chandler*, for example, a lease for the duration of the second world war was held void as being of uncertain maximum duration. In recent years, however, the principle of time certain has been under attack and courts have been willing to accept arrangements which on a proper construction could not be said to have a certain term. In *Ashburn Anstalt v Arnold*, an arrangement whereby a tenant occupied property indefinitely until the landlord gave three months notice was held to be a lease on the ground that the term could be rendered certain by action of one of the parties. This does seem to contradict the rule that a lease must be certain at the date of its commencement and it came as no surprise when, in 1992, the House of Lords in *Prudential Assurance v London Residuary Body* reaffirmed the rule that a leasehold term must be certain from the outset and it is not enough that the term can in fact be rendered certain by action of either the landlord or the tenant after the lease has commenced. This is a significant and welcome return to the orthodox position. Finally, one further point needs to be borne in mind when talking about time certain. It often happens that a tenant may occupy premises and pay a regular sum to the landlord in respect of that occupation. There may well be no written record of this arrangement. In these circumstances, a tenancy of a certain duration will be presumed from the facts. Thus, if money is paid weekly in respect of a week's occupation, a periodic tenancy of one week will be presumed and likewise if payment is made monthly or quarterly. Obviously, if a further week's, month's or quarterly payment is made, the lease will continue and can in this sense continue indefinitely so long as the payment is made. However, although such a situation appears to be a lease for an uncertain period, in fact it is a succession of periodic tenancies; that is, one week after one week or one month after one month and so on. These relatively short term periodic tenancies are common in residential lettings and should not be thought to contradict the principle of time certain.

The other external conditions for the existence of a lease are not so controversial although they may be just as difficult to identify in practice. The concept of exclusive possession is notoriously elusive as can be seen in the confused and confusing debate over the distinction between a lease and a licence. In essence, the existence of exclusive possession is a matter for the construction of the agreement between the parties in the light of their conduct in relation to the property, *Antoniades v Villiers*. Thus, if the occupier has been granted the exclusive right to use the property, even to the exclusion of the landlord, then there is a strong presumption that the agreement amounts to a lease. The only exceptions to this are in those circumstances identified by Lord Templeman in *Street* where, because of some special circumstance, exclusive possession may exist but a tenancy does not. An example is the service occupancy of *Norris v Checksfield* and cases where occupiers enjoy property through acts of generosity or friendship where there is no intention to create legal relations, as in *Heslop v Burns*.

Finally, we come to rent, the receipt of which is usually the main reason why the landlord has granted the tenancy in the first place. As noted above, under s 205 LPA, it is clear that rent is not an essential requirement of a lease, although certain types of tenancies such as those within the Rent Acts must be supported by rent to qualify for statutory protection. Indeed, that is why in *Street* Lord Templeman refers to rent, that being a case concerning the application of the Rent Acts. In fact, the existence of rent as an adjunct to a lease is so likely that, in the absence of an express promise by the tenant, a covenant to pay rent can easily be implied from the words of a deed. It is, however, a common misconception that rent has to be in monetary form. It can be in goods, services, or payable in kind. The only clear requirement is that the amount of rent must be capable of being rendered certain. Thus, in *Bostock v Bryant*, the obligation to pay fluctuating utility bills could not be regarded as rent, being an uncertain sum.

The defining features of the leasehold estate have been described above and reference to its versatility has been made. This versatility is reflected in the terminology of leasehold estates where 'term of years', 'lease', 'tenancy', 'periodic tenancy' and 'sublease' all describe situations within which the relationship of landlord and tenant can exist. That relationship has many advantages, both for the landlord and the tenant (eg simultaneous enjoyment of property, leasehold covenants, occupation or income generation) and that is why it has survived the many statutory reforms of the law of real property in the twentieth century.

Question 19

Are there any significant differences between the creation and the operation of legal, as opposed to equitable leases?

Answer plan

- sections 52 and 54 Law of Property Act 1925
- periodic tenancies
- section 2 Law of Property (Miscellaneous Provisions) Act 1989
- *Walsh v Lonsdale*
- registered and unregistered land
- leasehold covenants
- section 62 LPA

Answer

Under s 52 of the Law of Property Act 1925, all legal leases except those which are exempt under s 52(2) must be created by deed. This is the basic principle in respect of the creation of legal leases. The exception granted by statute is for those leases which take effect in possession for not more than three years without a fine. This is merely a complicated way of saying that leases for three years or less which entitle the tenant to go into immediate possession and which require only the payment of rent and not an initial lump sum are legal leases without the need for a deed. Thus, the periodic tenancy, where an occupier goes into occupation and pays a defined sum for a period usually of one week, one month or one quarter, will amount to a legal tenancy because the rent will be paid in respect of periods of less than three years. It matters not that, in fact, the periodic tenant may occupy for many years because in theory this is just a succession of periodic tenancies. Of course, this means that the tenancy can be determined by the giving of one period's notice but while it continues it is legal in character. In fact, the provisions of ss 52 and 54 are relatively simple but they only tell us how legal leases can be created. What of leases that take effect in equity only?

It is not often that equitable leases are deliberately created. They are usually the product of an unsuccessful attempt to create a legal lease; unsuccessful, that is, because the formalities of s 52 have not been observed. All leases start out as a result of a contract or agreement between the prospective landlord and the prospective tenant (cf below estoppel leases). In the normal course of events this contract will be executed by means of a deed and a legal lease will be created. However, there can be many reasons why this contract to grant a legal lease is never actually executed (ie no deed drawn up) and it is in these circumstances that an equitable lease can result. An equitable lease is in essence a failed legal lease which equity nevertheless treats as valid. In order for this to happen two conditions must be satisfied. First, the contract between the parties must be valid. Before the Law of Property Act 1989 this contract could either be in writing, or orally if supported by acts of part performance by the tenant (s 40 LPA). Now, however, under s 2 Law of Property (Miscellaneous Provisions) Act 1989 (which repeals s 40), all contracts for the disposition of an interest in land must be in writing (except leases for three years or less under s 52(2) LPA). Thus, before an equitable lease can exist, we must have an enforceable contract.

Secondly, this properly created contract must be specifically enforceable, for it is the specific enforceability of the contract that allows it to be regarded as an equitable lease. If the contract is specifically enforceable, this means that it would be executed by order of a court and, because equity regards as done what ought to be done, the unexecuted but enforceable contract will be regarded as an equitable lease, *Walsh v Lonsdale*. Of course, if the contract is in fact carried out, a legal lease by deed will be the result, but usually a dispute arises between the parties simply because there is no deed. A contract will be specifically enforceable if valuable consideration has been paid by the tenant, if damages for breach of contract would be an inadequate remedy and if the person seeking to enforce the contract has not themselves behaved inequitably. Usually these three conditions are easily satisfied (the first two almost by definition) and in most cases an equitable tenancy can be established. Furthermore, *Walsh* makes it clear that if in the circumstances there is a choice between a legal periodic tenancy (because the tenant is in occupation and paying rent) and an equitable tenancy on the same terms as the proposed but defunct lease by deed, the equitable tenancy will take priority as this gives efficacy to the parties agreement. So, for example, any intended covenants in the failed legal lease will take effect in the equitable lease, so far as this is possible.

It is plain to see, then, that the requirements for an equitable lease have changed somewhat since 1989, primarily because of the requirement of writing. There is, however, one small exception to this. It may still be possible to create a lease longer than three years entirely out of oral agreements providing that those oral agreements amount to a proprietary estoppel within the rules of *Taylor Fashions v Liverpool Victoria Trustees*. So, if a landlord assures an occupier that they have a tenancy and the occupier relies on that to their detriment, an estoppel tenancy may well result. This will be equitable and, even if over three years without writing, would be enforceable against the landlord.

However, despite the apparent ease with which a failed legal lease can yield up an equitable lease on the same terms, it is clear that legal leases do have significant advantages, not least because a purchaser of the freehold reversion will be aware of the existence of a legal tenancy. In registered land, legal leases will either be registered with their own title number (if over 21 years). In any event, the legal lease will be an overriding interest under s 70(1)(g) LRA if, having failed to be registered as a title, it is coupled with actual occupation or under s 70(1)(k) LRA if 21 years or less. Either way, a purchaser of the reversion will be bound by the legal lease. Likewise, in unregistered land, the deed (or fact of occupation under a legal periodic tenancy) will be obvious and, after all, in unregistered land legal rights bind the whole world. As much cannot be said, however, for equitable leases.

Equitable leases are not only difficult for a purchaser of the reversion to discover (although the requirement of writing in the 1989 Act may relieve this somewhat), they can also be easily destroyed on a sale of that reversion. Although these problems are, of course, mutually exclusive, they still generate uncertainty for all the parties to an equitable lease and their successors in title. Like all equitable interests, equitable leases are *prima facie* vulnerable to purchasers, that is, to purchasers of the freehold land over which the lease exists. In unregistered land, for example, the equitable tenant is required to register their interest as a Class C(iv) land charge under the Land Charges Act. Should they fail to do so, the equitable tenancy is not binding on any purchaser of the reversion of a legal estate for money or money's worth - s 4 Land Charges Act. This was just the position in *Hollington Brothers v Rhodes* and no amount of occupation, obvious or otherwise, can help. Moreover, if the equitable lease has resulted from proprietary estoppel, it is probably unregisterable as a land charge.(cf *Ives v High*). In that case, the old doctrine of notice comes into play and that is unsatisfactory for both the purchaser and the equitable tenant.

In registered land, the position is a little more satisfactory, at least for the tenant. Whereas the equitable tenant may protect their interest by way of notice as a minor interest, they may rely in the alternative on s 70(1)(g) LRA to gain an overriding interest as a person in actual occupation of the premises. Of course, this is all very well for the equitable tenant, but the purchaser of the reversion may well become bound by an interest that was informally created. Of course, in many cases the fact of occupation (and hence the equitable lease) may well be obvious and a purchaser is warned of the overriding interest, but that might not always be the case, especially with estoppel leases that can still be entirely oral.

Further difficulties with equitable leases also arise in the context of leasehold covenants. Generally, while covenants in equitable leases will be enforceable between the original landlord and the original equitable tenant (because of privity of contract), they may well be unenforceable between successors in title to those persons. Being an equitable lease (and despite contrary dicta in *Boyer v Warby*), the traditional view is that there is no 'privity of estate' between a successor to the landlord and an assignee of the tenant: there is no legal estate with which to be 'privy'. In fact, it is the landlord that suffers most in this situation because the burden of covenants entered into by the original tenant (that is the obligation to perform them) may well not be passed to an assignee of an equitable lease, unless they can be enforced as restrictive covenants under *Tulk v Moxhay*. Indeed, it is worse than this because the new equitable reversioner is under the burdens of the equitable lease as these are statutorily transmitted on a sale of the reversion by s 142 LPA. Thus, the new landlord can be sued on the original covenants of an equitable lease but unless *Tulk* applies he cannot sue the new tenant.

Finally, there are some provisions of the Law of Property Act relating to conveyances of land that apply only to conveyances of a legal estate. The most important of these in practice is s 62 LPA which is often used to imply easements into a tenancy in favour of the tenant; for example an easement of way. Unfortunately, s 62 is restricted to transfer of a legal estate and cannot be relied upon by an equitable tenant. Any easements would, therefore, have to be expressly created in their favour.

Ultimately, then, it is better for all parties if a legal lease is established. Not only is the equitable lease dependent on the availability of specific performance, its informal nature poses problems for purchaser and tenant alike.

Notes

The first two questions really require a thorough understanding of the nature of a lease and its method of creation. Apart from being relatively straightforward, such knowledge is required when dealing with problems from other areas, such as the mechanism of registered and unregistered land. Recent developments which may cause problems are the effect of s 2 Law of Property (Miscellaneous Provisions) Act on the creation of equitable leases and the controversy - hopefully now settled by *Prudential* - over 'time certain'.

Question 20

In 1985, Lord Templeman in *Street v Mountford* stated that the defining features of a lease were exclusive possession, for a term, at a rent. Is this still the case?

Answer plan

- the existence of rights v intention of the parties
- lodgers and tenants
- exceptions to exclusive possession
- *Antoniades v Villiers*; *Westminster CC v Clarke*

Answer

A lease is a proprietary right, an interest in land capable of binding third parties. Despite some suggestions to the contrary (eg *Errington v Errington & Woods*), a licence is a personal right, usually arising out of contract, which as a matter of principle is not capable of binding third parties under property law principles (*Ashburn Anstalt v Arnold*). It is from this basic distinction that so many practical consequences flow. Indeed, the great majority of cases on the lease/licence distinction have been the result of occupiers trying to claim the protection of the 1977 Rent Act, because the protection it offers is available to a tenant of a dwelling house only, not to a licensee. Of course, the ability of landlords to grant non-protected tenancies under the Housing Act 1988 may affect the volume of litigation before the courts on this subject, but the distinction between a lease and a licence forms the boundary between property and contract and will always be contentious.

Lord Templeman's judgment in *Street v Mountford* caused something of a stir. Not only did he propound an abstract test for distinguishing between a lease and a licence ('exclusive possession for a term at a rent'), he told us how to apply it. Firstly, there are certain exceptional situations where the occupier will have exclusive possession of the property but for special reasons no tenancy will result. One example is where a mortgagee goes into possession under the terms of her mortgage and another where the occupation is based on charity or friendship, as where there is no intention to create legal relations between the owner and the occupier. These exempted categories were explained at length in *Facchini v Bryson* and that they are alive and well is demonstrated by *Norris v Checksfield*. In that case, the occupier of a cottage was held to be a 'service occupant' and hence a licensee, although the Court of Appeal did warn that this was an exceptional situation justified only because the occupation of the cottage was for the better performance of the employee's duties. Secondly, apart from the exceptional situations, an occupier must either be a lodger (a licensee) or a tenant.

This practical distinction between a lodger and a tenant is crucial. A lodger is someone who receives attendance and services from the landlord, such as room cleaning or meals. Such a person will be a licensee, although as *Markou v Da Silvaesa* illustrates, a mere promise to provide such services is not sufficient. They must actually be provided. However, if it is true that an occupier is *either* a lodger or a tenant, this means that no other kind of 'occupation licence' can exist. If someone is not a lodger, they are a tenant. There is no intermediate category of licensee who, while not a lodger, is still not a tenant. Obviously, this has far reaching consequences for it restricts the options open to a landlord when seeking to make use of her property. It is the triumph of property law over freedom of contract and it is precisely this that subsequent cases have found difficult to accept. Indeed, many of the apparently inconsistent decisions of the Court of Appeal have resulted from attempts to identify some middle way, some form of occupation that can still give rise to a licence, but where the occupier is not a lodger. *Hadjiloucas v Creen* and *Brooker Estates v Ayers,* both decisions of the Court of Appeal quite soon after *Street*, are of this type.

However, under the influence of Lord Templeman in the House of Lords (eg *Antoniades v Villiers, Westminster CC v Clarke*) and Lord Donaldson in the Court of Appeal (eg *Aslan v Murphy*) a degree of certainty has emerged. Firstly, cases of multiple occupancy may give rise to licences in favour of the occupiers because of the absence of the four unities necessary to support a joint-tenancy of the whole premises. This is the result of *AG Securities v Vaughan*. So, if four people occupy a four bedroom house, but each sign different agreements, on different days and for a different rent, there can be no exclusive possession/joint tenancy because there is no unity of interest, title, or time. The house, as a whole, cannot be held on a tenancy. Each occupier may have a tenancy of their own rooms, with a licence over the common parts, but this may not give Rent Act protection as each separate room may not constitute a 'dwelling house'.

Secondly, there are certain types of public sector landlords who may be able to grant licences in circumstances where a private landlord could not. Examples are *Westminster CC v Basson*, *Ogwr BC v Dykes* and the House of Lords' decision in *Westminster CC v Clarke*. In these cases, the licence is allowed not because of the intention of the landlord - for that would be to return to *Somma v Hazlehurst* - but because of a policy decision *viz* that public sector landlords must not be hindered in the exercise of their statutory housing duties. Of course, in *Family Housing Association v Jones*, a right granted by another public sector landlord was held to be a tenancy, but it may be that this is explained by the fact that the housing in Jones was not done under statutory powers for the relief of emergency cases of homelessness. In some respect, the emerging 'public sector landlord' exemption from the rigours of *Street* is similar to the *Fachini* categories, justified by policy rather than principle.

Thirdly, Lord Oliver in *Antoniades* suggests that there may be circumstances where a landlord can genuinely reserve to himself the right to make use of the premises and, if such use is made, no exclusive possession is given. In effect, this is no more than a restatement of the distinction between exclusive possession and exclusive *occupation*: the former establishing the legal relationship of landlord and tenant, the latter describing a factual situation devoid of proprietary effect. An example might be where an academic lets his house to students but reserves the right to enter the house and use his library. This is, of course, open to abuse and in the light of his speech in *Antoniades*, it is doubtful whether Lord Templeman would agree that it is even a possibility. However, the door has been left open by Lord Oliver for future development in genuine cases.

Finally, all of the above is subject to the doctrine of pretences. Any clause, in any agreement, will not be given legal effect if it is not intended to be relied on by either party to the agreement but is merely inserted to avoid the grant of the tenancy that would otherwise arise. Thus, in *Antoniades* itself, an agreement providing for the separate occupancy of an unmarried couple in what was to be their home was held to be a tenancy because the separate agreements were clearly a pretence. It should be noted in this regard, that the doctrine of 'pretences' has replaced that of shams: a 'sham' transaction is where only one party does not intended a clause in a lease to have legal effect and, of course, a landlord always intends in these cases to deny, by means of a clause like that used as in *Antoniades*, the creation of a lease.

To conclude then, the case law after *Street* has finally taken a decidedly practical path where the emphasis is on identifying those factual situations which can give rise to a licence and those which can give rise to a tenancy. This may not be the most intellectually satisfying approach - after all, we have not defined 'exclusive possession' - but it is the most realistic.

Question 21

Nellie is the registered proprietor of freehold land comprising a large Victorian property in the centre of town. The house has four storeys, including a basement. Nellie has just inherited a small bungalow in the country and has decided to move out. She wishes to let the property but is determined not to have long-term tenants just in case she wants to return to the city. She divides the house into two self-contained, one-bedroomed, apartments on the first and second floors, and one self-contained two-bedroomed flat on the ground floor/basement. She agrees in writing with Ivor and Anne, a young unmarried couple, that they can occupy the two roomed flat and produces two documents which state in each that 'this agreement does not intend to create a term of years' and gets them to sign separately and on different days for a 'fee' of £30 per week each. She lets the first floor flat to Steven, an apprentice builder, who is to carry out repairs to the premises. Steven pays no money, but each week £15 is deducted from his wages. Nellie keeps a key to Steven's flat, primarily to inspect the building works at the weekend when Steven is away. The top floor flat is given to Nellie's son, Tony, a university drop out with nowhere else to go. Tony is not the most reliable individual, so Steven is asked to keep an eye on him and to make sure that he gets regular meals.

Nellie has now decided to move to the country permanently and sells the entire premises to Peter, a property developer. Peter wishes to evict all the occupants and redevelop the site.

Advise him.

Answer plan

- leases and licences
- *Antoniades v Villiers*
- *Street v Mountford*
- *Mikeover v Brady*
- *Aslan v Murphy*
- section 70(1) Land Registration Act 1925

Answer

This problem concerns the distinction between a lease and a licence. A lease is a proprietary right, whereas a licence is a mere personal arrangement between two parties (*Ashburn Anstalt v Arnold*). The practical difference this makes in this problem is clear. If the arrangements entered into by Nellie with her respective occupiers amount to leases, then they have the ability to bind Peter the purchaser when he acquires the freehold title. If, however, the arrangements are properly to be regarded as licences, then in principle they cannot bind Peter and the occupiers will have to vacate the premises.

In general terms, the distinction between a lease and a licence was summarised by Lord Templeman in *Street v Mountford*. A lease exists where an occupier has been granted exclusive possession of the property, for a term, at a rent. The answer is not to be found in the label attached to the agreement by the parties but in the nature of the agreement created by the parties. Not surprisingly, this formula is subject to some exceptions, notably those known as the *Facchini v Bryson* categories which relate to special, limited, factual situations where for some reason, external to the parties, no tenancy will exist even though exclusive possession has been granted. The main practical distinction resulting from Lord Templeman's formula is that an occupier must be either a tenant or a lodger, the latter being someone in receipt of attendance and services from the landlord and so without exclusive possession - *Markou v Da Silvaesa*. Finally, we must also be aware of the doctrine of pretences (see eg *Antoniades v Villiers*), whereby the court will examine an agreement between the parties to discover whether its terms genuinely reflect the actual relationship between the parties. Only if the agreement is 'genuine' in this sense will any clauses in the agreement excluding 'exclusive possession' be given legal effect.

a) Ivor and Anne

Clearly, the agreement between Nellie on the one hand and Ivor and Anne on the other is designed to allow them to occupy the premises and, from Nellie's point of view, to prevent the grant of a tenancy: this much is expressly stated in the documents which both Ivor and Anne sign. At one time, such an express statement of the parties 'intention' (query whether Ivor and Anne can really be said to share this intention) would have been enough to prevent a lease being granted - *Somma v Hazlehurst*. Now, after *Street*, it is clear that it is the nature of the relationship that is important and not what the parties decide to call that relationship. Thus, if this agreement amounts to a lease under the *Street* formula, it will be a lease irrespective of the label attached to it.

Clearly, Nellie has had some well informed legal advice, for she has made every attempt to prevent the couple enjoying exclusive possession. She has, in fact, attempted to deny them a tenancy by seeking to grant each of them a separate licence whereby neither of them has exclusive possession of the whole but each occupies in common with the other. The only way that Ivor and Anne can refute this is to establish that they have been granted exclusive possession jointly: in other words that they are joint-tenants of a leasehold interest. As was made clear in *AG Securities v Vaughan*, for a joint-tenancy of a leasehold estate to exist, the 'four unities' must be present: there must be unity of interest, title, possession and time and this is what Nellie has tried to prevent. In this case, as in *Vaughan* itself, the landlord has persuaded the parties to sign different documents on different days. It looks as if there is no unity of time or of title. In *Vaughan*, these facts, plus the different rents paid by the occupiers, clearly meant that no leasehold joint-tenancy of the whole property could exist. The parties were occupying separately not jointly. Moreover, even if *Vaughan* is not quite in point, because, in that case, the property was always intended to be for independent, ever changing, occupants, Nellie can clearly rely on the decision in *Mikeover v Brady*. In that case, a flat was let to two people by two separate agreements, each responsible for one half of the total 'fee'. Despite the fact that the occupiers wished to co-habit jointly (ie as a couple), the agreements were held to confer separate licences only. The facts of our case are very similar indeed.

Perhaps, however, there is one possibility. In *Antoniades v Villiers*, the appellants were a young couple, living together as if married in a joint home. This fact was known to the landlord. In the House of Lords, this arrangement was held to create a joint-tenancy of the leasehold estate, despite the fact of separate 'licence' agreements similar to those signed by Ivor and Anne. According to Lord Templeman, the landlord's attempt to deny the couple exclusive possession jointly was a pretence designed entirely to avoid the imposition of a lease. As such it would be ignored and the 'true' nature of the parties' bargain respected. If we follow *Antoniades* then, and assuming Nellie knew that Ivor and Anne wished to live together, this agreement may amount to a lease. Despite the fact that separate agreements were signed, and on different days, there will be a joint-tenancy of the leasehold estate because this was the true nature of the bargain.

If the couple do have a lease, then it would appear to be equitable. The agreement is in writing (not by deed and not legal) and probably amounts to a specifically enforceable contract. Assuming this, equity will regard this as an equitable lease under *Walsh v Lonsdale*. When the property is sold to Peter, presumably the couple are in actual occupation and would, therefore, have an overriding interest under s 70(1)(g) LRA. If the lease is not equitable, the arrangement may well amount to a legal periodic tenancy because of rent paid and accepted for the weekly term. If that were true, it would be overriding under s 70(1)(k) LRA. Of course, the lease is binding on Peter only according to its terms. He may terminate it on giving the appropriate notice unless it is protected by the Rent Acts.

b) Steven

Steven is in occupation of the first floor flat and, again, the nature of his occupancy is crucial in determining whether Peter can acquire immediate possession. Whether or not Steven has a tenancy may well depend on whether Steven's occupancy falls within one of the exceptional categories identified by Lord Templeman in *Street* as being occasions where even though exclusive possession is granted, no tenancy results. As a preliminary point, it might be thought that the apparent lack of rent destroys any chance of a tenancy. However, as confirmed in *Ashburn*, relying on s 205 LPA, the payment of rent is not essential for the existence of a tenancy. Lord Templeman's comments in *Street* should be read in context: viz that the case was concerned with the Rent Acts, under which tenancies do need to be supported by rent to qualify for statutory protection. In any event, we can argue forcefully that the weekly deduction from Steven's wages does amount to rent. There is no rule that 'rent' must be described as such, so long as the payment made is in respect of the right to occupy the demised premises.

Steven's problem is, however, that his occupation seems to be a 'service occupancy'. He appears to be in occupation of the premises for 'the better performance of his duties' as Nellie's employee/builder. A *bona fide* service occupancy clearly creates a licence and was one of the original *Facchini* exceptions. That it still can occur has been confirmed in the recent case of *Norris v Checksfield*. Subject to the warning in that case that the court must be astute to detect 'pretences', as where the occupant is given minimal employment duties to make it appear as if there is a service occupancy, our case seems to fall into this category. If anything, Steven is more like a caretaker than a tenant. Assuming, then, that Steven has a licence by way of service occupancy Peter cannot be bound by the agreement. A mere licence is binding only on the parties and Steven will have to quit.

c) As far as Nellie's son, Tony, is concerned, the circumstances also seem to give rise to a licence. There is every indication that Tony's occupation of the top floor flat can be put down to normal family considerations rather than the creation of a tenancy. As in *Heslop v Burns*, this is not a situation where the parties had an intention to enter into legal relations at all. This is within one of the *Facchini* excepted categories: viz occupation based on friendship, generosity or family arrangement. Moreover, if this were not enough, Nellie could even argue that Tony was a lodger and by definition not a tenant (*Street*). The facts suggest that Tony is in receipt attendance and services as provided by Steven, who may be regarded as Nellie's agent for these purposes. On this interpretation of the facts, Tony could be within *Markou v Da Silvaesa* and a licensee by virtue of a genuine lodger relationship. Once again, there is no possibility of Peter being bound.

So, to conclude, with the possible exception of the arrangement agreed with Ivor and Anne, Nellie has successfully avoided granting any leases over her property. Peter can obtain vacant possession. Finally, we can note that Nellie would have been well advised to have granted new style short term tenancies under the Housing Act 1988. These fall outside the Rent Acts and possession can be recovered easily. This would have avoided all the difficulties Nellie experienced.

Note

Question 3 and 4 are variations on the same theme: the distinction between a lease and a licence. There is a welter of caselaw here and it is easy to get lost. A firm grasp of *Street* and *Antoniades* and *Vaughan* is a good base point. There are, however, always new cases (see the latest issue of the *Student Law Review*) and examiners do tend to concentrate on novel points. The role of the public sector landlord is currently the most litigious aspect of this area.

Question 22

'Although complicated, the law governing the enforceability of leasehold covenants between the original parties to a lease and their successors in title is theoretically coherent and workable in practice'.

Do you agree?

Answer plan

- an outline of the legal framework
- the relationship to the registration systems
- the purpose of the rules
- proposals for reform

Answer

In 1988, the Law Commission produced a Report and a Draft Bill (No 174) containing various proposals for the reform of the law of leasehold covenants. In their view, the need to iron out the idiosyncrasies, the illogicalities and the plain injustices of the present law justified a fundamental reordering of its rules. To this end, the Law Commission set out to resolve what they believed to be two of the most fundamental problems. First, the principle of continuing liability throughout the entire term of the lease for the original landlord and tenant and, secondly, the notoriously elusive concept of covenants that 'touch and concern' the land.

The law of the enforceability of leasehold covenants today revolves around privity of contract, privity of estate and statutory magic. Indeed, the basic principles are clear enough. The original parties to a lease will be bound throughout the entirety of the term to perform the covenants they have agreed to, whether those covenants be personal or not. Thus, both the original landlord (*Stuart v Joy*) and the original tenant (*Arlesford Trading Co v Servansingh*) can be sued for failure to perform the leasehold covenants by the person who enjoys the benefit of those covenants irrespective of the time the breach was committed or by whom. This is the principle of continuing liability and it flows from the very nature of a lease as a contract. Of course, it is open to the original parties of a lease to stipulate expressly that their liability shall be limited to the period in which they enjoyed possession but as the Law Commission point out, this is quite unlikely especially for a tenant in what is typically a landlord's market. The continuing liability of the landlord and tenant is a primary one, so that they may be sued on the covenants even though the plaintiff has an obvious remedy against the person actually committing the breach, such as an assignee.

These rules can cause hardship to either landlord or tenant but it was the position of the latter that caused the Law Commission greatest concern, especially as resort to original tenants by landlords faced with an impecunious assignee seemed to be on the increase. In their view, not only did the continuing liability of the tenant distort the public perception of the nature of the landlord and tenant relationship (ie that liability is co-extensive with possession) it could also cause hardship to tenants who, many years after parting with possession, found themselves liable to perform repairing or other obligations undertaken many years ago and now remaining unperformed by some tenant over whom they had no control: as where the current tenant is a third or fourth assignee. Indeed, the continuing liability even extends to variations of the original covenants, as where the rent is raised by a later rent review in which the original tenant plays no part, as in *Centrovincial Estates Ltd v Bulk Storage*. Likewise the original tenant's liability continues if the lease is extended by the exercise of an option to renew contained in the original lease (*Bayton v Morgan*) and even if the lease is extended by statute, as where an assignee gains the benefit of statutory holdover, *Herbert Duncan Ltd v Cluttons* (but see contra *City of London Corporation v Fell*). Of course, the original tenant can always obtain an express indemnity from an assignee, and in any event one will be implied in most cases, (s 77 LPA 1925, s 24 LRA 1925, or *Moule v Garrett*) but this is useless if the assignee is bankrupt, as may well be the case if the original tenant is being sued.

The Law Commission's view of all of this was to disregard the policy behind the principle of continuing liability (that a tenant should take care to assign to a worthy successor) and to propose that when a tenant assigns a leasehold interest, they would be released automatically from all liability in respect of any future breaches of the covenants. The only exception would be where an assignment by the tenant is conditional on the landlord's consent, in which case the landlord could impose a condition whereby the original tenant would guarantee the performance of the covenants by the immediate assignee. However, unlike the situation now, any continuing liability could not extend beyond one assignment and it would truly be a guarantee, such that the landlord would have to look to the assignee first in the event of breach.

Strangely, however, the Law Commission did not feel that it was as pressing to protect the landlord from continuing liability under their covenants. Thus, under these proposals, a landlord would remain liable for breaches of covenants committed by his successors unless he served a notice on the tenant indicating his desire to be released. Should the tenant disagree, the matter would be resolved in Court with the landlord seeking to establish that it would be reasonable to release him from further responsibility. Although this does seem an unbalanced approach, and does in fact contradict the Law Commission's own view that leasehold covenants should only bind parties while they are obtaining the benefit of the property, it does recognise the reality of the stronger bargaining position of landlords in most situations. In one related respect, however, these proposals do seem to lose coherency. There is no proposal to change the accepted effect of s 141 LPA that a landlord who assigns the reversion loses the right to sue in respect of past as well as future breaches of covenant, *Re King*. Although it could be argued that there is nothing objectionable to the present rule in itself (for it places the right to sue in the hands of the person actually enjoying the reversion), it does mean that the original landlord remains liable throughout the term of the lease yet enjoys the benefits of the lease only while in possession. The Law Commission's proposals could have dealt more consistently with this problem.

The second major area of difficulty identified by the Law Commission is the requirement at common law that a covenant must 'touch and concern the land' (*Spencer's Case*) (and the equivalent under statute that it must have 'reference to the subject matter of the lease', ss 141, 142 LPA), before it can bind successors in title. At present this a precondition of the enforceability of leasehold covenants between persons other than the original parties (who are bound in contract to perform all covenants). So, if privity of estate exists between plaintiff and defendant, the assignee of a tenant will acquire the benefit and burden of all those covenants that touch and concern the land, *Spencer's Case*. Likewise, the benefit and the burden of all of the original landlord's covenants will be passed to an assignee of the reversion if they have reference to the subject matter of the lease.

Obviously, such a central concept needs to be applied consistently and, if possibly, to have a core meaning. Unfortunately, this has proved very difficult in practice. Some help has been provided recently by the House of Lords in *Swift Investments v Combined English Stores* where Lord Oliver developed a three stage test, viz:

a) whether the covenant could benefit any estate owner as opposed to the particular original covenantee,

b) whether the covenant affected the nature, quality, mode of user or value of the land and

c) whether the covenant was expressed to be personal.

However, this is somewhat circular and it is obvious that whether a covenant 'touches and concerns' will still be a matter for judgment in each individual case. It is this element of inconsistency and uncertainty that prompted the Law Commission to propose a radical reform: the abolition of the distinction between covenants which do and covenants which do not touch and concern the land.

This is clearly consistent with the principle of limited tenant liability, for it is premised on the belief that a tenant should remain liable only for such time as they enjoy the benefits of possession. If it were otherwise, purely personal covenants - such as to pay the rates of other property *Gower v Postmaster General* - would be enforceable for the entire term of the lease. Of course, the immediate liability of any successor in title will be increased if these proposals are accepted and this is where the Law Commission have failed to explain fully their reasoning. The purpose of the 'touching' requirement is both to ensure that promises benefitting the land are capable of fulfilment by persons other than the original parties but also that those which have no relation to the land (as land) should not be, even if they happen to be in a proprietary instrument (the lease). The recent example of *Hua Chiao v Chia Chua* is a case in point. Here, a landlord's covenant to return a tenant's deposit at the end of a lease was held not to 'touch and concern' and therefore not enforceable against an assignee of the reversion. As a matter of principle, this must be correct given that the assignee of the reversion had not received the tenant's deposit which had been paid to the original landlord. The Law Commission's difficulties in this regard do, indeed, seem to be caused more by the fact that it is impossible to define the concept of 'touching and concerning' than an analysis of whether the rational behind the requirement is still compelling. Until it can be established that there are good reasons for making all covenants in leases binding on successors in title - other than it is too difficult to make a distinction - there should be no change in the present law.

Finally, we come to those issues which although not addressed by the Law Commission in detail, still cause problems. For example, it is uncertain whether an assignee of the reversion is liable for breaches of covenants committed by the original landlord before assignment. As a matter of principle it would seem that he should not be, but dicta in *Celsteel v Alton* suggests otherwise. Again, there is a certain inequality in the fact that a landlord loses the right to sue on the covenants when he assigns his reversion (*Re King*), but according to *City & Metropolitan Properties v Greycroft*, a tenant retains the right to sue the landlord after assigning the lease, at least in respect of breaches of covenant committed while he was in possession. All of this, however, pales into insignificance in the light of the problems that arise when the lease is merely equitable or where a legal lease has been assigned only in equity (ie not by deed, *Julian v Crago*). In such cases, although the original parties are bound to each other in contract, there can be no privity of estate between successors in title to those parties. This can cause serious difficulties, especially for a landlord. Thus, whereas ss 141 and 142 Law of Property Act 1925 operate to transfer the benefit of covenants and the burden of covenants respectively to the equitable assignee of the reversion (as they do with legal leases), the assignee of the equitable tenant does not come under the burden of the covenants due to lack of privity of estate. This is even more disadvantageous to the landlord when we appreciate that the benefit of an original equitable tenant's covenants can be transmitted to an assignee by a simple contractual assignment on the basis that benefits of a contract can be assigned. Thus, we reach the position where an assignee of the tenant can sue an assignee of the landlord but not vice versa. Of course, there is some relief for the landlord by virtue of the fact that restrictive covenants may bind under the rule in *Tulk v Moxhay* and also that the landlord may have the remedy of forfeiture. However, forfeiture is a drastic remedy as it brings to an end the lease (and the income generated by it) and *Tulk* does not help with important positive covenants such as covenants to repair. One solution would be to regard the parties as being in privity of estate if they were parties to either a legal or an equitable lease and indeed such a solution was proposed by Lord Denning in *Boyer v Warby*. This has not yet commanded widespread acceptance and for the present there is an unfortunate distinction between the running of covenants in legal leases and the running of covenants in their equitable counterparts.

Admittedly, it is easy to highlight the difficulties that surround the law of leasehold covenants. Perhaps the final word should be a note on some important achievements. The simple fact that covenants can endure for the benefit of land irrespective of who owns that land is part of the attraction of the leasehold estate as a means of property ownership. The unique ability of leasehold covenants to bind successors in title even with all these faults is such that they still stand outside the system of registration in both registered and unregistered land. They present a self contained mechanism for the private management of land use and, as such, considerable thought should be given to wholesale amendments which might distort their purposes and destroy their usefulness.

Question 23

a) Lawrence is the registered proprietor of a large industrial site on the edge of Camford. In 1970, he lets Unit 1 to Alex on a 21 year lease by deed containing covenants that Alex shall not use the premises for the purpose of the manufacture of sports equipment, shall not assign or sublet the property without Lawrence's consent and shall carry out all reasonable external and internal repairs to the property. Seven years later, Alex assigns his interest, with Lawrence's consent to Billy, a car manufacturer. Billy's business suffers in the recession and he sublets to Clive, a bicycle manufacturer, without Lawrence's knowledge.

b) Unit No 2 is let to Mildred on a ten year lease by deed for the purpose of establishing a pub on the site to service the estate during working hours. Mildred covenants not to open after 7.00 pm and to sell only beer manufactured by Lawrence in his brewery. In return, Lawrence covenants not to carry on any catering business elsewhere on the site. Unfortunately, Mildred turns into an alcoholic and must leave the premises for the sake of her health. She assigns her lease in writing to Norman, who finds that the only way to make a profit is to open until 11.00 and sell a wider range of beers. Meanwhile, Lawrence has sold the entire site to Polly, who starts to manufacture chocolate in Unit 3. Polly finds she can make quite a profit selling chocolate cakes to the site workers at lunchtime.

Polly has discovered about Clive and the roof of Unit 1 is leaking. The police are concerned about drunkenness on the estate at night and Norman is about to sue for breach of covenant.

Answer plan

- meaning of 'privity of estate'
- requirement of 'touching and concerning': *Swift Investments*
- sections 141, 142 Law of Property Act 1925
- *Spencer's Case*
- *Re King*
- *Tulk v Moxhay*

Answer

This question concerns the operation of the rules relating to the enforceability of leasehold covenants, both between the original parties to the lease and their respective successors in title. In this case, both the original landlord, Lawrence, and the original tenants Alex and Mildred have assigned their leasehold estates. In general, the law in this area is a mixture of contract and property law. Obviously, the original parties are bound to each other in contract to perform the covenants contained in their lease. Thus, in this problem, Lawrence can sue Alex, Lawrence can sue Mildred and Mildred can sue Lawrence in contract on all the covenants, whether or not they concern the land. This liability continues throughout the life of the contract, that being the term of the lease, although due to the wording of s 141 LPA 1925, a landlord will not be able to sue the original tenant after he has parted with the land as that right is statutorily transferred to the new landlord (*Arlesford Trading Co v Servansingh*).

Of course, for practical purposes, the present landlord, Polly, will wish to enforce the leasehold covenants against the present tenants (and vice versa) and in this respect the issue turns on whether the benefit of the covenant (the right to sue on it) has passed to the plaintiff and the burden of the covenant (the obligation to perform it) has passed to the defendant. In simple terms, both burden and benefit will have passed to successors in title of the original landlord and tenant so as to enable an action on the covenant if: (i) there is privity of estate between the parties; and (ii) the covenant touches and concerns the land. In the case of the landlord, these common law conditions are now found in slightly modified form in ss 141 and 142 LPA 1925.

Before we consider the particular facts in detail, it is wise to determine, as a matter of principle, whether these covenants 'touch and concern' the land. In other words, whether they are so intimately connected with the land that they are not personal to the particular covenanting parties. Only if they do 'touch and concern', can the covenants be enforceable between successors. The requirements for determining whether a covenant does 'touch and concern' have recently been re-stated by the House of Lords in *Swift Investments v Combined English Stores*, viz:

a) whether the covenant could benefit any estate owner as opposed to the particular original covenantee,

b) whether the covenant affected the nature, quality, mode of user or value of the land and

c) whether the covenant was expressed to be personal. In our problem there are six covenants in all.

(i) The covenant by Alex that the premises shall not be used for the manufacture of sports equipment. This is a covenant restrictive of the user of premises and prima facie touches and concerns the land. It seems to fall within the *Swift* formula, see eg *Williams v Earle* where the property was restricted to domestic use only.

(ii) The covenant by Alex not to assign or sub-let without consent - clearly acceptable, as in *Goldstein v Sanders*.

(iii)The covenant by Alex to undertake all reasonable repairs - clearly acceptable as in *Martyn v Clue*.

(iv)The covenant by Mildred not to open after 7.00 pm. Although at first sight, this may seem to be a merely personal covenant, it is clear that it is intended for the benefit of other units on the site. It is not for Lawrence's personal benefit and clearly affects the mode of user of the land within the *Swift* formula. It seems to touch and concern.

(v) The covenant by Mildred to buy beer only from Lawrence - this also touches and concerns the land and is identical to the covenant in *Clegg v Hands*.

(vi)The covenant by Lawrence not to open a catering business. Once again, this covenant affects the mode or user of land retained by Lawrence and is intended to benefit land granted by him. It is an anti-competition covenant and is also acceptable.

In result, then, all these covenants touch and concern the land and are *capable* of passing benefit and burden, as appropriate to successors in title.

a) Unit 1

It is necessary in respect of unit 1 to determine a number of issues. Firstly, which parties are within 'privity of estate', for it is only between these parties that 'touching' covenants can run under the leasehold rules. 'Privity of estate' exists where there is a relationship of landlord and tenant under a legal lease or, in other words, where the particular plaintiff and particular defendant are now landlord and tenant of the same legal estate. In our case, Polly is in privity of estate with Billy. There is no privity of estate between Polly and Clive because Clive is a sub-tenant. (In fact, Clive is Billy's tenant and in privity of estate with him). So, presumptively, Polly can sue Billy.

Secondly, does Polly have the right to sue on the covenants, made by Alex to Lawrence, after purchasing the reversion: has the benefit run to her? The answer to this is clear. Under s 141 LPA 1925, the benefit of every covenant 'having reference to the subject-matter' of the lease is attached to the reversion and passes with it. The requirement of 'having reference to the subject matter' is taken to be synonymous with 'touching and concerning'. In other words, Polly has the right to sue any person with whom she is in privity of estate (Billy) and who is subject to the burden of the covenant. Thirdly, to whom has the burden run? The position here is clear, following *Spencer's Case*, that 'touching' covenants are binding on a successor in title to the original tenant in favour of anyone with whom they are in privity of estate. Again, this is Billy.

So, as far as Unit 1 is concerned, Polly can sue Billy on all three covenants if they have been breached. That, of course, is a matter of construction, although it is reasonably clear that Billy has broken the covenant against sub-letting and the covenant to effect reasonable repairs. If bicycles are 'sports equipment' then the third covenant is also broken. We should note here that Billy is liable for breaking the covenant against the manufacture of sports equipment, even though the actual breach is caused by Clive. Billy is liable throughout his term, and it is immaterial that the breach was actually committed by his tenant. Polly will have various remedies to choose from, including an injunction to restrain cycle production, money damages and perhaps even forfeiture of the lease if there is a right of re-entry.

Finally, we should also note that even though Clive and Polly do not share privity of estate, Polly may well be able to enforce any restrictive covenants against Clive under the rule in *Tulk v Moxhay* that normally operates in disputes between freeholders (who also are not in privity of estate with each other). Under *Tulk*, restrictive covenants can be enforced against any occupier providing they (here, the subtenant) have notice of the covenants (unregistered land) or are within s 23(1)(a) LRA (registered land). Also, of course, if Polly does forfeit against Billy, Clive's sub-tenancy will also be determined, *Shiloh Spinners v Harding*.

b) Unit 2

As above, there is no doubt that Polly, as purchaser, has the benefit of the covenants made to Lawrence: this is the effect of s 141(1) LPA. Correspondingly, however, Polly also has the burden of any covenants made by Lawrence, such as the covenant not to carry on any catering business on the site. This is the effect of s 142(1) LPA, operating for the burden in the same way as s 141 does for the benefit. Thus, Polly can sue Mildred on the covenants not to open after 7.00 pm and not to sell beer other than the landlord's and Mildred's liability continues for the term of the lease even though in fact the breach is committed by Norman. Likewise, Mildred can sue Polly on the covenant to prevent breach of the covenant against catering if as a matter of construction it has been breached. Of course, however, if she is able, both the new landlord and the new tenant will wish to secure a direct remedy against the person actually acting in breach.

In this respect, there are some difficulties. For Polly to sue Norman, the burdens of the covenant must have passed to Norman. However, even though the original lease is by deed (and hence legal) the assignment is only in writing. It is not, therefore, correctly assigned (s 52(1) LPA) and cannot take effect as a legal assignment. Following *Purchase v Lichfield Brewery*, this equitable assignment of a legal lease cannot pass the burdens to Norman and Norman is not liable under leasehold covenant rules. In essence, there is no privity of the legal estate. Of course, it is possible for Polly to seek an injunction against Norman preventing the breach of any restrictive covenants under the *Tulk* rule, provided that the equitable assignee has notice of them. Both of the covenants affecting Norman's land are indeed restrictive and, given that Norman should have seen the original lease before taking an assignment of it, he will have notice of the covenants contained therein. In other words, despite the fact that these covenants cannot be enforced under the 'leasehold rules', they will be binding under *Tulk*.

The position in respect of Norman's attempt to sue Polly is not so complicated. We have seen above that Polly is affected by the burden of the covenant made by Lawrence and there is good reason to suppose that Norman may well be entitled to the benefit of it. Although the right to sue cannot exist because of lack of privity of estate, it is possible that, as a matter of contract, the benefit of the covenant will have been assigned to Norman when he purchased the lease. This is a matter of construction of the assignment form Mildred, but it is a distinct possibility that the benefit of any covenants would have been assigned to Norman personally under normal contractual principles. If that were the case, Norman could sue Polly on this covenant.

Notes

For further reference on the difficulties of leasehold covenant law, see *Thornton* (1991) Legal Studies on proposals for reform and present problems.

Question 24

Assess critically the remedies available to landlords for breach of covenant by their tenants. What factors may influence a landlord when deciding which remedy to pursue?

Answer plan

- forfeiture: s 146 Law of Property Act 1925
- injunction
- distress
- action for arrears of rent
- action for damages

Answer

One of the great advantages of the leasehold estate is that it allows two or more persons to use and enjoy property at the same time. In the typical case, the tenant will enjoy occupation and physical use of the property even to the exclusion of the landlord, but the landlord will reap the benefits of allowing that exclusive occupation in the form of rent and profits. It is, of course, essential for this duality to function that both parties are able to preserve the value of their respective interests in the property. This is the function of covenants in leases, which may take many forms depending on the needs and priorities of the particular landlord and tenant.

From the landlord's point of view, he will wish to ensure that the value of the property and its marketability as an income generating asset is preserved. Thus, there may be covenants restricting the user of the premises by the tenant, obliging the tenant to keep the premises in repair, requiring the landlord's consent before any assignment or sublet is undertaking and, of course, obliging the tenant to pay rent. Obviously, these covenants are designed to secure different objectives and it should come as no surprise that the landlord's remedy for breach of covenant by the tenant may well depend on the particular type of covenant that has in fact been broken. In many cases for example, the landlord will be content to secure performance of the covenant, as with repairing covenants, or simply the payment of outstanding rent. In others, the covenant broken may be so fundamental, or the breach so serious, as to suggest to the landlord that he should end the lease, thereby ridding himself of an unreliable tenant. Indeed, the law itself recognises that certain remedies are more appropriate to achieve certain ends and there are a whole range of statutory provisions which supplement or restrict the landlord in both the choice of remedy and the manner in which he may pursue it.

By far the most powerful weapon in the armoury of the landlord in the event of a breach of covenant is the remedy of forfeiture. A successful forfeiture of the lease effectively brings the lease to an end. It is, in other words, a remedy which can result in the tenant's estate in the land being terminated and, as such, it is not surprising that the right of the landlord to forfeit the lease is strictly controlled by statute. In general terms, in order for forfeiture to be available the lease must contain a right of re-entry. This is a stipulation that the landlord is entitled to re-enter the premises should the tenant fail to observe their covenants. All professionally drafted leases will contain such a right and one will be implied in all equitable leases, *Shiloh Spinners v Harding*. Subject to what will be said below, the existence of a right of re-entry gives the landlord two potential paths to a successful forfeiture. First, the landlord may physically re-enter the property by obtaining actual possession of it. A typical example being the changing of locks. Secondly, and more frequently, a landlord may seek to exercise his right of re-entry through an action for possession in the courts. At one time, a landlord had a free choice about which path to take but this is now modified by statute, mainly to protect the tenant from an over-zealous landlord using unrestricted force. Thus, a right of re-entry under a residential lease 'while any person is lawfully residing in the premises' must take place through court action, s 2 Protection from Eviction Act 1977. Any attempt to physically re-enter will result in criminal liability. Likewise, even if the lease is non-residential (or otherwise outside the scope of s 2), it is only peaceful physical re-entry that is permitted and the landlord must avoid committing offenses under the Criminal Law Act 1977. In short, this means that physical re-entry is possible only when the premises are held under a business lease and are unoccupied.

That, however, is not the end of the statutory code relating to forfeiture. In all cases where the landlord is seeking to forfeit because of a breach of a covenant, other than a breach of a covenant to pay rent, the procedure specified in s 146 Law of Property Act 1925 must be strictly followed. (Forfeiture because of breach of a covenant to pay rent is dealt with under separate rules.) Section 146 requires a landlord to serve a notice on the tenant specifying the breach of covenant of which complaint is made, requesting compensation if desired, advising the tenant of their rights under the Leasehold Property (Repairs) Act 1938 if appropriate, and requesting that the covenant is remedied if that is possible. If the covenant is capable of remedy, and this depends upon the test laid down in *Expert Clothing v Hillgate House*, the landlord must give the tenant a reasonable time to make amends before proceeding to forfeit by re-entry or court action. Only if the covenant cannot be remedied (is 'irremediable'), such as where the tenant has committed a once and for all breach of a negative covenant (*Scala House v Forces* and *Cooper v Henderson*), can the landlord proceed to forfeit with reasonable speed. Even then, however, the landlord's remedy is controlled. If the landlord decides to proceed by way of action it is clear that the tenant has a right to relief from forfeiture under s 146(2) LPA. This will be granted if the tenant has performed the covenants or the court considers that it would be just and reasonable to allow the lease to survive despite the breaches of covenant (see *Shiloh Spinners v Harding*). Likewise, it is now clear after the House of Lord's decision in *Billson v Residential Apartments* that even if the landlord proceeds to forfeit by physical re-entry, such as changing the locks as in that case, the tenant can still apply to the court for relief under s 146(2). This recent 're-interpretation' of s 146 emphasises once again that forfeiture is a drastic remedy, almost a remedy of last resort.

Forfeiture for breach of the covenant to pay rent is also controlled, although the procedure varies slightly according to whether action is taken in the County or the High Court (depending on the amount owed) and the inherent jurisdiction of the court (High Court), as well as statute (County Court), is the source of a tenant's right to relief. In essence, the landlord must make a formal demand for rent, unless this is excluded by the express terms of the lease or by statute, as where more than six months is in arrear and 'distress' (see below) would be inadequate, s 210 Common Law Procedure Act 1852. After this, in both County and High Court, the tenant has a statutory right to have proceedings stayed by payment of rent interests and costs upto a specified time before the hearing date, although in the High Court this right arises only if six months rent is in arrear. However, the High Court has an inherent jurisdiction to grant relief for forfeiture if less than six months is owing and payment is rendered before trial and may grant relief subsequent to a possession order (or physical re-entry, *Howard v Fanshawe*), if the tenant pays within six months and probably longer in exceptional cases, *Di Palma v Victoria Square Property*. In the County Court, there is a statutory right to relief if payment is made within four weeks of a possession order and the court has a discretion to grant relief upto six months after possession is obtained, s 138(3), (9A) County Court Act 1984. The rational behind these generous provisions is, of course, that the landlord has let the premises in order to generate income and should not be entitled to bring that arrangement to an end when that income is paid.

Indeed, taking all cases of forfeiture together, it is clear that the remedy may well be the most powerful in result, but it is also the one that the courts control most closely. It will be the remedy that the landlord resorts to in cases of serious and sustained breach of covenant but in other circumstances an attempt to forfeit is likely to be met with a successful claim for relief. The Law Commission has accordingly proposed a reform of the law of forfeiture which would essentially rationalise and assimilate the procedures for forfeiture for rent and non rent covenants and abolish forfeiture by way of physical re-entry. They have also proposed reform, or rather abolition, of another of the remedies available to a landlord for breach of covenant. The remedy of distress allows a landlord to seize certain of the tenants goods present on the property and sell them for the purpose of realising the arrears of rent. It is a remedy for non payment of rent pure and simple and cannot be used in respect of breaches of any other covenant. With the exception of tenancies controlled under the Rent Acts and similar legislation, distress is a remedy by way of self help requiring no court process. It is, however, bounded by traditional and often confusing common law conditions. There are, for example, many classes of privileged goods that cannot be seized (eg tools of the trade, goods in actual use) and there are common law conditions dictating when distress may be levied (eg not on a Sunday, between dawn and dusk). All in all, despite the increased use of distress in times of recession, the Law Commission's proposed abolition of the remedy would not cause significant hardship to landlords and would remove one more right of self-help and the attendant dangers of abuse. At the moment, its most important consequence is that distress and forfeiture are mutually exclusive. However, should the landlord simply be concerned with rent and not wish to go to the trouble of distress or use the threat of forfeiture (which of course may often produce the rent), he may bring a simple action for arrears of rent up to the maximum of six years in arrear allowed under the Limitation Act.

Finally, for covenants other than the covenant to pay rent there remain two other possible remedies. Firstly, the landlord may sue for damages for breach of covenant which in general terms will follow the normal contractual rules and will place the landlord in the position he would have been in had the breach not been committed. The exception is damages for breach of a covenant to repair which are limited by s 18 Landlord and Tenant Act 1927 to damages no greater than the loss of value in the reversion. Secondly, it may be possible for a landlord to obtain an injunction to prevent continued breach of a restrictive covenant under the rules of *Tulk v Moxhay*. In reality, this is just an example of the general rule that equity may intervene to restrain conduct which is contrary to explicitly undertaken obligations.

Unfortunately, however, despite some dicta to the contrary in *SEDAC v Tanner*, it seems that no order of specific performance can be obtained to compel a tenant to perform a positive covenant to repair (*Hill v Barclay*), despite this being one of the landlord's most valuable benefits.

It is indeed true then, that there is a range of remedies available to the landlord in the event of breach of covenant by the tenant and that the choice of these remedies will depend ultimately on the type of covenant that has been breached and the purpose of the landlord in seeking to enforce it. If the landlord merely wishes to recover rent there is a range of actions. If, however, the aim is to terminate the tenancy and recover possession the remedy of forfeiture is available but severely restricted. In essence it will only be available to a landlord when the tenant has behaved in such disregard of the leasehold covenants that they have effectively taken themselves outside the landlord and tenant relationship.

Notes

A very general essay question. Students can improve this answer by discussing Law Commission recommendations for the reform of leasehold covenant law.

Question 25

Lyn is the freehold owner of a large warehouse and a block of offices on the harbour in Cityport in an area of unregistered land. In 1980, he leases the warehouse to Tim, an electrical goods importer, by deed for 20 years. Tim covenants to keep the premises in good repair, not to use the premises for residential occupancy, not to employ Zola (Lyn's deadly rival) in any capacity and to provide Lyn with a new television set every three years. The lease contains a right of re-entry. In 1987, Tim goes out of business and was forced to assign the lease to Albert by deed, a property developer. Unknown to Lyn, Albert begins to convert the warehouse into modern flats and employs Zola as his architect. Meanwhile, Lyn has let the offices to Dolly for use as company headquarters on the same terms as the lease to Tim plus covenants by Dolly not to assign or sublet without Lyn's consent and not to carry on the trade of insurance brokerage, Lyn's own profession. Dolly discovers that she could have obtained a better deal in the centre of town and sublets to Enid, a financial consultant. Unfortunately, Enid is implicated in a city fraud and fails to pay rent to Dolly, who in turn cannot pay Lyn. Discovering this, Lyn changes all the locks on the office block late one night and refuses to let either Dolly or Enid gain entry.

Lyn now comes to you for advice and he has just learnt of the proposed residential development. He is outraged that Zola is on his property. He would also like a new television.

Answer plan

- enforceability of leasehold covenants
- touching and concerning
- sections 141 and 142 LPA
- forfeiture: s 146 LPA, *Billson v Residential Apartments*
- other remedies in brief

Answer

This question revolves around two central issues. First, the enforceability of the covenants contained in the leases made by Lyn and subsequently assigned or sublet by the original tenants, and secondly, the remedies available to a landlord in the event of breach of covenant, particularly that of forfeiture.

1) The warehouse

The first point is something that Lyn should bear in mind should all other remedies prove to be unavailable. Tim, the original tenant, will be liable throughout the term of the lease as a matter of contract. Thus, if all else fails, Tim can be sued for the breaches of the covenants, even though the acts in breach were those of Albert. The only restriction on this is where the original contract (ie the lease) limited Tim's liability expressly to the period of his possession of the demised premises: there is no evidence of this in our case.

It is clear, however, that Lyn may be able to enforce the covenants against the persons more directly responsible as he and Albert, the assignee, share privity of estate. The original lease was by deed, hence legal, and the assignment is by deed. For all intents and purposes, therefore, Lyn and Albert are as landlord and tenant. This makes Lyn's position much stronger for it means that under the rule in *Spencer's* case, Albert will be subject to the burden of all covenants that touch and concern the land. In this case, there are four covenants in all and each must either be justified by previous authority as 'touching and concerning' or must pass the general test put forward by Lord Oliver in *Swift Investments v Combined English Stores*, viz:

a) whether the covenant is capable of benefiting any estate owner as opposed to the particular original covenantee,

b) whether the covenant affects the nature, quality, mode of user or value of the land and

c) whether the covenant is expressed to be personal.

In this problem, the covenant to repair is of no difficulty, *Parker v Webb*, and the same is true of the covenant against residential occupancy: both clearly 'touch and concern'. There might, however, be thought to be some difficulty with the remaining two covenants and, certainly, the covenant to provide a new television set is clearly personal to Tim in his capacity as an importer of electrical goods. It is not related to use of the land as such. However, in *Lewin v American and Colonial Distributors*, a covenant not to allow a named individual to be connected with any business carried on upon the land was held to touch and concern as it was intended to affect the mode of user and value of the land. The covenant in our case is not quite of this kind and could be distinguished from that in the *Lewin* case. It will be a matter for argument because this covenant prevents the covenantor from employing Zola in any capacity and does not seem to be restricted to an activity carried on on the land. This covenant might be too wide and unconnected with the land for it to touch and concern.

Thus, it seems that Tim, the original tenant is liable in respect of the television as a matter of contract law and probably not liable in respect of Zola: after all Tim has not employed him and the covenant probably does not run to Albert. Albert, however, is subject to the repairing obligation and the restriction against residential occupancy. Obviously, it is these last two covenants that Lyn will be most concerned with and he has several remedies available - eg damages, injunction. More than likely, however, he may well seek to forfeit the lease under his right of re-entry.

There is no doubt that in principle Albert is subject to forfeiture as the right of re-entry is enforceable against him. Being attached to a legal estate, it is itself a legal right and binding on Albert. However, the right of forfeiture for covenants other than to pay rent - and here we are dealing with breach of a covenant against residential occupation (see below for the repairing covenant) is controlled by statute, irrespective of whether forfeiture is by action in the courts or by physical re-entry. Under s 146 LPA, in all cases of forfeiture, the landlord must serve a 'section 146 notice' specifying the breach which is complained of, requiring compensation and requiring the tenant to remedy the breach if it is capable of remedy. Any attempted forfeiture without following this procedure is void (*Re Riggs*). It is crucial, therefore, for Lyn to serve such a notice. Furthermore, when the notice is served, Lyn cannot go on to forfeit by action or physical re-entry without giving the tenant a reasonable chance to remedy the covenant, if it is capable of remedy. It is crucial to know, for this reason, whether the covenant is indeed capable of remedy. The appropriate test for this purpose was discussed in *Expert Clothing Service & Sales v Hillgate House Ltd* and boils down to whether the harm to the landlord could be remedied. In the case of 'negative covenants' eg as here with the ban on residential occupancy, this is difficult as once the action is done, the covenant is broken, *Scala House v Forbes*. Only if the breach of a negative covenant is 'continuing' will it be regarded as sufficient to stop the offending action and thereby avoid forfeiture. Under, *Expert Clothing*, a positive covenant (such as to repair) can more easily be remedied by carrying out the required task.

Having served a s 146 notice and given a reasonable time for remedy (if appropriate) Lyn may be able to forfeit by physical re-entry, as this is not a residential property (cf Protection of Eviction Act 1977 s 2). However, after *Billson v Residential Apartments*, also a case where work was done to property without consent, it is clear that even physical re-entry does not destroy the tenant's right to relief from forfeiture under s 146(2) LPA. Such relief can be granted even if a covenant is technically irremediable as the law leans against forfeitures. It is a matter for the courts' discretion in the circumstances of the case, *Shiloh Spinners v Harding*. Lyn would be wise, therefore, to seek forfeiture by action in the courts if Albert does not desist from the conversion work and pay compensation. The effect of a successful forfeiture would be, of course to bring the lease to an end. Finally, it may be that due to the redevelopment work, the warehouse is not kept in good repair. If this is the case, Lyn might be better advised to sue for damages for breach of the repairing covenant as the procedure for forfeiture for breach of repairing obligations is complicated by the requirements of the Leasehold Property (Repairs) Act 1938. This gives the tenant added protection under s 146 LPA and a longer time to fulfil repairing obligations. Forfeiture for lack of repair will not be necessary if forfeiture for the non-observance of the domestic occupancy covenant is successful.

2) The offices

The position here is similar to that above, with the exception that the breach of one covenant has been caused by the action of a sub-tenant. The obvious point is, of course, that Dolly is bound by all the covenants as a matter of contract (being the original covenantor) and, if it is true that her lease also contains a covenant to provide a television set, she must do so. On the other hand, it is also clear that there is no privity of estate between Lyn and Enid. Enid is a subtenant and is in privity of estate only with her own landlord, Dolly. Thus, the burden of the covenants cannot run to Enid.

However, this does not mean that Lyn is left without a remedy apart from the contractual action against Dolly. In the first place, Lyn can enforce any negative covenants which touch and concern the land (as with the covenant restrictive of user) by injunction under the rule in *Tulk v Moxhay* provided that Enid has notice of them (as is most likely, *Gosling v Woolfe*). Secondly, however, Lyn can proceed to forfeit the headlease for breach of covenant, although if forfeiting for breach of the covenant not to sublet, the procedure outlined above has clearly not been followed. There has been no 'section 146 notice'. Even if there had been, *Billson* makes it clear that relief from forfeiture can still be granted even where the landlord has forfeited by physical re-entry of the premises (changing the locks) instead of by action in the courts. Furthermore, under s 146 LPA a subtenant may apply for such relief in an action by the reversioner against the head tenant. Thus, although breach of the covenant not to sublet cannot be remedied (it is a once-and-for-all breach of a negative covenant - *Scala House*), Lyn has not followed the correct procedure which was designed to give the tenant or subtenant the chance to claim relief.

Alternatively, Lyn could choose to forfeit for non-payment of rent, although again certain procedural limitations exist. For example, it is clear that unless expressly excluded by the lease, a landlord must issue a formal demand for rent if less than six months rent is owing. We do not know if Lyn has done this. Moreover, Dolly has a right to have the proceedings stayed on payment of all arrears and costs and, even after re-entry, the court has a discretion to grant relief from forfeiture, *Howard v Fanshawe*. In general, the court looks very carefully at attempted forfeiture for non-payment of rent as immediate payment plus costs will always remedy the situation. In this respect, threatened forfeiture is a costly way of recovering rent and Lyn would be well advised to use the normal action for rent recovery.

Notes

These last two questions concern the remedies available to a landlord in the event of breach of covenant, with particular reference to forfeiture. In this respect *Billson* must be thoroughly understood as must the operation of s 146 LPA. These two questions illustrate the most likely issues that can arise, although sometimes questions about the determination of tenancies can also appear, eg by effluxion of time, notice, unity of title etc.

Licences and Proprietary Estoppel

Introduction

In one sense, there is no necessary reason why the law of licences and the law of proprietary estoppel should be considered together. 'Licences' are one way in which a person may enjoy some right or privilege over the land of another and much of the dispute in this area concerns the theoretical and practical distinction between 'licences' and 'easements'. 'Proprietary estoppel', on the other hand, is now regarded as a method for the creation of certain rights and privileges over land. Viewed in this way, proprietary estoppel is a mechanism that may give rise to licences, easements, leases or any other kind of right connected with the use and ownership of land and should be considered in its own right. However, that said, it is true that many of the cases and most of the textbooks consider licences and proprietary estoppel together. This is because 'licences' seem to be the most common result of the application of proprietary estoppel to a given set of facts. Whether this is theoretically justified or practically necessary is an issue that will be explored in this chapter, but for the moment the conventional form of exposition, which groups these matters together, will be used.

Licences then, involve a permission from the owner of land, given to another, to use that land for some purpose. This can be to do anything from attending a cinema, parking a car or occupying premises to erecting an advertising hoarding. The range of activities that can be covered by a licence are, indeed, virtually limitless and we have already explored this issue in one respect in considering the distinction between leases and licences. Crucially, however, the traditional view of licences is that they are not proprietary in nature: in other words, they are not interests in land, but rather personal rights *over* land. As a consequence, the right conferred by a licence can be enforced only against the person who created it. It does not run with the land and, unlike easements and restrictive covenants, cannot be enforced against a purchaser of the land over which the licence exists. The licence is a matter of contract, not property law. In recent years, this fundamental theoretical distinction has been attacked and many examination questions now ask students to analyse whether the status of licences has changed as the use of land has changed.

Checklist

In dealing with both problem and essay questions on licences, students will need to have a firm grasp of what it means to say that something is an interest in land, as well as an understanding of the law of easements and general principles of equity concerning constructive trusts. Case law is particularly important.

Proprietary estoppel is the name given to a doctrine or set of principles whereby an owner of land may be held to have conferred some right or privilege connected with the land on another person. Typically, the right or privilege conferred will arise out of the conduct of the parties, usually because of some assurance made, which is relied upon by the person claiming the right. In other words, proprietary estoppel is a mechanism whereby rights in or over land may be created informally. In this respect, it is close to the doctrine of constructive trusts considered in Chapter 3 and many cases use these doctrines interchangeably. This is not necessarily accurate although the precise ambit and differences between the two doctrines have not yet been worked out. In this area, case law is vital as this is a judge-made doctrine, so typical of a court of equity. There are parallels with promissory estoppel in the law of contract, although proprietary estoppel is a much more powerful doctrine. The former is a defence to an action on a contract, the latter is a means of acquiring rights over land belonging to another. It is a sword as well as a shield.

Question 26

To what extent have the courts recognised contractual licences as interests in land? Why is the issue important?

Answer plan

- definition of an interest in land: *National Provincial Bank v Ainsworth*
- definition of a licence: *Thomas v Sorrell*
- types of licences and purposes of licences
- the supposed need to bind third parties

- judicial developments: *Errington v Errington; Binions v Evans; Re Sharpe; Midland Bank v Farm Pride Hatcheries; Ashburn Anstalt v Arnold; Kewal Investments v Arthur Maiden*
- theoretical considerations

Answer

A licence is classically defined in *Thomas v Sorrell* as a permission to use land belonging to another which, without such permission, would amount to a trespass. It is, in other words, the consent of the estate owner to the use of their land by another. Importantly, as Vaughan CJ makes clear in *Sorrell*, the traditional view of licences is that they 'properly passeth no interest nor alters or transfers property in any thing'; in other words, licences are not proprietary in nature but personal to the parties that created them. In effect, that they are not interests in land and therefore not within the scope of the 1925 property legislation and are incapable of binding third parties when the licensor (the grantor of the licence) passes the affected land on to a third party.

However, such a traditional view has, in recent years, been subject to attack and various cases and theories have sought to explain why licences are, or should, be regarded as interests in land in the full sense. The aim is often to ensure that subsequent transferees of the burdened land are bound. Not least, this is due to the multitude of purposes that licences can serve. The law reports are replete with cases covering such matters as entry by ticket to a cinema (*Hurst v Picture Theatres Ltd*), permission to use local facilities for a conference (*Verrall v Great Yarmouth BC*), permission to erect an advertising hoarding (*Kewal Investments v Arthur Maiden*) and even permission to occupy premises for residential accommodation (*Ogwr BC v Dykes*). Indeed, it is in respect of this last category - so called occupation licences (but see Chapter 5) - that much of the debate has taken place, for if it is possible to grant licences to occupy as a residence, it is in the interests of the licensee to claim that the licence can in fact bind any transferee from the licensor.

This multipurpose application of licences is reflected in the traditional categorisation that is often placed upon types of licences. All categories are noted here, although it must be borne in mind that it is really in respect of the last two that the debate about the proprietary nature of licences has taken place. First, there are 'bare licences', being the most simple form of permission to use land given voluntarily by the owner of property. Typically, such licences allow the 'licensee' to carry on some limited activity on the 'licensor's' land, as where permission is given to hold a fete. It is intrinsic to this type of licence that the permission may be withdrawn at any time and, because given voluntarily without consideration, does not give the licensee any claim to damages or other legal remedy. Secondly, there are those licences grouped together because they are 'coupled with an interest in the land'. In essence, these licences comprise the implied permission which a person obtains and which enables them to enjoy some right previously granted over the land, as where a person is granted the right to fish, cut turf or gather wood, as in *James Jones & Son v Earl of Tankerville*. To some extent, however, the label 'licence' is misleading, for the licence is merely incidental and ancillary to the right which has actually been granted over the land. Thus, where as in the above examples the right granted may also be proprietary in nature, as with the profit of piscary (fish) and the profit of turbary (to cut turf), it is the right granted that is important and not the licence which facilitates it. So, the licence will last for as long as the profit is granted and be enforceable against whomsoever the profit is enforceable against, being merely an ingredient in the greater right. Likewise, should the grantee (and licensee) be unlawfully denied the right granted, the normal remedies will be available to prevent interference with the right, such as injunction.

As noted above, however, it is with the third and fourth categories of licence that the question whether they amount to an interest in land has been most commonly posed, that of contractual licences and licences arising by estoppel. Contractual licences are in principle little different in nature from bare licences save that contractual licences are granted to the licensee in return for valuable consideration moving to the licensor; the purchase of a cinema ticket is a good example. Crucially, of course, such contractual licences are governed by the ordinary rules relating to remedies for breach of contract and it is now clear that either an injunction will be granted preventing the licensor from revoking the licence before its contractual date of expiry (*Wintergarden*

Theatres v Millennium Productions Ltd) or even a decree of specific performance requiring the licensor to permit the activity authorised by the licence to take place (*Verrall v Great Yarmouth*). It is obvious that the effect of the availability if these remedies may, in appropriate circumstances (depending on the contract and the conduct of the parties), make the licence *de facto* irrevocable throughout the contractual time period (eg the theatre performance). Of course, this is in reality only an issue between the original licensor and licensee but the fact that such licences could be irrevocable during their contractual period *and* that they related to land did raise the inevitable question of their effect on third parties. Put simply, the question is asked whether, given that a contractual licence is irrevocable between the licensor and licensee throughout its contractual period, the licensor can nevertheless defeat the licence by conveying the property to a third party during that period. Of course, the licensee may well have a good claim in contract, but that is not the same as allowing the licensee's rights to use the land to continue against the third party for the remainder of the period.

In the event, under the influence of Lord Denning's Court of Appeal, two strands of thought developed which sought to explain why a licence could bind a third party and, perhaps, why it should be regarded as a new species of interest in land. On the one hand, in *Errington v Errington*, Lord Denning regarded a contractual licence as binding on a third party who received the property which was subject to the licence by a will, her husband being the original licensor. In this case, the reasoning was explicit that since the licensee could restrain revocation of the licence for its period against the licensor, there was no reason why the licence could not continue against a third party who was not a *bona fide* purchaser of a legal estate for value in the property. This does, of course, assume that licences are *capable* of binding third parties as only if they actually are does it matter whether the third party is 'equity's darling'. The reasoning for the decision is unclear, although it seems that the contractual licence was supported by 'an equity' which transformed it into a proprietary right. Unfortunately, the court in this case did not make it clear why a previous House of Lords decision (*King v David Allen & Sons, Billposting*), which had expressly decided that contractual licences could not bind third parties, could be ignored.

The second line of attack on the traditional view came with the Court of Appeal in *Binions v Evans*. In that case, a purchaser of land subject to what looked like a contractual licence, expressly agreed to take the land subject to that licence. The purchaser later sought to evict the licensee. Two of the Court of Appeal actually decided that no licence was involved at all: rather the occupier had a life interest under a settlement which was protected under the Settled Land Act. Lord Denning, however, took a different view and decided that the purchaser was bound to give effect to the licence having purchased the property subject to it and that such licence was protected by the imposition of a constructive trust on the purchaser. In the case itself, it is not clear whether Denning MR regards these as separate or complimentary grounds for the decision but subsequent decisions (eg *Bannister v Bannister*, *Re Sharpe*) have tended to rely on the constructive trust argument as a means of protecting the licence against a third party. However, as we shall see, this does not necessarily mean that the contractual licence has become an interest in land.

This seems to have been the position, cloudy though it was, until the decision of the Court of Appeal in *Ashburn Anstalt v Arnold*. In that case, Fox LJ re-examined thoroughly the question of licences as interests in land and, relying on the House of Lords in *King* and *National Provincial Bank v Ainsworth*, re-affirmed the traditional view of the law. In his view, *Errington*, in so far as it decided that a licence was an interest in land, was *per incuriam*, because of the existence of the binding authority of *King*. In any event, in Fox LJ's view, *Errington* could have been decided on at least three other grounds (the existence of an estate contract binding a non-purchaser, a *Rosset* type equitable right of ownership, or estoppel against the widow). Indeed, Fox LJ's judgment makes it clear that *as a matter of principle* licences are not interests in land and cannot bind third parties for that reason. However, turning to *Binion*, Fox LJ accepted that in appropriate cases a contractual licence may take effect behind a constructive trust, binding on the purchaser, if the purchaser has so conducted himself that it would be inequitable for the licence to be denied. Such a trust does not exist, however, merely because the purchaser bought the land was 'subject to' the licence, but only if there was unconscionable conduct on the part of the purchaser (eg paying a lower price as a result of the promise to respect the licence). In any event, the licence is only protected behind a *personal* constructive trust binding on this particular purchaser because of their particular conduct: it has not thereby assumed the status of an interest in land.

This latest view is, without doubt, a thoroughly orthodox approach to the problem and it serves to highlight the fundamental distinction between interests in land and purely personal interests which just happen to relate to property. It has been followed subsequently (in *Kewal Investments*) and now seems to represent the law. In fact, now that the house of Lords has in *Street v Mountford* and other cases asserted that residential occupation usually gives rise to a lease and not a licence, there is a certain symmetry to the picture. Further, to be entirely fair to Lord Denning and the other judges following his lead, their attempt to confer proprietary status on mainly occupation licences came at a time when landowners were able to avoid granting leases. In this respect, attempts to protect occupation licences could be seen as an attempt to protect what were really leases and, after *Street*, would be regarded as so. Indeed, if one takes Lord Wilberforce's definition of an interest in land in *Ainsworth* ('before a right or interest can be admitted into the category of property, or of a right affecting property it must be definable, identifiable by third parties, capable in its nature of assumption by third parties and have some degree of permanence or stability'), it is obvious that there is some circularity in the whole issue. What these cases show us is that the distinction between licences and interests in land is a real and immovable one, but what amounts to either a 'licence' or an 'interest in land' in any given case depends ultimately on the facts of that case. The categories are boxes, which have pre-determined consequences, but what goes into those boxes is a matter of judgment.

Notes

This is a standard examination question, although it cannot be completed successfully without knowledge of recent case law. The distinction between the ability of a proprietary right to bind a third party and the purely personal way in which a licence may bind someone because of a purely personal constructive trust is most important.

Question 27

In 1990, Bluebell acquired registered title to a small cottage on Dartmoor, formerly part of a large farm and quite close to the old farmhouse. Being fond of animals she acquires several horses and asks Farmer Cowslip whether she can keep them on his land. He agrees, but only if he may use the horses to hire to tourists who stay on his farm. Farmer Cowslip also provided riding holidays for tourists, using his own horses, and Bluebell agreed that if there was insufficient space in the farmhouse, she would accommodate any extra tourists and provide them with breakfast and an evening meal if desired. Bluebell also pays Farmer cowslip £20 per month to park her car in an old barn on the farm. She also regularly collects firewood from the fields for her only source of heating is an old wood burning stove. In 1991, Farmer Cowslip proposes marriage to Bluebell but she refuses. Farmer Cowslip takes great offence and immediately threatens to turn Bluebell's horses out, although he does continue to use them for his riding business. In anger, Bluebell refuses to accommodate any of Farmer Cowslip's tourists and evicts those that are currently in occupation. They subsequently sue Cowslip for a ruined holiday. Cowslip's response is to sell the barn and fields to Grockle Holidays plc who immediately refuse Bluebell the right to park her car or gather wood.

Bluebell comes to you for advice as her car has broken down due to standing in the cold and she cannot live in the cottage without her source of fuel. She hopes to be able to sell the cottage to her friend, Daisy, who would also like to keep horses. It also emerges that Grockle plc knew of Bluebell's activities and paid Farmer Cowslip a much reduced price for the land it has purchased. You discover subsequently that Farmer Cowslip is the major shareholder in Grockle plc.

Answer plan

- identification of rights over the land: licences or proprietary interests
- effect of licences between the original parties: remedies
- effect of licences on third parties

- constructive trusts and the protection of licences
- the creation of new licences binding on a 'third party'

Answer

This problem concerns the creation of rights over land, the identification of the nature of those rights and the consequences which flow from subsequent dealings with the land over which those rights exist. In essence, as we are asked to advise Bluebell, it is necessary to determine a) whether she has any right to insist that her horses be accommodated and whether this right can be enforced against Farmer Cowslip; and whether the benefit of the right can subsequently be passed on to Daisy; b) whether Bluebell is under any liability in respect of the displaced tourists and the refusal to house further tourists; c) whether Bluebell has any rights to park her car and collect wood and whether these are binding on Grockle plc; and d) whether Grockle's conduct and the involvement of Farmer Cowslip suggest any other remedy for Bluebell.

a) The horses

There seems little doubt that Bluebell and Farmer Cowslip have entered into a contract whereby Bluebell agrees to allow the horses to be used for Cowslip's business in return for which Cowslip allows Bluebell to keep the horses on his land. However, the nature of the rights created by this contract are the crucial factor, for that may determine their enforceability and status in respect of third parties.

The contract is purely oral and, if it to be argued that this contract confers some sort of proprietary interest on Bluebell, there are going to be difficulties in fulfilling the formality requirements of s 2 Law of Property (Miscellaneous Provisions) Act 1989. In fact, the only possibility of a proprietary right is that Bluebell has some lease of the land (cf *University of Reading v Johnson-Houghton*), in the form of a periodic tenancy, which would be binding on Cowslip according to its terms and could be assigned to Daisy in the normal way by deed (*Crago v Julian*). However, the nature of Bluebell's right to keep horses, and the circumstances in which it was created, militate against the granting of any proprietary interest. Indeed, it is likely that her right is in the nature of a contractual licence over Farmer Cowslip's land. Moreover, presumptively a contractual licence is revocable during its term by the licensor, although the licensee (Bluebell) would have a claim in damages. On the other hand, however, it is clear from *Wintergarden Theatres v Millennium Productions* that if, on construction of the contract, a contractual licence was intended to be irrevocable during its period of operation, equity will intervene to restrain breach of that contract by the licensor by way of injunction or specific performance as appropriate. Whether the remedy is available to Bluebell will depend on many factors, not least her own conduct. Her willingness to continue to allow her horses to be used (ie that she kept her side of the contract) will be important, although her apparent refusal to cater for the very tourists who would ride will count against. It will be a matter for the court. As far as Daisy is concerned, it has always been true that the benefit of a contract can be expressly assigned and there is no reason why Bluebell cannot transfer to Daisy such rights as she has against Cowslip under the contractual licence for the accommodation of her horses.

b) The tourists

The precise nature of Bluebell's liabilities here will depend on the exact terms of the contract she made with Farmer Cowslip. It may well be that she is in breach of contract in evicting the tourists before the end of their holiday and in refusing to accommodate future arrivals. In such a case, Farmer Cowslip will have a right to sue Bluebell in contract and recover the loss caused by the action against him by his disgruntled clients. What is quite clear, however, is that the tourists have no short term lease over their rooms in Bluebell's cottage. Under *Street v Mountford*, there is no doubt that these occupiers are lodgers and therefore not tenants. There is the provision of board and services within *Markou v Da Silvaesa*. The tourists may, of course, have a contractual licence to occupy the cottage, although it is difficult to see on the facts how they could be in direct contract with Bluebell. If they were, and were occupying on a contractual licence from Bluebell, *Tanner v Tanner* suggests that an injunction could be obtained to prevent eviction for the duration of the licence. However, not only is this the least likely remedy sought by the transient tourists, the *Tanner* case is fundamentally different in that it concerned a long term occupier who was denied continued occupation by the licensor in very inequitable circumstances.

c) Car parking and collecting wood

The issue of the car parking and the collection of wood raise rather more difficult issues, both as to the nature of the rights granted and because of the involvement of a third party who purchased the land over which the rights existed.

As to the car parking, it is clear from *Newman v Jones* that it is perfectly possible to have an easement giving a right to park on a neighbour's land. However, it seems that this can occur only if the easement is to park generally and not in a defined space: exclusive possession of the servient land cannot amount to an easement (*Grigsby v Melville*). In any event, even assuming that this could be an easement, the requirements of formality needed to create a legal or equitable right have not been met and there is little possibility of an estoppel easement. All in all, this looks as if Bluebell has been granted a contractual licence to park her car which, of course, is enforceable against Cowslip as the licensor. However, it is now clear from *Ashburn Anstalt v Arnold* that licences as such are not interests in land and cannot therefore bind a subsequent purchaser of the land. They are not proprietary in nature. So, subject to what will be said below, at first sight it looks as if Bluebell's right to park her car cannot be enforced against Grockle.

The right to collect wood does, however, pose different problems. There is no doubt that it is possible for a person to be granted a profit a prendre to collect wood for the purpose of fuel, otherwise known as a profit of estovers (*AG v Reynolds*). Profits are, of course, proprietary rights and any licences attached to the profit to enter onto another's land for the purpose of exercising the profit take the character of the superior right's proprietary status, *James Jones v Earl of Tankerville*. However, it is also clear that in order for the profit to exist - and hence be capable of binding a third party such as Grockle - it must be created in due form. In this case, there is no deed of grant to support a legal profit and no written contract to support an equitable profit.

Bluebell's only hope is, perhaps, to plead the creation of a profit by estoppel, similar to the creation of an easement by estoppel in *Celsteel v Alton*. If that were the case, the profit would constitute an overriding interest against the servient land (s 70(1)(a) LRA 1925) and be binding automatically on Grockle plc. If, on the other hand, no estoppel profit can arise, Bluebell's only hope is to prove that it was never the intention of the parties to grant her a profit but, rather, that she has a mere licence to collect wood. Obviously, a mere licence cannot bind Grockle plc as such - not being an interest in land - but she may gain some comfort from the principle of constructive trust considered below.

d) Grockle and Farmer Cowslip

Although it is clear that the licence to park the car (and to collect wood if established as a licence) cannot bind Grockle as a matter of property law, there is the possibility that the purchaser will be bound by a personal constructive trust, imposed to give effect to the licences, because of the purchaser's inequitable conduct. That even a licence can gain protection in this way is accepted in *Ashburn Anstalt v Arnold*, for its essence is that equity imposes an obligation on the conscience of a particular purchaser. The nature of the right is not crucial. The circumstances in which such an obligation will be imposed are obviously varied and it is not enough that the purchaser simply promised to give effect to the licences (*Ashburn*, criticising *Binions v Evans*). In our case, the fact that the purchaser paid a lower price because they knew of the existence of the licences may well be important, although as we know from *Midland Bank v Green* (in other context), undervalue and knowledge that rights will be defeated do not necessarily amount to inequitable conduct. It will in essence be a matter for the court. If a constructive trust is imposed, it will ensure that Grockle plc permit the continuance of the rights of Bluebell.

Finally, two further points should be noted. First, as with a) above, Bluebell may transfer the benefit of any contract to Daisy irrespective of the nature of the rights created by the contract. That is a matter of contract law. It is not clear, however, whether the transfer of the benefit of the contractual rights to a third party will affect the court's decision to impose a constructive trust on the purchaser of the land over which those rights exists. Secondly, it may be possible to argue that there is no third party purchaser on the grounds that Grockle plc is just Farmer Cowslip in another guise. If that were the case, because Cowslip is the majority shareholder, no question of the enforcement of licences against third parties arise. It is more likely, however, that given the separate legal personality of companies and their owners, that Cowslip's majority shareholding will be relevant to the question of the imposition of the constructive trust on the 'third party' rather than in deciding that there was no third party at all, see *Jones v Lipman*.

Notes

This question illustrates just how easy it is for questions to raise issues concerning licences and easements. In some senses, a licence is what a person obtains if they cannot claim an easement: either because the right is not capable of being an easement or because of some formality defects.

Question 28

'The law of proprietary estoppel has changed dramatically in recent years. From being a fairly limited right available to a plaintiff in confined circumstances, it has developed into a panacea for all occasions. It is now the last resort of the desperate plaintiff, who far too often succeeds.'

Do you agree?

Answer plan

- the general operation of proprietary estoppel and its relationship to formality requirements
- the five probanda: *Willmott v Barber*
- the changing definition of proprietary estoppel: *Taylor Fashions v Liverpool Victoria Trustees*
- the role of proprietary estoppel in the modern law

Answer

In 1989, the Law of Property (Miscellaneous Provisions) Act was passed in order to bring more clarity and more certainty into the creation and disposition of interests in land. In effect, s 2 of that Act replaced s 40 of the Law of Property Act and stipulated that a contract for the disposition of an interest in land should now be in writing. Crucially, s 2 abolished the doctrine of part performance whereby purely oral contracts could, if acted upon, give rise to an interest in land. In simple terms, then, s 2 brought more formality to the creation of interests in land and effectively provides, in conjunction with other rules, that legal rights must be created by deed or registered disposition (see the exceptions for short leases and the doctrine of prescription) and equitable interests by written contract. It is in such a context, where statute requires more formality for the creation of proprietary interests, that the doctrine of proprietary estoppel should be examined.

The exact purpose or role of proprietary estoppel is, not surprisingly, a matter of some debate. On the one hand, it can (like its brother promissory estoppel) provide a defence to an action by a landowner who seeks to enforce his strict rights against someone who has been promised some right or liberty over the land. For example, an action in trespass by the landlord can be met by a plea of estoppel in that the landowner has so conducted himself as to forfeit the remedy claimed. However, proprietary estoppel is much more than this, for there is no doubt that if successfully established it can generate property interests in favour of a claimant, if it would be equitable to so do. As is typically stated, proprietary estoppel is both a shield and a sword, *Crabb v Arun DC*. In essence, then, proprietary estoppel may be seen as a method of creating rights in or over land without writing or formal contract. It is the creation of rights arising from the action of equity on an individual's conscience.

The doctrine of proprietary estoppel is not a modern development, although it certainly has come to the fore in recent times. In *Willmott v Barber*, Fry LJ laid down what was to be regarded for many years as the five 'probanda' of proprietary estoppel or, in other words, the five conditions that needed to be established before a claimant could be awarded a right to another's land arising informally. The five conditions were that firstly, the claimant should have made some mistake as to their legal rights; secondly, that the claimant must have expended some money or done some act on the faith of the mistaken belief; thirdly, that the true landowner must know of the existence of their own right and that it is inconsistent with the right claimed by the claimant; fourthly, the landowner must know of the claimant's mistaken belief as to their legal rights; and fifthly, that the landowner should have encouraged the expenditure by the claimant, either directly or by abstaining from enforcing their legal right.

It is obvious that these five conditions are fairly strict: they limit the circumstances in which equity will intervene to award a right to the claimant and circumscribe the circumstances in which rights connected with property may be created informally. Indeed, this formulation is appropriate when the purpose of proprietary estoppel is to limit the ability of the 'true' owner of land to rely on their formal title in circumstances where it would be inequitable to do so. However, over a period of time it became clear that courts were prepared to accept a plea of proprietary estoppel when one or more of Fry LJ's probanda were missing (eg *Berg Homes v Grey*). To all intents and purposes, this was because the emphasis of proprietary estoppel shifted from preventing the true owner from relying on their strict legal rights over land, to a doctrine which asked whether the claimant had any positive right to that land. In short, the focus shifted from the landowner to the claimant, wherein the latter's actions and perceptions became much more central to the issue. Of course, there are still cases where Fry LJ's formula is used in full (*Coombes v Smith*) but essentially the modern position is that put forward in *Taylor Fashions v Liverpool Victoria Trustees*. In that case, Oliver J made it clear that proprietary estoppel is not limited to cases where the landowner knows of their rights, or their extent, but is indeed a flexible doctrine, springing from equity which should not be unduly restricted by rigid rules.

In essence, the position after *Taylor Fashions* is that a person may be entitled to claim rights in or over land formally belonging to another where it would be unconscionable to deny those rights. Effectively, this means that the claimant must prove an assurance - express or implied - by the landowner as to the claimant's position in relation to the land; reliance on that assurance by the claimant; and detriment by the claimant as a result of relying on the assurance. Indeed, so general and flexible are these criteria that sometimes little evidence will be needed in order to support an estoppel. In *Greasely v Cooke*, for example, the Court of Appeal held that if it is clear that assurances have been made, and detriment suffered, it is permissible to assume that reliance has occurred. Likewise, in *J T Developments v Quinn*, it became clear that an estoppel could arise even though there was no intention to create binding obligations, as where the parties had attempted to negotiate a contract in respect of land but failed. Numerous examples now exist of successful claims of proprietary estoppel and cases such as *Re Basham* illustrate that it is an all purpose remedy resorted to as much by claimants seeking to avoid the formality requirements otherwise imposed for the creation of property rights as by judges seeking to achieve a 'just' result in the case before them.

In some senses, then, proprietary estoppel is the embodiment of the equitable jurisdiction: it allows for the creation of property rights without needing to fulfil the strict requirements of statute, in cases where it would be unfair to do otherwise. Such flexibility is, indeed, reflected in the way that the court's 'satisfy' the estoppel or, in other words, the flexibility they have to grant the most appropriate remedy to the claimant. For example, if the claimant successfully establishes an assurance supported by detrimental reliance, the estoppel so established may be satisfied by awarding the fee simple to the claimant (*Dillwyn v Llewellyn, Pascoe v Turner*), or the grant of an easement (*Celsteel v Alton*), or a life interest (one view of *Bannister v Bannister*), a right of occupation until expenditure is repaid (*Dodsworth v Dodsworth*), a complete re-adjustment of the parties rights over the property (*Voyce v Voyce*), a re-adjustment of testamentary dispositions (*Re Basham*) or a licence to use the property (one view of *Inwards v Baker*). As one can see, the range of remedies is open-ended and, importantly, does not necessarily have to result in the grant of a proprietary interest at all, as where a licence is granted.

All in all, both in terms of establishing the estoppel and in the court's choice of the appropriate remedy, this doctrine is flexible enough to meet most situations. It is not surprising, therefore, that it can be regarded as a panacea for all ills and certainly has been used as such by the courts (eg *Re Basham*). Moreover, in that it allows rights over property to be created by entirely informal means, it provides an easy escape route for the claimant who has failed to observe the statutory requirements for the creation of proprietary rights at large. That said, no-one should or could deny the value of a doctrine which seeks to resolve matters according to the conscience of the parties involved rather than the strict forms required. This is a necessary adjunct to any legal system which stipulates formalities as a means to certainty. The trick is, however, not to go too far. There is merit in certainty, especially in relation to transactions concerning land and policy considerations should not be forgotten when considering the informal and flexible doctrine of proprietary estoppel.

Notes

This question is interesting as it gives the good student an opportunity to explain how proprietary estoppel is related to the general formality requirements of land law. It also illustrates the wide, and as yet undefined, reach of estoppel. However, it can also be answered competently by a good knowledge of case law, especially post *Taylor Fashions*.

Question 29

'The law of proprietary estoppel has altered fundamentally the distinction between licences and proprietary interests in land. To all intents and purposes, to make such distinctions is no longer practically necessary or theoretically justified'.

Discuss.

Answer plan

- the nature of proprietary estoppel
- its relation to estoppel licences
- estoppels and third parties
- the need for theoretical clarity

Answer

In recent years, the courts' resort to proprietary estoppel as a means of resolving disputes over property has increased dramatically. Of course, this in itself is worthy of note but not truly startling: the fact that the courts are prepared to intervene more readily where they perceive unconscionability shows that 'equity' remains a developing body of law able to meet in part the demands of the late twentieth century. Indeed, since *Taylor Fashions v Liverpool Victoria Trustees* de-constructed the law of proprietary estoppel, by making the conditions for a successful claim less rigid, the doctrine has moved into new fields, as both *Voyce v Voyce* and *J T Developments v Quinn* illustrate. Indeed, it may be that proprietary estoppel emerges as the main counterweight to the relatively new formality requirements contained in s 2 Law Of Property (Miscellaneous Provisions) Act 1989. However, the development of this doctrine supposes not only that there are clear (or relatively clear) principles which can separate the legitimate from the spurious claim, but also that the consequences of a successful invocation of proprietary estoppel are clearly understood. In this last respect, the jury is still out.

It is clear from *Taylor Fashions* that an estoppel will arise in favour of a claimant if they can prove an assurance, relied upon to their detriment. It is also clear from *Crabb v Arun DC* that once the court has decided that the equity is established, it may seek to 'satisfy' it in a way appropriate to the case before it, in essence using its discretion. The recent case of *Voyce v Voyce* where the court unscrambled the complicated property dealings of the parties and imposed a solution outside of the parties intention shows that the court's power is wide and unfettered by the actual expectations of the parties. However, none of this settles the question of the nature of proprietary estoppel *per se*, all it does is tell us that the court may use the doctrine to achieve such result as it thinks fair and reasonable in the circumstances. In particular, the question has arisen in the context of licences which on the now confirmed traditional view (*Ashburn Anstalt v Arnold*) are not interests in land. In simple terms, if the result of the courts' deliberations are that one of the parties has a licence over the other's land, generated or protected by estoppel, does this amount to an interest in land. Or, to put it another way, is the estoppel itself an interest in land that can bind third parties in the normal way appropriate to proprietary interests in registered or unregistered land, such that it can confer such a status on what would otherwise be a purely personal licence to use the land.

The answer to this question is by no means clear for there is little specific guidance in the case law. This is not surprising given that the courts are more concerned with reaching practical solutions to practical problems without delving into the theoretical niceties of the nature of proprietary estoppel. In general, however, two distinct trends may be distinguished. Firstly, there is some support for the view that licences generated by estoppel, or protected by estoppel, are themselves interests in land. This seems to be another way of saying that an estoppel *per se* has a proprietary character. Support for this view may derive from *Ives v High* and from *Inwards v Baker* where dicta suggest that estoppel, once arisen, may bind a third party. In unregistered land, this is through the mechanism of notice (*Ives v High*) and in registered land presumably through occupation giving rise to an overriding interest under s 70(1)(g). Certainly, if this view is correct, it seems that estoppel has been elevated to an interest in land *per se* and one could argue, in the context of licences, that the decision in *Ashburn Anstalt v Arnold* (that licences are not interests in land) is limited to contractual licences only. However, there are difficulties. First, a distinction should be made between estoppel which creates a right between A and B and estoppel which protects a pre-existing right (created by A and B) against C. It is only the first of these scenarios that gives rise to the problems we are considering. For example, in *Ives v High*, one explanation of the case is that A and B had by their action created an easement binding on A's land and, when the land was sold to C, C so acted as to be estopped from denying the right. In effect, this has nothing to do with the transfer of existing rights to a third party because the third party is bound by estoppel because of their own actions. In other words, C is bound by their own estoppel, not that which existed between A and B. Secondly, there is only fragile evidence that an estoppel itself has ever been held binding against a third party. The acid test would be whether an estoppel generated licence has ever had this effect, because as we know that pure licences cannot bind third parties, it is the estoppel that would be instrumental. The evidence is, however, equivocal. It is true that in *Inwards v Baker*, the court indicated that the claimant should be awarded a licence to occupy which could bind third parties and the same solution was adopted in *Greasely v Cooke*. Likewise, in *Re Sharpe* the court accepts that the estoppel (the 'equity') can bind a trustee in bankruptcy. However, it is also true that both *Inwards* and *Cooke* can be justified on other grounds (that the claimant should have had a life interest under a settlement, see *Dodsworth v Dodsworth*) and in *Williams v Staite* (another oft cited case in support of this view) the matter was assumed rather than argued.

Indeed, after the decision in *Ashburn*, it may be that the more traditional approach should be preferred. This sees proprietary estoppel not as a right in itself, but rather as a method of creating rights: a means to an end, not the end itself. If such a view is taken, estoppel can be regarded as a process whereby rights are created, rather like a contract or a deed but, of course, much less formal. For such a view, it is not the fact of estoppel that is relevant but, rather, the right that is created. So, for example, if the estoppel gives rise to a lease, a freehold, an easement or any proprietary right, then there is no doubt that a third person buying the land over which the right takes effect will be bound by it: they are bound in the same way that any lease, freehold or easement would bind. The essence of the matter is that the estoppel has generated a proprietary right and it is the right that is binding not the estoppel. The one distinction between this and the normal way in which such rights bind third parties may be that estoppel generated rights operate within the systems of registration in a different way. Thus, a 'normal' equitable easement in both registered and unregistered land is required to be registered to be binding (minor interest and Class D(iii) respectively), but an equitable easement generated by estoppel can be binding without its 'owner' having to take positive steps: being an overriding interest in registered land (*Celsteel v Alton*) and through notice in unregistered land (*Ives v High*). The difference is mainly because of the informality in the creation of the right and the practical fact that the 'owner' may not know they have a right until the court actually 'concretises' it in a dispute. The corollary of this is, however, that if the estoppel gives rise to a licence, then it is not, indeed cannot, be binding on a third party because licences as such are not proprietary rights.

Of course, this view of estoppel - as a method of creating a right, not a right itself - may be criticised on the ground that the position of the 'owner' is precarious if the land is transferred *before* the court announces what right they have. The answer is relatively clear. If the new owner of the burdened land does not object to the exercise of the estoppel generated right (ie generated by their vendor) then no issue arises. If, however, the new owner does object, court action will ensue and the court has the opportunity of concretising the estoppel in such a way so as to ensure that the right is binding ie by establishing a proprietary interest. This is result oriented, but that is the nature of proprietary estoppel.

In conclusion, then, whether proprietary estoppel has altered the fundamental distinction between personal rights and proprietary rights depends on the view one takes of the doctrine. Is an estoppel in itself a right, or is it merely a method whereby rights are created, some of which will be proprietary, some of which will be personal? One thing is, however, clear. Proprietary estoppel has certainly relaxed the formality that is necessary for the creation of proprietary rights and, in that sense, there is certainly some truth in the question.

Notes

This is a difficult question as it raises an issue to which the courts have not yet given a conclusive answer: viz the nature of proprietary estoppel. Help can be obtained from academic comment; see in particular, Battersby (1991) Conv, Moriarty 100 LQR 376, Dewar 49 MLR 74.

Question 30

In 1991, Alberto, Benito and Claudio live in Nos 1, 2 and 3 Abdication Street respectively, an area of registered land. Each house has a large garden, although Alberto has concreted over his and uses it to store spare parts connected with his car repair business. Last year, Alberto asked Benito (in No 2) whether he would mind if Alberto constructed a small shed to store some more valuable equipment even though this meant siting some foundations in Benito's garden. Benito readily agreed and helped Alberto construct the shed. A little later, before the shed is complete, Alberto promised that Benito could store some of his (Benito's) own goods in the shed. Benito also asked if Alberto would mind if his wife's mother, Tosca, parked her cycle in the shed.

Alberto readily agreed, not realising that Tosca drove a very large motorcycle which would occupy considerable space. Meanwhile, Claudio has been negotiating with Benito over the purchase of some land at the back of Abdication Street owned by Benito. Benito is unwilling to sell, but permits Claudio to occupy the land pending the negotiation of a long lease. Benito asks Claudio to pay him £300 per month as 'a down-payment' for the lease, but when Claudio comes to pay, Benito tells him to keep his money as Benito has decided to sell and will give him a full price later. Claudio subsequently seeks planning permission from the local council to build a pizza parlour on his new land and gets Alberto's and Benito's guarantee that they will not oppose planning permission. However, just as he is about to instruct a local builder, Benito informs him that he has sold the property to Bigburger Inc.

Alberto is distraught at the prospect of a large takeaway restaurant behind his house and manages to sell to Hank. Hank has just discovered Tosca's motorcycle in the shed and has removed it, along with Benito's property. In retaliation, Benito is about to knockdown that part of the shed that stands on his land. Claudio wants to know whether he can enforce his rights against Bigburger Inc.

Discuss.

Answer plan

- what rights, if any, are created by the actions of the parties: proprietary estoppel
- what are the nature of those rights: how is the equity satisfied
- how, if at all, do those rights affect subsequent purchasers of the land

Answer

This problem essentially revolves around two central issues, although their application to the particular facts of the individual circumstances of Alberto, Benito and Claudio may vary. First, it is necessary to determine the nature and extent of any interests created by the actions of the brothers in favour of each other. Secondly, and depending on the answer to the first question, whether any or all of those interests are rights binding on the subsequent purchasers of the plots, Hank and Bigburger Inc.

a) Alberto and the shed; Benito and the storage: Tosca and her motorcycle

As a preliminary matter, it is apparent from the facts of the problem that none of the arrangements of the parties have been recorded in writing. This immediately raises the problem that unless the activities fall within one of the recognised exceptions to the formality requirements found in s 2 Law of Property (Miscellaneous Provisions) Act 1989, then such interest as may have arisen will be void. Further, although it is not absolutely certain (see *Street v Mountford*) there is little evidence that any of these arrangements -particularly those relating to storage in Alberto's shed - were intended to or do amount to a lease. If that were the case, if the lease were less than three years, the absence of writing would be immaterial (s 54(2) LPA 1925) and it would be binding on Hank according to its terms as an overriding interest under s 70(1)(k) LRA 1925.

The absence of writing means that Alberto, Benito and Tosca may all have to rely on proprietary estoppel if they are to claim rights. It is then another matter whether these rights will be binding on subsequent third parties. Alternatively, these rights could arise from contract and be in the nature of contractual licences.

i) The shed

Clearly, Benito the owner of the land over which the shed will intrude has agreed that Alberto can build that shed in the full knowledge that use of his own land will thereby be diminished. In such circumstances, Alberto will have a reasonable chance of establishing that Benito is bound by proprietary estoppel from demolishing the shed. In the language of *Taylor Fashions v Liverpool Victoria Trustees*, Benito made an assurance to Alberto (albeit in response to Alberto's request) that the shed could be built, which was relied upon by Alberto to his detriment. The fact that Benito assisted in the building can only reinforce this presumption. In such circumstances, following cases such as *Crabb v Arun DC* and *Ives v High* (and subject to what will be said below in respect of Benito's claim of storage), it is unlikely that Benito will be able to renege on his promise and destroy the shed. Equity will intervene by way of an injunction.

What is not clear, however, is what will happen if either or both of the properties are sold. There is authority that the *benefit* of the estoppel cannot be transferred to a successor in title (*Fryer v Brook*) because it is merely personal to the promisee, although this appears to have been contradicted by Lord Denning in *Ives v High*. In our case, then, it is unclear whether the estoppel that exists in favour of Alberto can be passed on to Hank when he purchases the land. However, Hank might argue that the benefit of the right has been expressly assigned to him under the contract of sale (ie as a personal transfer of a personal right). Likewise, if Benito were to sell his house (although there is no evidence here), it is unclear whether the estoppel binding on him could be made to bind a subsequent purchaser. The matter is considered in more detail below.

ii) The storage of Benito's goods

The position here is somewhat complicated. On one view of the facts, Alberto has simply agreed that Benito can store his goods in his shed. This may have been done as a personal favour - in which case Benito has a bare licence - or it may have been done as a counterpart to Benito's promise and assistance with the shed - in which case it may be a contractual licence. If it is a bare licence, it seems that it is revocable at will by Alberto (*Thomas v Sorrell*), although if it is contractual it may irrevocable by Alberto according to its terms (*Wintergarden Theatres v Millennium Productions Ltd*). However, in either case, it is clear that a contractual licence as such cannot be binding on a third party (Hank), *Ashburn Anstalt v Arnold*.

An alternative view is, however, that there has been some form of estoppel generated in Benito's favour by Alberto's conduct in relation to the storage. It would be necessary to establish that there was an assurance reliance and detriment (*Taylor Fashions*), although it might well be difficult on the facts of the case as there appears to be little in the way of detriment suffered by Benito in reliance on the promise. However, if the estoppel is made out, Benito could go on to argue either: a) firstly, that the estoppel should be satisfied by the granting of an easement of storage in his favour. This would be binding on Hank, a subsequent purchaser, as an overriding interest under s 70(1)(a) following the judgment in *Celsteel v Alton*. We know, however, from the law of easements, that a right to storage may be incapable of being an easement because it amounts to exclusive possession of the servient tenement (*Copeland v Greenhalf, Grigsby v Melville*); b) secondly, therefore, Benito could argue that the estoppel itself is capable of binding a third party, irrespective of whether it generates an easement or a licence. If this is the case - that an estoppel is an interest in land - it might be binding on the purchaser Hank as an overriding interest, possibly under the catch-all s 70(1)(g).

iii) The shed and the storage

In the above analysis, we have assumed that the shed building and the storage were separate events. It might be possible to argue that they are so interconnected that, at least for Alberto and Benito, they must be taken together. Hence, by analogy with *Ives v High*, it could be argued that if Alberto wants the benefit of the shed, he must be subject to the burden of the storage of Benito's goods. This would, of course, prevent either of the original parties from reneging on their agreement. Whether the 'burden' of Alberto's obligations could be passed to Hank is another matter. There is no evidence that Hank purchased Alberto's land with express knowledge of Benito's rights (or in an inequitable manner), so as to subject him to a personal constructive trust within *Ashburn Anstalt v Arnold*. Alternatively, however, if Hank seeks to make use of the shed, it is just possible that the court would stipulate that if he wished to take the benefit, then he must be subject to the burden. The problem with this is, however, that we could apply it to every subsequent purchaser of the two plots with the effect that purely personal rights could evolve into proprietary obligations.

iv) The motorcycle

The position over Tosca's motorcycle is very similar to the position above in respect of Benito's goods and it may well be difficult for Benito to establish anything other than a bare or contractual licence to support the parking/storage. Moreover, if we were to approach this issue on a benefit/burden analysis, it may well prove decisive that the 'benefit' is to be conferred on someone other than the person who is subject to the burden of the shed: viz the benefit is Tosca's but the burden of submitting to the shed falls on Benito. This makes it highly unlikely that Hank would be bound by this obligation when he purchases Alberto's land. The right is essentially personal and the analogy with benefit and burden is not very appropriate.

b) Claudio and the plot of land and Bigburger Inc

The first matter is to determine the nature of Claudio's interest, if any, in the plot of land that Benito has sold, and then to see whether this interest is binding on the purchaser, Bigburger Inc.

Clearly, Claudio and Benito start off by negotiating the terms of a lease, as that is the clear intention of the parties following Benito's initial refusal to sell the land. Equally clearly, there is no doubt that Claudio and Benito fail to reach agreement on the terms of the long lease. On the other hand, Claudio is let into occupation by Benito on the grounds that he can occupy pending successful conclusion of negotiations and provided that he pays £300. At first site, this may appear to raise the possibility of a periodic tenancy. If this could be established then Claudio would have an overriding interest against the purchaser Bigburger (s 70(1)(k) LRA 1925), who would be bound by the terms of the lease. Unfortunately for Claudio, however, it appears from *Javid v Aqil* that occupation and payment of rent (and there was none here, merely offered) will not give rise to a periodic tenancy if the occupation can be attributed to negotiations pending the grant of a 'real' lease. This is Claudio's position and he will be a tenant at will which, despite its name, is not a tenancy at all. It is not a proprietary right and cannot be binding on Bigburger Inc.

Circumstances then take a different turn. Benito makes it clear that he will now sell to Claudio and Claudio, acting in reliance on this, begins to make plans for his small restaurant. Benito even re-enforces this by promising not to oppose a planning application. This may be, then, raise a proprietary estoppel in Claudio's favour, providing he can establish assurance, reliance and detriment in the normal way. On the facts, Benito will argue that he simply made an offer to sell which he has now withdrawn, whereas Claudio will argue that he has relied on the promise to such an extent as to raise an estoppel in his favour. The answer is one of judgment, but certainly Claudio does not appear to have suffered the same degree of detriment as the promisees in other cases such as *Re Basham, Pascoe v Turner* and *Inwards v Baker*. His claim is, therefore, quite weak. However, were it to be accepted that Claudio had an estoppel in his favour, there is every chance that this could be binding against Bigburger. Either the court will satisfy the equity with the award of a proprietary right (eg the freehold, *Pascoe*) which could be binding on the purchaser as an overriding interest under s 70(1)(g), Claudio being in actual occupation; or, the estoppel itself can be regarded as an interest in land which will bind Bigburger in the same way.

Notes

This is similar to question 4, being the practical application of the problems there raised.

Easements

Introduction

Easements comprise those rights which one landowner may exercise over the land of their neighbour. Common examples are the right of way, the right of light and the right of support. It is essential to the understanding of the law of easements that the student appreciates that every easement has two aspects: one landowner will enjoy the benefit of an easement and another will be subject to its burden. This is just another way of saying that easements exist over a servient tenement for the benefit of a dominant tenement. However, it is important to remember the dual nature of an easement as this will make problems concerning the transmission of easements to third parties easier to understand. It is often said that easements can either be 'positive' or 'negative' in character. The former are those which allow the dominant tenement owner (the person who has the benefit) to do some thing on the servient land, such as enjoy a right of way, while the latter prevent the servient tenement owner (the person subject to the burden) from doing some thing on their own land, such as building new premises. However, it is obvious that most easements have a positive and negative aspect, depending on which position you look at it from, and the distinction is not of great practical use. Its one advantage is that it illustrates that many so-called negative easements are similar to restrictive covenants and perhaps their subject matter would be more appropriate to the latter than the former.

Checklist

Questions on the law of easements can come in either problem or essay form and the student should be aware of the following issues:

A) The nature of easements
B) The creation of easements
C) The distinction between legal and equitable easements
D) The transmissibility of easements to third parties, both benefit and burden
E) reform of the law of easements

Question 31

Is there any consistent policy evident in the rights which the courts have recognised as easements?

Answer plan

- *Re Ellenborough Park*
- positive and negative easements
- relationship to restrictive covenants
- public policy

Answer

An easement is essentially a right of property that is enjoyed or exercised over land belonging to another. In one sense, the law of easements can be regarded as the private law equivalent to public planning law as where an easement prevents the owner of land from doing something on his own property. For example, if land is subject to an easement of light, this effectively prevents the owner of that land from building so as to obstruct that light. However, easements are not only negative in nature. Many easements authorise a neighbour to use the land subject to the easement in a way that would otherwise be a trespass. Thus, a right of way enables the owner of the easement to walk across his neighbour's land. Indeed, this distinction between 'positive' and 'negative' easements is perhaps one of the most important factors in the law of easements for it is often said that the law should be wary of accepting new negative easements, as in *Phipps v Pears* where it was alleged (and rejected) that the servient owner was under a negative easement preventing him for demolishing his premises. In fact, it is inherent in the nature of all easements that they comprise both a positive and a negative aspect, for what the dominant owner is allowed to do, the servient owner must suffer. In this sense, irrespective of whether the easement is positive or negative, all easements comprise a benefit and a burden. The land subject to the easement (the servient tenement) bears the burden of that easement whilst the owner of the land entitled to enjoy the easement (the dominant tenement) has the benefit of it. It is important to remember this duality when considering questions of the transmissibility of the benefits and burdens of easements to subsequent purchasers of the dominant or servient land.

The traditional starting point for a discussion about the essential characteristics of an easement is the judgment in *Re Ellenborough Park*. This gives us a four-fold test. Firstly, there must be a dominant and a servient tenement. Secondly, an easement must accommodate, that is benefit, the dominant tenement. Thirdly, the dominant and servient tenement owners must be different persons and fourthly, the easement must be capable of being the subject matter of a grant. If the alleged right satisfies these conditions, it is most likely to be recognised as an easement irrespective of the name given to it by the parties that created it. The only small caveat to this is that occasionally certain rights which fulfil these criteria are not accepted as easements on grounds of public policy. It is rare, however, for an alleged easement to be disallowed on this ground explicitly and it is more likely that a judge will prefer to base his decision of lack of fulfilment of one of the flexible *Re Ellenborough* criteria.

The essential duality of an easement is evident from the first condition. It is crucial that if an easement is to exist there must be a dominant and servient tenement. The easement must burden land but it must also benefit land and in technical terms the easement cannot exist in gross (*Hawkins v Rutter*). The easement runs with the land, both the benefit and the burden.

The second condition established by *Ellenborough* is that the easement, or rather the alleged easement, must confer a benefit on the dominant tenement: it must accommodate it. Easements are proprietary rights and therefore confer benefits on land, not persons, *Manson v Shrewsbury Railway*. Rather like covenants that touch and concern the land, easements must benefit the user of land, the value of land or the mode of occupation of land. This particular requirement can be manifested in several ways. Thus, the servient tenement must be sufficiently proximate to the dominant tenement to be able to confer the benefit on it, *Bailey v Stevens*. However, the most widely cited example of an alleged easement that was disallowed as not conferring a benefit on the dominant tenement was the personal advantage in *Hill v Tupper* where the owner of a canal granted the plaintiff the right to put pleasure boats on the canal. This was deemed not to be sufficiently connected with the land so as to amount to an easement. It is not, however, authority for the proposition that mere commercial advantages cannot be easements. *Moody v Steggles* makes it clear that an easement which benefits a trade or occupation carried on on the land, such as a public house, is permitted, as where a pub sign is hung on adjacent property. Of course, the distinction here is sometimes difficult to draw and with such flexible criteria consistency cannot be guaranteed. On the other hand, this criterion does give judges a certain amount of hidden discretion to exclude those rights which for matters of policy should not fall within the ambit of easements. In *Hill*, for example, it may well have been against the public interest for a particular individual to have exclusive rights to a waterway. The same cannot be said for the easement in *Moody*.

As indicated above, an easement has a dual aspect. It confers both a benefit and a burden. It is essentially a right in another's land. For that reason, the third *Ellenborough* condition is that the dominant and servient tenements must not be both owned and occupied by the same person, *Roe v Siddons*. Indeed should the dominant and servient tenements come into the ownership and possession of the same person, any easement over the servient land will thereby be extinguished. In effect, this means that a man cannot have an easement against himself, although due to the operation of the rule in *Wheeldon v Burrows* an easement may be created in such a situation when part of the merged land is sold off. The rule is, however, that the dominant and servient tenement must not be both owned and occupied by the same person and so there is nothing to stop a tenant having an easement against their landlord as in *Wright v Macadam* (and vice versa).

Finally no right may amount to an easement unless it is capable of forming the subject matter of a grant or, in other words, an easement must be capable of being expressly conveyed by deed. This appears to be an all engrossing condition, itself having several different manifestations. First, there is the obvious point that an easement cannot exist unless there is a capable grantor, that is somebody legally competent to create an easement, and a capable grantee. So, for example, no easement can exist where purportedly granted or received by a limited company having no power to grant or receive easements under its articles of association. Secondly, it is clear that all rights that are capable of forming the subject matter of a grant must be sufficiently definite. In the case of an easement, therefore, the right must be capable of clear description and precise definition so, for example, in *Re Aldred* a right to a good view could not exist as an easement. Similarly there is no easement of privacy (*Browne v Flower*) and no easement to receive light generally as opposed to a right to receive light through a defined window. It is, however, with the final element of this condition that consistency gives way to flexibility and, to some extent, judicial discretion. Only those interests actually lay in grant that are capable of lying in grant or, in other words, that the right must be within the general nature of rights recognised as easements or be rights by close analogy thereto. This does not mean of course that new easements for new times cannot exist. Thus, there has been an easement to use a letterbox as (*Goldberg v Edwards*) and an easement to use an airfield as in *Re Bolton Paul*.

In essence, however, it does mean that the courts will strike down alleged easements which do not appear to the particular judge to be within the class of rights that should be recognised. Of course some general principles have developed and it is often said that no new easement will be recognised that requires the servient owner to spend money, *Phipps v Pears*. Again, according to *Phipps*, the law will look unfavourably on claims to an easement which give the dominant tenement owner the right to prevent the servient tenement owner from doing something on his land. These so called negative easements are more properly to be regarded as within the sphere of restrictive covenants. It is also said that no right will be recognised as an easement which gives the dominant tenement owner the right to use exclusively the servient tenement. So in *Copeland v Greenhalf* no easement could exist to store tools of the trade on the servient land and in *Grigsby v Melville* a right of storage in a cellar could not be accepted. Similarly the right to park in a defined space in a carpark cannot be an easement although as *Newman v Jones* makes clear, there can be an easement to park generally on a piece of land. The position here is, however, somewhat policy orientated. For as *Macadam* shows, the particular facts of a case may require the granting of an easement so as to facilitate commodious living. In that case, the tenant successfully claimed an easement of storage of coal in a small part of the landlord's coal shed. There is no real distinction that can be sensibly drawn between this and *Copeland* and *Melville*, other than to say that the court in *Macadam* believed that the tenant deserved the right claimed. Such flexibility is inherent in the *Ellenborough* conditions and it would be unfortunate if the development of the law of easements was stultified by too exacting and rigorously applied conditions.

At present, the *Re Ellenbourgh* rules provide an outline outside of which a judge cannot go but inside of which he may recognise an easement or not according to the circumstances of the case, the needs of the property and indeed the behaviour of the parties. In this sense of course, the law is uncertain as it becomes difficult if not impossible to predict whether a new right will be regarded as an easement However, to some extent many issues which formerly would have fallen within the range of easements are now dealt with under the law of restrictive covenants and local planning regulations. Of course, the easement has one great advantage. Not only is it proprietary like the restrictive covenant (so therefore capable of binding third parties), it may, unlike the restrictive covenant, be legal and bind those third parties automatically in unregistered land and as an overriding interest in registered land. The powerful effects of easements on servient lands and on successors in title to those lands means that care has to be taken when considering any proposed reform in the definition of these rights.

Notes

This has to be one of the most boring questions any examiner can ask in any subject. It is straightforward, textbook based and easy to score a 'safe' mark. Any attempt at criticism will be rewarded as most students repeat verbatim the same answer, as above. It is difficult not to.

Question 32

Apart from easements established by long user, by what methods can easements be created? Is there any significant difference between legal and equitable easements?

Answer plan

- legal and equitable easements
- distinction between grant and reservation
- express creation
- implied creation: necessity; *Wheeldon v Burrows*: s 62 LPA

Answer

Easements are essentially a species of right that one landowner enjoys over the land of another. They are proprietary in the sense that they attach to the land rather than to the owners of the land. Moreover, like restrictive covenants easements have a dual aspect. They both confer a benefit on one piece of land to be enjoyed by the owners for the time being thereof and they impose a burden on land which must be accepted by the owners for the time being of the servient land. It is intrinsic in this duality that the benefit and the burden of an easement can be transmitted independently. Thus, it is quite possible for the benefit of an easement to be passed onto several owners of the dominant tenement even though ownership of the servient tenement remains in the hands of the person who granted the easement. Likewise, it may be only the servient land that is transferred, or both. Indeed, the ability of easements to bind third parties is one reason, perhaps the most important, why it is necessary to have clear rules governing both the creation of easements and the conditions which must be fulfilled before an easement can be regarded as legal or equitable.

All easements are either created expressly, impliedly or by long user under the law of prescription. However, this tells us nothing about whether the easement will be legal or equitable and we must start therefore with a consideration of these requirements. In general terms, an easement can qualify as a legal interest only if it is held as an adjunct to a fee simple absolute in possession or as an adjunct to a term of years absolute in possession, s 1 LPA 1925. More important in practice, however, is the rule that easements are only legal if they are created by statute, by deed, or by the process of prescription (or long user). All other easements must be equitable. We are not concerned here with the creation of easements by prescription and the creation of easements by statute speaks for itself, as where a local or private Act of Parliament gives certain rights to the person for whose benefit the Act was passed. The requirement of a deed for a legal easement is also reasonably straight forward, as this ensures that its existence is easily discoverable by a prospective purchaser of the servient land. However, although all other easements must be equitable, that does not mean that equity requires no formality at all. Thus, under s 2 Law of Property (Miscellaneous Provisions) Act 1989, a contract for the creation of an interest in land (eg an easement) must be in writing signed by both parties. So, rather as is the case with equitable leases, if the parties have a written agreement to create an easement which can be regarded as specifically enforceable under *Walsh v Lonsdale*, equity will treat an equitable easement as existing. However, it is no longer true that mere oral promises or agreements can create equitable easements, save only where the easement is created by proprietary estoppel, as in *Ives v High*. These then, are the formality requirements. What are the consequences of an easement being legal or equitable?

For the most part, the consequences concern the effect of the easement on third parties, particularly purchasers of the servient land. In fact, the position is relatively straight forward. In unregistered land, all legal easements will bind any subsequent owner or occupier of the servient land under the general rule that legal interests bind the whole world. In registered land, the legal easement may well have been noted on the servient tenement title at the time of its creation and will be binding for that reason. However, under s 70(1)(a) LRA 1925, legal easements are overriding interests and so automatically bind all subsequent transferees. This is as it should be, because most legal easements will be evident to a potential purchaser and he should take his land aware of their existence. Of course, the same is not always true of equitable easements and so the conditions for binding purchasers of the servient land are different. In unregistered land, most equitable easements are Class D(iii) Land charges and they must be registered as such in order to bind a subsequent purchaser. If they are not registered, they will be void, *Midland Bank v Green*. The exception to this seems to be equitable estoppel easements which according to Lord Denning in *Ives* are not within

Class D(iii) land charges because that category includes only those equitable easements which could once have been legal but are rendered equitable by the 1925 legislation. Estoppel easements are, of course, purely equitable and according to *Ives* bind a purchaser through the doctrine of notice. In registered land, equitable easements are minor interests and must be registered as such. Again however, estoppel easements may be exempt from this requirement and may in fact take effect as overriding interests under s 70(1)(a). This is the effect of *Celsteel v Alton* which decided that estoppel easements openly enjoyed were not excluded from s 70(1)(a). Although this has been criticised by the Law Commission, the reasoning is the same as in unregistered land: *viz* that owners of equitable easements arising by estoppel may well not understand that they have such a right and so cannot be expected to protect it by registration. These rules, then, reasonably clear in application, determine when an easement will be legal or equitable and the consequences that flow from that. What we must now discuss are the circumstances in which easements can be created, or rather the practical methods by which they come into existence.

Generally speaking, and putting prescription on one side, the creation of easements is either by express or implied grant or express or implied reservation. A grant is where the owner of the servient tenement grants an easement to the owner of what will become the dominant tenement. A reservation is the opposite. It is where the transferor of land reserves to themselves an easement over the land they are transferring. In very broad terms, it is easier to grant easements to somebody else than it is to reserve easements to oneself because of the rule that a man cannot generally derogate from his grant.

Turning first to reservation. If A sells land to B, A may expressly reserve to himself an easement over the land sold. The easement will be legal if it is reserved in a deed and it will be equitable if it is reserved in a written document. Likewise, however, it is clear that an easement can be impliedly reserved by the vendor in these circumstances. Thus if A sells land to B, but the only access to the land retained by A is over the land sold to B, an implied reserved easement of necessity will exist in A's favour, as in *Pinnington v Galland*. However, in order for an easement of necessity to be reserved in this fashion, it must be true that the land retained by the vendor would be unusable without the easement claimed and no easement will be allowed where it is merely inconvenient to use another route, as in *Re Dodd*. It should be noted that impliedly reserved easements may also be legal or equitable. The easement is implied into a sale by A to B in favour of A. If, therefore, the sale is by deed the easement is implied into a deed and is legal. If the sale is by written document for valuable consideration, the easement is implied into that document and will be equitable. In other words, the easement carries the character of the document into which it is implied.

Turning now to easements by grant, as where one landowner (A) expressly grants an easement to his neighbour B, either by deed or in writing, or where A sells some land to B and as part of that sale grants B an easement over the land retained by himself. In the first case of course, the easement is expressly granted and will be legal or equitable according to the form it takes. In the second case, the easement may well be expressly granted, as part of the sale. However, it is this second scenario, the sale of land by A to B that most often gives rise to implied grant. In fact, implied grant can take one of three forms, although in all cases the principle is the same: that an easement is implied into the grant of land by A to B so that the land sold becomes the dominant tenement and the land retained becomes the servient tenement. As with reservation, if the easement is implied into a deed, the easement will be legal and if it is implied into a written transfer it will be equitable. Firstly, it is clear that easements may be impliedly granted by way of necessity. So if the land granted cannot be used except by, say, access over the land retained by the vendor, an easement of necessity will exist. Or, as in *Wong v Beaumont*, an easement of ventilation by necessity was held to exist when the land granted was intended to be used as a restaurant but could not be so used without a ventilation shaft over the land retained by the vendor. Generally speaking, it is easier to claim an implied grant of an easement of necessity than it is an implied reservation but, as *Re MRA Engineering* shows, a real necessity must exist, not merely a more convenient use of the land.

Secondly, easements may be impliedly granted under the rule in *Wheeldon v Burrows*. As we know, no easement can exist where the dominant and the servient tenement are owned and occupied by the same person. However, it often happens that a landowner will use one part of his land for the benefit of another, as where a landowner walks across a field to get to his house. These are sometimes known as quasi-easements because they would be easements had the land been in separate ownership or possession. So, if it should happen that the owner of the entire plot of land should sell the quasi-dominant part of his land, in the previous example the house, or in other words the land benefited by the right, the rule in *Wheeldon v Burrows* stipulates that he will have impliedly granted that right to a purchaser. This rule, which is based upon the idea that a person cannot derogate from their grant, can be expressly excluded and of course he cannot grant as easements any rights which are incapable of being easements. Furthermore, it appears from *Wheeldon* itself, that the rights that are impliedly granted must have been used by the vendor at the time of the grant for the benefit of the part sold (for example, the path must be being used), and the easement must be continuous and apparent and/or necessary for the reasonable enjoyment of the part granted. (It is most likely that the second and third conditions are alternatives and they were so treated in *Wheeldon*). Providing, however, that these conditions are fulfilled, the purchaser of that part of the common owner's land which is the dominant part will acquire those easements impliedly granted in the conveyance of the land. Again, the right may be legal if the conveyance of the land was by deed or equitable as in *Borman v Griffith*, where the grant of the land was under an equitable lease. Furthermore, if the common landowner grants the dominant part to X and at the same time grants the servient part to Y, it is clear that the rule in *Wheeldon* operates to give X an easement over Y's land, as in *Swansborough v Coventry*. Although the rule in *Wheeldon* does not apply to reservations of easements, it is obvious that any owner of land who intends to sell that land in parts may well find his own land bound by easements he has impliedly granted. It is, in fact, a very powerful means of creating easements.

Finally, we come to third method by which easements may be impliedly granted. That is under s 62 LPA 1925. At the outset however, it should be noted that s 62 only applies to conveyances which are defined in the Law of Property Act as transfers by deed. Thus, s 62 can operate only to create legal easements because it only operates when there has been a transfer of land by deed or its registered land equivalent, the registered disposition. Section 62 is a very wide ranging statutory provision and it has many purposes beyond the creation of easements. Moreover, it is clear that it is not limited to rights which are continuous or apparent or reasonably necessary as in *Wheeldon*. The only requirement is that the right is capable of being an easement. The factual situation of s 62 is, however, quite different from *Wheeldon*. If a landowner has two or more plots of land and then conveys by deed one of those plots to a purchaser, the purchaser will be granted by s 62 all of those rights that were previously enjoyed with the land. This is straight forward enough, but s 62 will convert into easements all of those rights enjoyed for the use of the land sold, even though prior to sale they were merely precarious, in the sense of being exercised by permission only. According to *Sovmots Investments v Secretary of State for the Environment*, it is essential for the operation of s 62 that the land owned by the vendor was in prior diversity of occupation before the sale. Practically, this means that before the land is sold to the person acquiring the easement, it must have been used by either a tenant or a licensee of the vendor who enjoyed rights over that land. If then the land is conveyed to that person by deed, that person will be impliedly granted the rights previously enjoyed. So in *Goldberg v Edwards*, a licensee enjoyed a right over her landlord's land and when a new tenancy by deed was granted to her, that licence was transformed into an easement (see also *Wright v Macadam*). This has potentially devastating consequences for the landowner, although s 62 can be avoided by an express contrary stipulation. The requirement of prior diversity of occupation does of course limit the effects of its operation, but a land owner must be careful. Of all of the cases of implied grant, it is the most far removed from the intention of the parties.

Notes

Although a long question, it is relatively simple. Most textbooks deal with this issue thoroughly, although Gray is again very good.

Question 33

In 1990, Matilda, the owner of three adjacent terraced houses, title to which were registered, decided to realise some capital and resolved to sell two of her properties whilst remaining in the third. In the conveyance of No 10 to Aaron, Matilda promised to allow Aaron to park his ten foot yacht in her garden, in return for which Aaron allowed Matilda to site a satellite dish on his roof. Matilda also agreed orally that Aaron could hang a small sign advertising his boat building business (which was based on the river some four miles away) on her end wall. When negotiating a sale of No 12 to Jacob, he insisted that he be·given the right to temporarily store some building materials in Matilda's garden (next to the yacht) should he run out of space in his builder's yard opposite. This was agreed in the conveyance.

Matilda has just sold her house (No 11) to Ben who is unhappy with the elaborate sign that Aaron had erected and with the yacht taking up most of his garden. Aaron, however, has just retired and sold his business, the yacht and house to Sarah who is threatening to remove the satellite dish unless the yacht and the sign are allowed to stay. Meanwhile, Jacob has been storing materials on a permanent basis in the garden of No 11 and Ben decides to remove them.

Discuss.

Answer plan

- the nature of easements
- creation of easements
- legal and equitable easements and third parties

Answer

This problem concerns the acquisition of easements and their effects on persons who subsequently come into possession of the servient and dominant land. In essence, there are two separate problems here, as the relationship of Matilda's property to each of the premises she has sold should be considered independently. Of course, in all cases, it is first necessary to determine whether the alleged right is capable of existing as an easement, then whether any easement that does exist is legal or equitable and then finally its effect on a purchaser of the dominant or servient tenement as the case may.

a) Matilda and Aaron, and the subsequent sales of both houses

In this situation, there are three rights which it is alleged may amount to easements: the erection of the satellite dish in favour of Matilda's property, and the parking of the yacht and erection of the sign on Matilda's property in favour of Jacob's property. Can these interests amount to easements for, if they cannot, they amount only to personal licences between the original parties which cannot bind on successors in title (*Ashburn Anstalt v Arnold*). Clearly, in respect of all rights, there is a capable grantor and grantee, there are two properties which could be the dominant and servient tenements and both tenements are not owned or occupied by the same person. Thus far, there is no difficulty with the requirements for a valid easement laid down in *Re Ellenborough Park*. However, some difficulty may exist in the need to show that the alleged rights benefit the dominant tenement *qua* tenement and whether they fall within the general nature of rights capable of being created as easements. This issue, and the nature of any right satisfying the *Ellenborough* formula, will be considered in respect of each right.

i)   The erection of the satellite dish is perhaps the least contentious. There seems little doubt that such a right is of benefit to the dominant tenement in much the same way as the easement to run telephone lines over neighbouring land accepted in *Lancashire & Cheshire Telephone Exchange Co v Manchester Overseers*. It is clear that there is no necessary reason to deny the existence of new easements, provided they do not contradict the *Ellenborough* principles. There is no expenditure required of the servient owner and no exclusive occupation of his premises and the right is sufficiently definite. It would seem to be able to qualify as an easement.

Indeed, assuming that to be correct, the facts of this problem make it quite clear that the right was expressly reserved by Matilda when she sold the house to Aaron. There is, then no difficulty over its creation and, because it is expressly reserved in a conveyance (ie a transfer by deed), this is a legal easement. What happens when the servient land is sold to Sarah? Being registered land, it is quite likely that the burden of the easement would have been registered against Aaron's title (Land Registration Rule 1925 r 41) when he became registered proprietor. In any event, even if it were not, legal easements in registered land are overriding interests under s 70(1)(a) LRA. In either case, therefore, Sarah is bound to give effect to the easement allowing siting of the satellite dish. It should be noted finally, that when Matilda conveys the dominant tenement to Ben, the benefit of the easement is transferred to Ben under the general rule that a benefit of an easement becomes annexed to each and every part of the legal estate and passes with it.

ii) Can Aaron (and then Sarah) claim an easement of parking of the yacht?

This particular claim raises difficulties for the owners of the alleged dominant tenement. There is no doubt that an easement of parking does exist, *Newman v Jones*. However, it is also clear that easements in general must not amount to exclusive user of the servient land (*Copeland v Greenhalf*) and for this reason it is highly unlikely that a right to park in a defined space can be an easement. The easement of parking in *Newman* was in respect of a general area of land and not a regular spot. Likewise in *Grigsby v Melville* a right of storage in a cellar was thought to connote exclusive use such as to oust an easement and the case where storage was permitted (*Wright v Macadam*) should be seen in the context of a dispute between a powerful landlord and a badly treated tenant. Unfortunately, therefore, it seems that this right amounts only to a personal permission between Aaron and Matilda: in other words a contractual licence. So, even if the benefit of this contract has passed to Sarah, the burden of it is incapable of binding a successor in title of the alleged servient tenement, *Ashburn Anstalt v Arnold*.

iii) The sign

Once again, this presents certain problems. There is no doubt that erecting a sign on a neighbour's property can amount to an easement, as in *Moody v Steggles*. It matters not that this is to advertise some commercial activity on the land, so long as the activity is intimately connected with the land and not a 'pure' commercial venture, as in *Hill v Tupper*. Moreover, there is, it would seem, no objection in principle to a grant of an easement to a landowner on the occasion of a conveyance of property X (the house), where the easement is to benefit property Y (the boat yard). After all, easements can be created by deed between landowners irrespective of any sale, as where a freeholder grants a right of way to his neighbour.

However, every easement must accommodate the dominant tenement and in this case, when the land was sold to Aaron, the business is carried on on property some four miles away. It is well known that while the dominant and servient tenement need not be adjacent, there must be proximity between them, *Pugh v Savage*. This will be a question of fact in each case. However, even if the right is capable of existing as an easement, there is a further problem. How has it been created? This is not a case of implied grant (there is no necessity, no claim under s 62 and no quasi-easement within *Wheeldon v Burrows*) and, in any event, the intentions seems to have been to create the easement expressly. However, we are told that the intended right is not expressly included in the conveyance to Aaron and it cannot, therefore, be legal: not being by deed (more accurately, not by registered disposition as this is registered land). Of course, easements can be expressly granted by other means, but then they will be only equitable but, yet again, there are formality problems. In order to be equitable, it is clear that the easement would have to have been granted by a valid contract which, if specifically enforceable, equity would treat as an equitable easement, *Walsh v Lonsdale*. However, this contract is not in writing as required by s 2 Law of Property (Miscellaneous Provisions) Act 1989 and there is no possibility of an equitable easement by this route. The only hope is that Aaron can claim an easement by proprietary estoppel, in similar circumstances to that in *Ives v High*. Clearly, there seems to have been a promise made and we are told that Aaron erects an elaborate (and hence expensive?) sign. This may be detrimental reliance. Further, it is no objection to the existence of an estoppel that it did indeed arise out of a failed explicit bargain, *Voyce v Voyce*. If an estoppel is established, a purely oral equitable easement may exist. In such circumstances, Sarah will have obtained the benefit of the easement under the normal rule that it is annexed to the land and Ben, the purchaser of the servient tenement, may well be bound by the estoppel easement because of the decision in *Celsteel v Alton*. Albeit subject to much criticism, this case tells us that an equitable easement arising out of an estoppel may amount to an overriding interest under s 70(1)(a) LPA. As such, it binds the purchaser, Ben, automatically.

b) Matilda, Jacob, the building materials and Ben

Once again, the initial question to be answered is whether the right to store is capable of being an easement. As noted above, it is an essential characteristic of an easement that it does not amount to exclusive use of the servient tenement. Thus, in *Copeland v Greenhalf* and *Grigsby v Melville* a right of storage was not admitted into the category of easements. However, we are told here that the right expressly granted was a right to store temporarily when the need should arise. This may be completely different as there are many easements (eg a right to use a lavatory, *Miller v Emcer Products*) which when being exercised by the dominant tenement owner on the servient land exclude any other use by the servient owner. One view is that the right of temporary storage is analogous to the right to park generally on a piece of land and, in any event a right to store trade produce has been accepted as an easement in *AG of Southern Nigeria v John Holt and Co*. Thus, it is a matter for argument whether this can exist as an easement. Of course, if it does, it seems that Jacob is going beyond its explicit terms and, of course this can be restrained by injunction. Finally, if the easement does exist, it is clear that it has been expressly created by the conveyance (ie by deed/registered disposition) and is therefore legal. As with the legal easements considered above, this will bind Ben, the purchaser of the servient tenement whether as being registered against his title or as an overriding interest under s 70(1)(a) LRA.

Question 34

Elizabeth is the owner of a large farm in Huntshire, title to which is unregistered. Last year, she built a small bungalow on her lower field for her retirement and asked her daughter, Anne, to look after it in the meantime. Anne moved in with her boyfriend,

Mark. The only access to the bungalow is along a dirt track over the farm proper or by boat along the river Garter which flows through the property. Last week, Anne and Mark had a serious row and Anne has moved out. Elizabeth, who was never fond of her daughter's boyfriend, agreed with Mark in writing that he can occupy the premises for five years at £800 per month and an initial sum of £2000. However, before any rent is paid, Mark meets another woman and moves in with her. Fortunately, soon after, Elizabeth is able to sell the bungalow to John by registered disposition for a large profit. Two months later, she decides to retire to Jamaica and sells the rest of the farm to Norman.

John has just re-surfaced the dust road in order to obtain access for his car. Norman, seeing the chance for a small profit, has asked John for £1000 to use the new road. John seeks your advice as to whether he should pay.

Answer plan

- the creation of easements by implied grant, s 62 LPA
- equitable or legal?
- affect on third parties of new easement

Answer

This question involves complicated issues about the creation of easements and their effect on third parties. In general, the position is simple enough. Legal easements must be created by deed, prescription or statute and equitable easements by written document under s 2 Law of Property (Miscellaneous Provisions) Act 1989 or by the law of proprietary estoppel, *Ives v High*. It is, of course, essential to determine whether any easement is legal or equitable for this may determine its ability to bind a purchaser of the servient land. However, in this problem, there is the further complication that there appears to be no express grant of the alleged easement. Such sales of the land as there are make no mention of any rights of way. Thus, we are thrown back on the creation of easements by implied grant: either by necessity, under s 62 LPA or the rule in *Wheeldon v Burrows*. However, whatever method, if any, is appropriate to this case, one important feature needs to be kept in mind. Under implied grant, the easement is said to be implied into a sale of the dominant tenement. That is, it is as if the grantor - who usually retains the servient tenement - did include the easement in the conveyance. Thus, it necessarily follows that if an easement is impliedly granted, it takes its legal or equitable character from the grant into which it is implied. So, implied grant can give rise to legal and equitable easements depending on the quality of the transfer to the owner of what becomes the dominant tenement.

Clearly then, John, the purchaser of the bungalow will wish to assert an easement of way over the road which passes over the farm of which it was formerly a part. The only way to determine whether the easement exists is consider the position of the three occupants in turn: Anne and Mark, Mark and then John. Moreover, if such an easement exists, it falls to be determined whether the easement binds Norman, the purchaser of the allegedly servient land and, even if it does, what the precise scope of the easement is.

i)   Anne and Mark

When Anne and Mark occupy the bungalow, it is clear that they do so at the invitation of the owner, Elizabeth. There is no express grant of an easement to them. Moreover, it appears from the facts that they do not occupy the premises by virtue of a grant of any estate. There is no sale of it to them and there is no lease of it to them. They appear to be licensees occupying with the consent of the owner under a family arrangement wherein there is no intention to create legal relations, *Street v Mountford* and *Heslop v Burns*. There is, therefore, no grant into which an easement can be implied. In any event, in order to create an easement where none already exists, there must exist a dominant tenement that is itself proprietary in nature. A licence is not proprietary and no easement can be created by the creation of such a personal right.

ii) Mark

When Anne leaves the property, the status of the remaining occupant, Mark would appear to change. As we are told,

Elizabeth the owner, agrees by writing that Mark can occupy the premises. This is clearly an attempt to create a lease in Mark's favour, although the lease is not legal, not having been created by deed. Neither can it qualify as a legal periodic tenancy because no rent has been paid and, in any event, a premium (or 'fine') has been taken, s 52(2) LPA. This is, in effect, an equitable lease under a specifically enforceable contract within *Walsh v Lonsdale*. This has one immediate consequence in that s 62 LPA cannot be used to establish the implied grant of an easement. Section 62 applies to 'conveyances' which, under s 205(1)(ii) LPA, does not include a contract to grant an estate. So, there is no scope for the implied creation of an easement by this method. This leaves us with two alternatives: creation by *Wheeldon v Burrows* (which can apply to contracts, *Borman v Griffith*) or by virtue of necessity.

As to the rule in *Wheeldon*, this applies where an owner grants part of their land and, because of the rule that a person cannot derogate from their grant, is taken to impliedly grant easements necessary for the proper enjoyment of that land. In the normal case, these impliedly granted easements were rights which the owner themselves exercised for the benefit of the plot sold, being a burden on the plot retained. In our case, this would be if Elizabeth had used the path to get to the bungalow and then granted an estate to Mark. This is not a case, however, where the vendor was exercising such quasi-easements before partition: it is a case where the person to whom the land was sold was exercising those rights. It is doubtful whether *Wheeldon* can apply in these circumstances because the rule appears to be that as well as the easements being necessary for the reasonable enjoyment of the property (and/or continuous and apparent) they must 'have been and are at the time of the grant used by the owner of the entirety for the benefit of the part granted'. This does seem to rule out implied grant by *Wheeldon* in cases such as this unless we can say that Mark, prior to the sale, was exercising the alleged easement on behalf of the owner of the entirety. Perhaps this is possible on the facts given that Mark seems to have been a 'housesitter'. If it is, then an impliedly granted equitable easement will result and this will be binding on Norman, the purchaser of the servient tenement, only if it is registered as a Class D (iii) Land charge. There is no evidence that it has been so registered and so would be void against Norman.

Assuming, however, that there is no new novel application of *Wheeldon* so as to support an easement, has one arisen by necessity? There is no doubt that an easement of way can arise though necessity, as in *Pinnington v Galland*, but as *MRA Engineering Ltd v Trimster Co Ltd* confirms, an easement of way can be implied only where the land cannot be used at all, and not simply where it would be convenient. Moreover, in the Privy Council decision of *Manjang v Drammeh*, Lord Oliver relied on the Scottish decision in *Menzies v Breadalbane* as authority for the proposition that if access to land was available by water, this could negate an easement of way over *terra firma*. There is some doubt, then, over whether an easement of way by necessity could exist. Even if it did, it is impliedly granted to Mark in an equitable lease and is itself equitable. It would be void against Norman for lack of registration as a Class D (iii) land charge.

iii) John

If John is to claim an easement, it seems that once again it will be by virtue of an implied grant. In his case, he has been sold the bungalow by registered disposition and so has acquired legal title in the normal way. Being a conveyance of the legal estate, John can claim the benefit of s 62 LPA.

Under s 62, a purchaser of a legal estate in the land will be impliedly granted, as easements, all those rights previously enjoyed with the property that are capable of being easements, providing there is no express provision in the conveyance to the contrary and providing that there was diversity of occupation between the alleged dominant and alleged servient tenement prior to the grant (*Sovmots Investments Ltd v Secretary of State for the Environment*). In this case, there clearly was diversity of occupation (Elizabeth and Mark) and there is no contrary intention. Of course, this case is somewhat different from the usual situation where the person to whom the land is granted was the very person enjoying the right prior to that grant. However, the words of s 62 seem wide enough to cover the situation as here where the grantee acquires land but the right that is translated into an easement was in fact exercised by somebody else. The point of s 62 is, indeed, that rights benefiting the granted land are not personal but proprietary. If then an easement is impliedly granted under s 62, the easement will necessarily be legal.

Norman, the purchaser of the servient land will be bound by it as legal easements in registered land are overriding interests, s 70(1)(a) LRA.

Question 35

Lowlife Properties Ltd is the registered proprietor of a large industrial estate in the centre of Littleton which they have been using as a company headquarters. Last year they decided to split the estate into smaller properties and sell them off. The estate was split into three Units, with Lowlife keeping Unit 3. Prior to the sale, the employees of Lowlife habitually ate their lunch on the grass outside what is now Unit 2 and parked their cars and walked across the forecourt of what is now Unit 1 to get to work. Likewise, all the water pipes for the estate cross the land of Unit 3, as does an overgrown path, the only access by foot. Last month, Unit 1 was sold to Kirk, a hairdresser, by registered disposition. Unit 2 was let to Scot, a fashion designer, on a seven year lease by deed, containing a covenant not to assign or sub-let without the landlord's consent.

Initially, Scot objected to the noise created by Lowlife's employees at lunchtime, although he agreed to drop his objections when Lowlife agreed to lower the rent. Kirk does not like the employees looking in at the people in his salon as they walk to work, so he fences off the parking area. However, most of Kirk's customers come by foot and he has tidied up the footpath. Lowlife is expanding fast and threatens to cut off the water supply if its new employees cannot park their cars. It has blocked off the path in retaliation. Scot's business has now floundered and he eventually obtains Lowlife's consent to assign to McCoy, who manages to negotiate a lower price because of the lunchtime gatherings. Lowlife now plan to sell to Megacorp who seek your advice as to the problems they may encounter.

Answer plan

- nature of easements
- creation of easements: *Wheeldon v Burrows*
- inequitable conduct and constructive trusts

Answer

In this case, the difficulties that Megacorp, the potential purchaser from the original owner of the entire estate, are two-fold. In the first place, they may be subject to binding easements in favour of the plots granted to Kirk and Scot (and assigned to McCoy) and secondly, they may well wish to claim the rights once enjoyed by Lowlife on behalf of their employees.

a) The water supply and the footpath

These are rights which will be claimed as easements by both Scot (and then McCoy) in respect of Unit 2 and Kirk in respect of Unit 1. The first issue to address is whether these rights are capable of existing as easements, within the formula established in *Re Ellenborough Park*. There seems to be little difficulty here: rights of way, whether limited to foot or not, are among the most common easements and a right to receive water through a pipe running on the servient land was accepted in *Goodhart v Hyett*.

However, what is not so straightforward is establishing how these easements are created, for there is no evidence here of an express grant. In fact, this appears to be an instance of the operation of the rule in *Wheeldon v Burrows*, whereby the owner of land will be taken to have impliedly granted to a purchaser of part of it, all those rights capable of existing as easements, which the owner enjoyed for the benefit of the land sold and exercised over the land retained. The requirements of such an implied creation seem to be that there must have been user by the common owner at the time of the grant, and the rights claimed must be reasonably necessary for the proper enjoyment of the land granted and/or continuous and apparent. In respect of the right to water supply, there is no difficulty with these conditions as (presumably) the water serviced all parts of the estate before sub-division, the reasonable necessity is obvious and, if required, continuous and apparent user will be deemed from the existence of water pipes. It is debatable, however, whether the same is true of the footpath. It is reasonably necessary, being the only access by foot, but being 'overgrown' there may be some argument that it was neither in use at the date of the grant nor, if required, continuous and apparent. This is simply a matter for argument, although if the path is well-defined, albeit overgrown, it will probably satisfy both conditions. The conclusion is, therefore, that both these easements have been impliedly granted to the purchasers Kirk and Scot, against the property retained by Lowlife. As both grants were themselves legal, the easement implied into them will be legal. As such, they will be binding on Megacorp as overriding interests under s 70(1)(a) LRA. Likewise, the benefit will be passed to McCoy, successor in title to the dominant tenement, as an adjunct of his estate.

b) The right to park and walk

As above, there is no difficulty with a right of way existing as an easement and, indeed, in *London and Suburban Land and Building Co v Carey* it was made clear that in principle (although not on the facts of that case), a right to park on an access way for the purpose of unloading etc could be an adjunct to the right of way. However, there has been considerable controversy over whether a right to park can, of itself, amount to an easement, not least because it seems to amount to exclusive user of the premises to the exclusion of the servient owner (see *Copeland v Greenhalf*). In *Newman v Jones*, an easement of parking was permitted, but only if the right was exercised generally and not in respect of the same defined places (see also *Sweet & Maxwell Ltd v Michael-Michaels Advertising*). Megacorp should be advised that only the claim to general parking may be upheld.

There is, however, a more pressing problem than this, for it is difficult to see how the easement has been created. The easement is alleged to exist in respect of the plot retained by the original vendor, Lowlife. Thus, if at all, it must have been by way of reservation when he sold the alleged servient tenement. There is no express reservation, s 62 cannot apply (it applies to grants only) and neither can *Wheeldon v Burrows*, which itself was a claim to an implied reservation of easement which failed. The only possibility is that Lowlife - and then Megacorp - could claim a reserved easement of necessity. Unfortunately, it is trite law that reserved easements of necessity are, not least because it was within the power of the vendor to expressly reserve a right. The only situations where there is a real possibility of success is when the retained land would be unusable without the impliedly reserved easement. This is clearly not the case here. So, if Lowlife have no easement, there is nothing to pass to Megacorp and they will have to re-negotiate with the adjoining landowners.

c) Lunchtime activities

Once again, there are serious difficulties if it is alleged that an easement was reserved for Lowlife when the land was let to Scot. As above, there is no express reservation and clearly no ground for a claim of necessity. In any event, it is highly unlikely that such a right could exist as an easement. It is not something which benefits the dominant tenement as such, being related to a right of recreation, *Re Ellenborough Park*.

However, just because this right cannot exist as an easement is not the end of the matter. It seems from the facts of the problem, that after he had acquired his estate in the land, Scot agreed to allow the lunchtime activities to continue and received consideration for it. In other words, there seems to have been a contract between Lowlife and Scot so as to create a contractual licence to use the area at lunchtime. This right, which is purely personal between the parties, nevertheless can be enforced against Scot while he is in possession as an original party to the contract. Licences are, however, not interests in land and cannot in principle bind successors in title (*Ashburn Anstalt v Arnold*). As a matter of property law, then, the obligation to allow the activity cannot be passed to McCoy when he buys the lease. However, it may well be that McCoy is bound to give effect to the licence because of his conduct at the time of the assignment. The lease cannot be assigned without Lowlife's consent and presumably they negotiated with McCoy and Scot about whether to agree. Indeed, we are told that McCoy obtains the lease for a reduced price because of the lunchtime activities. This does suggest that McCoy will be bound to give effect to the contractual licence because it would be inequitable for him to deny it. A constructive trust will be imposed upon him personally - not as a matter of property law - to give effect to the licence, *Binions v Evans, Ashburn Anstalt v Arnold*. It should be noted finally that, because this licence arose out of a contract between Scot and Lowlife, the benefit of the contract (ie the right for employees to go on Unit 2) can be expressly assigned under normal contractual principles. Thus, Megacorp should ensure that this right is transferred to them.

Notes

The above problems put into practice the issues considered at the beginning of this chapter. Usually, the questions will mix issues of the nature of easements, their creation and transmissibility to third parties. In this respect, creation and transmissibility must be distinguished, even though factually they may appear to be the same, as with *Wheeldon* and s 62.

Freehold Covenants

Introduction

In Chapter 5 on leases, we examined the law surrounding the operation of leasehold covenants. However, it is not only landlord and tenant that may wish to enter into promises affecting the mode of user of their property. Freeholders may also wish to control the use which neighbours may make of their land, as where owners of residential property may wish to preserve the non-business character of their area or the owners of an industrial estate may wish to limit the type of activity carried on there. Obviously, however, freeholders do not stand in a relationship of privity of estate with each other and the rules of leasehold covenants are inapplicable. Consequently, a set of principles have developed - mainly in connection with restrictive covenants - which govern the running of covenants between freeholders. Like leasehold covenants (and easements), each covenant comprises a 'benefit' and a 'burden' and it is always necessary when considering problems in this particular area to remember that before a plaintiff can sue a defendant on a particular covenant, the benefit must have passed to the plaintiff and the burden must have passed to the defendant. Indeed, it can quite easily happen that the benefit has passed, but the burden has not, or vice versa, and it is imperative when dealing with these issues to consider benefit and burden separately.

Checklist

Thus, students must be familiar with the general principles of covenants - such as the meaning of 'touching and concerning' - the requirements for the transmission of the benefit of covenants both at law and in equity, the requirements for the transmission of the burden in equity and the requirements of registration under the system of registered and unregistered land. In addition, some questions may ask whether the strictness of these rules - particularly in relation to the burden of a covenant - can be circumvented in any way, for example, by use of the principle in *Halsall v Brizell*. Finally, we should note that the rules discussed below apply whenever there is neither privity of estate or contract between the plaintiff and defendant. This is usually in disputes between freeholders, but may also occur between a landlord and a sub-tenant or a landlord and a tenant on an equitable lease: in neither case is there privity of estate and so these rules are relevant.

Question 36

Consider whether the rules relating to the running of freehold covenants adequately ensure that successors in title can enforce the benefits obtained by an original covenantee.

Answer plan

- the meaning of 'benefit' and the original covenantee; s 56 LPA
- 'successors in title': s 78 LPA
- benefit at common law: s 78 LPA
- benefit in equity: Annexation: *Federated Homes v Mill Lodge:* assignment:
  building schemes

Answer

Nowhere is it more true than in the law of real property that no man is an island. The use by one person of his or her land can seriously affect quality of enjoyment, the mode of user, or the occupation of their neighbour. This is obvious and it should come as no surprise therefore that the law of real property has developed rules and principles that allow one landowner to control the use to which his neighbour may put their own land. This can be achieved through the law of easements or through the law of covenants in leases. It can however also be achieved where the neighbouring landowners are freeholders through the mechanism of restrictive covenants. The law relating to freehold covenants applies in all of those circumstances where no privity of estate exists between the parties, that is where the plaintiff and defendant do not stand in the relationship of landlord and tenant. However, like covenants in leases, covenants between freeholders also have a dual aspect. Thus, each covenant will confer a benefit on one person and a corresponding burden on another. Indeed, it is a curiosity of the law of real property that rules relating to the transmission of the benefit of a freehold covenant, that is to somebody who buys the land from the original covenantee (the person to whom the covenant was made) are entirely independent from the rules relating to the transmission of the burdens of the covenant, that is to a person who buys land from the original covenantor (the person who made the promise). It is quite possible therefore for the benefit of a covenant to run to a successor in title of the original covenantee but for the burden of that covenant to have been destroyed or to bind only the original covenantor, and vice versa.

This particular question, however, asks us to consider the position of the benefit of covenants. In general terms, before the benefit of any covenant can pass to a successor in title of the original covenantee, that covenant must be one that touches and concerns the land. This area of law is concerned with the transmission of proprietary rights not merely personal advantages. Thus as with leasehold covenants, it is always essential to determine whether the covenant falls within the definition of Lord Oliver in *Swift Investments v Combined English Stores*. These are a reasonably flexible set of criteria and do allow the Court considerable discretion in deciding whether a covenant touches and concerns. It is a useful requirement as there is an overriding policy objective not to clutter up title to land by obligations that are merely transient, uncertain or personal in nature. The touching and concerning requirement helps to achieve this. Assuming, however, a covenant can touch and concern the land, then it is possible for the benefit of that covenant to pass either at law or in equity. In general terms, the difference is one of remedy. At law, damages are the appropriate remedy for breach of covenant while in equity an injunction for breach of a negative covenant is more appropriate and specific performance of a positive covenant will be normal. It is also true that the requirements for the passing of benefit at law are generally stricter than the requirements for the passing of the benefit at equity. This is of course, another example of the relaxed view of equity in property matters. It is also clear that both the benefit of positive and negative covenants can pass at law or in equity. A positive covenant is one which requires the person burdened to expend money in its fulfilment (*Hayward v Brunswick*) whilst a negative covenant is one which prevents the burdened owner from doing something on his land such as carrying on a trade or business or some particular trade or business. Turning first to the transmission of the benefit at law. Apart from the requirement that the covenant touches and concerns the land, there seem to be three further conditions.

Firstly, the persons seeking to enforce the covenant must own some legal estate in the land. Prior to s 78 of the LPA the person seeking to enforce the covenant at law had to own the same legal estate as the original covenantee. So, if the original covenantee was a freeholder, the successor had to be a freeholder. Section 78 has, however, made it clear that the successor need only have some legal estate, such as where the original covenantee being a freeholder lets the land to a successor on a lease by deed. This has clearly made the transmission of the benefit at law slightly simpler. Secondly, it is clear that the covenant must benefit the land of the original covenantee. In most cases, it will be enough that the covenant touches and concerns the land because from this, the fact of benefit will be presumed. However, in theory it is open to somebody disputing the fact that the benefit has run at law to claim that the land of the original covenantee never could have benefited from the particular covenant made and therefore cannot pass to a successor in title, see *Wrotham Park Estates*. Thirdly, and most importantly of all the covenant must have been annexed to the land in order for the benefit to run with the land. In this respect, the decision in *Federated Homes v Mill Lodge Properties Limited* has made the position much simpler. According to the Court of Appeal decision in that case the benefit of every covenant whether positive or negative and whether in law or in equity will be annexed to the land and indeed to every part of it, providing the deed of covenant mentions the land expressly or by implication. It is true that later cases (*Roake v Chadha*) have made it clear that this statutory annexation can be excluded by clear contrary intention. However, the decision in *Federated Homes* has clearly provided successors in title to original covenantees with a safe and certain method of claiming that they are entitled to the benefit of a covenant. It is true that the decision in *Federated Homes* has been subject to much criticism. For example, that s 78 does not precisely say what the Court of Appeal allege and that it is a decision favouring certainty at the expense of individuality. Nevertheless, until over-ruled by the House of Lords which seems most unlikely this decision will govern the running of covenants at law.

Indeed, if we now turn to the position in equity we will see that *Federated Homes* has had an impact here also. Once again, assuming that the covenant touches and concerns the land, the person seeking to enforce the covenant must have some estate or interest in the land although of course this may now only be equitable. If that is established it seems that there are three methods that the benefit may transfer in equity. The first of these is under the rule of statutory annexation that we have just considered in relation to covenants at law. As noted then, *Federated Homes* applies with equal vigour to the annexation of covenants in equity, so a covenant will be statutorily annexed to each and every part of the land providing it is clear from the covenant what land is intended to be benefited. Indeed, the efficacy of the *Federated Homes* principle is such that the other two methods of transferring the benefit in equity may now be largely redundant, except perhaps in the limited circumstances of express contrary intention (*Roake*) or when the advantages of a building scheme are required. The building scheme is the second method by which the benefit may be transferred. This is a rule based upon common intention and practicality. It allows a common vendor (such as a property developer) to transfer the benefit of the covenants received by him from every purchaser of a plot of land to every other purchaser of a plot of land. It is an attempt to create mutually enforceable obligations. Of course, there is nothing unique in this because under the normal rules, the benefits of the covenants made by early purchasers will be automatically transmitted to later purchasers who buy part of the retained land. However the advantage of a building scheme is that it allows the benefit of later purchasers' covenants to be given to earlier purchasers even though the time factor is out of synchronisation. The requirements for a valid building scheme were laid down in *Elleston v Reacher*. There must be a common vendor, the land must be laid out in definable plots, the benefits must be intended to be mutually enforceable, and these must be the conditions upon which all purchasers buy. These are, however, not inflexible and later cases such as *Re Dolphins Conveyance* and *Baxter v Four Oaks* illustrate that the benefit will run under a building scheme even though all of the requirements have not been met. It should be noted, however, that a building scheme does not affect the running of the burden of covenants and if the obligations are to be truly mutually enforceable the normal steps for transmitting the burden of restrictive covenants must be followed. Usually this will mean registration of the covenants against the title of all purchasers.

Finally, the third method of transmitting the benefit of covenants is the assignment. It is trite law that the benefit of a contract (ie a covenant) may be expressly assigned. So, for example, if a purchaser of the covenantee's land is expressly assigned the benefit of that covenant, he or she will be able to enforce it. However, this method does have some disadvantages. It seems that this is a method of transferring the benefit personally. So, following *Re Pinewood* if there has been an assignment of the covenant to the first successor of the original covenantee, a chain of assignments is required. Assignment is a personal not a proprietary method of transfer. Of course, after *Federated Homes* such a method is largely redundant and in all cases of the transmission of the benefit in equity the plaintiff (ie the successor in title) is at the mercy of the Court when seeking a remedy. Equitable remedies are discretionary and it is quite possible that a person who is in principle entitled to enforce covenants may not gain the remedy of injunction or specific performance if they do not come with clean hands.

It should be apparent from the above that it is relatively straight forward to transmit the benefit of a covenant both at law and in equity. The decision in *Federated Homes* has made this even more likely and the only real limit seems to be that the covenant must touch and concern the land. Of course having the benefit of a covenant is useless unless there is somebody who is subject to the burden. In this respect, the rule that the burden of only restrictive covenants may run and then only in equity is a real limitation on the practical enforcement of covenants. It means that in all cases where the original covenantor has parted with their land, only restrictive covenants will be relevant and then only that the rules of equity will be in play. As we have seen, these give rise to only a discretionary remedy and the successor in title to the original covenantee will have to establish a bona fide claim if they are to succeed.

Notes

A long but straightforward question. Essentially bookwork.

Question 37

Do you agree that the rules allowing the imposition of covenants on freeholders and their successors in title is too restrictive?

Answer plan

- the original covenantor
- successors in title and s 79 LPA
- requirements of registration

Answer

It is a general principle of English law that while the benefit of a contract can be assigned to a third party, the burden of a contract cannot. In the law of real property, this can cause serious difficulties for it means that when an owner of land makes a promise by covenant to do or not to do something on their land (in other words imposing a burden on that land) then any successor in title to that original covenantor may well be able to acquire the land free of the burden placed upon it. Obviously this is of great advantage to the successor to the original covenantor, but it is of no use to those persons who enjoy the benefit of the covenant, for they may see the benefits which they so carefully extracted destroyed on the first sale of the burdened land. Fortunately, the law of real property has mitigated the harshness of the contractual rule by providing that in some circumstances burdens attached to land by way of covenant may assume a proprietary nature and may be passed onto any person who subsequently acquires that land.

As is well known, the position is relatively straight forward if the covenantee and their successors and the covenantor and their successors stand in the relationship of landlord and tenant. Then the matter is governed by *Spencers* case and the doctrine of privity of estate. If, however, the covenant was made between freeholders or concerns persons not otherwise in privity of estate, such as a landlord and a sub-tenant, the rules commonly known as the rules of freehold covenants come into play. Not surprisingly, the rules allowing the transmission of burdens in non-privity of estate cases are quite strict as it is a general policy requirement that title to land should not be unduly cluttered. In essence the starting point for a discussion of the transmission of the burden of freehold covenants must be the decision in *Tulk v Moxhay*. In that case, concerning a restrictive covenant not to build in Leicester Square, it was decided that if a covenant touched and concerned the land and was restrictive in nature it could as a matter of conscience and equity be binding on any purchaser of the land burdened by the covenant who had notice of its existence. Although the principles have developed considerably since *Tulk*, the limits put on the doctrine by that case still exist. Thus it is clear that burdens of covenants may only run in equity. This is an equitable doctrine with all of the attendant problems associated with equitable rights including the fact that remedies are discretionary. Moreover despite some attempts, it is now clear that only the burden of restrictive or negative covenants may run in equity.

The conditions for the transmission of the burden are as follows. Firstly, the covenant must touch and concern the land and therefore pass the test in *Swift Investments v Combined English Stores*. Secondly, the covenant must be negative in nature and this is a question of substance not a question of form, normally resolved by asking whether the owner of the burdened land is required to expend money. Thirdly, the doctrine takes effect in equity only thus opening up the possibility that the equitable interests (ie the negative covenants) may be defeated by a sale to a purchaser of a legal estate for value. Of course, in many cases these hurdles are not formidable and most well drawn restrictive covenants will satisfy these initial tests. If they do, there are further matters which must be satisfied before a burden will run to a successor in title. Firstly, and most importantly of all, the covenant must have been made for the benefit of land owned by the covenantee. In other words, the burden cannot run unless it is a burden that benefits land of the covenantee. Like easements there must be a dominant and servient tenement. In effect, this means that not only must the original covenantee have owned land at the time the covenant was created but also that the particular covenant must have been capable of benefiting that land. This is a question of fact although the onus is on the person seeking to deny the covenant to prove that the land of the covenantee was not in fact benefited *Wrotham Park Estates v Parkside Homes*. The meaning of benefit is crucial in these circumstances and according to *Re Gadd's Transfer* it has several components. Next, it is necessary to establish that the burden of the covenant is annexed to the land. Words of annexation can, of course, be used. So, for example, a covenant expressed to be for X and his heirs and successors in title would effectively annex the covenant to the land. However, such long windedness is no longer needed because of s 79 of the LPA. This provision effectively incorporates words of annexation into every deed of covenant. The net effect is that the burden of restrictive covenants will be automatically annexed to the land unless the deed of covenant expressly contains a provision to the contrary. The position is effectively the same as that achieved for the benefit of the covenant under s 78 of the LPA as interpreted in *Federated Homes v Mill Lodge*.

Assuming these conditions are established, the covenant now has a proprietary nature. This means that the burden of the covenant can in principle bind successors in title to the original covenantor's land. However, as we have noted above these restrictive covenants take effect in equity and like all equitable rights they are capable of being defeated by a sale to a purchaser of a legal estate for value. Before 1925, as *Tulk* itself makes clear, a purchaser of the covenantor's land would only be bound by restrictive covenants even if they had passed the above tests if he purchased that land with notice of the covenants. Now, of course, notice has been replaced by registration, both in registered and unregistered land. Thus in order for a proprietary restrictive covenant to bind a purchaser, it must be registered in the relevant way. In registered land, the covenant must be protected by an entry as a minor interest on the register, usually by way of notice. In unregistered land the restrictive covenant is classified as a Class D(ii) land charge and must be registered accordingly. It should be noted, however, that the requirement of registration is needed only to bind purchasers of the legal estate. Thus, because these covenants are already proprietary, if the covenantor's land comes into the possession of somebody who is not a purchaser of a legal estate (such as a squatter or an equitable tenant or a person receiving the property by way of gift) then a restrictive covenant whether registered or not will be binding.

These then are the conditions upon which the burden of a restrictive covenant may be binding. As is obvious, the rules are quite strict applying only to restrictive covenants and only being in equity and usually subject to a requirement of registration. Obviously the burden of positive covenants cannot run and of course this can cause hardship. For this reason there are a number of avoidance devices that may be used. None of these are entirely satisfactory and it is only if the Law Commissions proposals for reform are adopted that the situation will substantially change.

Question 38

Victor was the freehold owner, registered with absolute title, of five shops in the Kings Road, Oxtown. No 1 sold electrical goods, No 2 general household goods, No 3 was a pet shop and Nos 4 and 5 were empty. Two years ago, Victor sold No 4 to Eve, who covenanted that she would not carry on any trade other than a dressmaker at No 4. Just after, he sold No 5 to Polly who covenanted 'with Victor and the owners for the time being of the shops in Kings Road' that he would use No 5 for no other purpose than the breeding and wholesale of pedigree budgerigars and would erect and maintain a fence to protect his neighbours in the event of an escape. Last week, Victor let No 1 to Albert on a four year lease in writing, who immediately sub-let to Bill. At the same time, he sold No 2 to Claude by registered disposition who turns the premises into a garden centre. Victor has since discovered that his original tenant of No 3 left the property some months ago and is now occupied by Desmond, a squatter, who is selling second hand clothes and electrical goods.

In the course of her dressmaking, Eve has invented a new sewing machine and has begun a small scale manufacturing and retail outlet from her premises. Meanwhile. Polly found that bird-breeding was not profitable and has turned to rabbit breeding. Unfortunately, this gets out of hand and the Kings Road is overrun with rabbits escaping from No 5. Claude's entire stock is threatened.

Advise the occupants of the Kings Road as to their respective rights and obligations.

Answer plan

- position of the original covenantors and covenantees
- running of the benefit at law and in equity
- section 78 LPA and *Federated Homes*
- section 56 LPA
- rights of squatters

Answer

This question concerns the operation of covenants in situations where there is no privity of estate between the original covenantor and the original covenantee and their respective successors in title. However, as is made clear from the facts of this problem, there is no issue here of the running of the burden of the covenant: both the original covenantors (Eve and Polly) are still in occupation of the burdened land and it is against them that an action for breach of the covenants will be directed. Turning first to the nature of the these covenants. The covenant by Eve is clearly restrictive in nature and without doubt touches and concerns the land. Likewise, Polly's covenant to keep only budgerigars is restrictive and because it affects the mode of user of the land (*Swift Investments v Combined English Stores*) it also touches and concerns. Polly's second covenant - to erect and maintain a fence - does touch and concern but it is positive in nature requiring expenditure by the owner of the burdened land. However, the fact that one covenant is positive may not be crucial in all respects in this case as it is only the burden of positive covenants that cannot flow to successors in title. There is nothing to prevent the benefit of a positive covenant passing in the same way as that of a restrictive one.

Firstly, we need to determine who the original parties to the covenants are, for they will be able to sue on the benefit of the covenant against Polly and Eve (the original covenantors) irrespective of any question of the passing of the benefit under 'land law' rules. It is simply a matter of contract. Clearly, Victor, the original freeholder (and now the landlord of No 1 and owner of No 3) has the benefit of all covenants by both Polly and Eve, being an original covenantee: he can sue on all the covenants at law and on those covenants in equity where he is still in possession of the land, *Chambers v Randall*. Of course, the remedy at law will be damages and they will be nominal if Victor does not possess the land at the time of the breach. In practice he will wish to obtain an injunction for breach of both restrictive covenants and a decree of specific performance in respect of the positive covenant to build a fence. This will require him to sue in equity and, therefore, he should sue as freeholder of No 3. It is clear also, however, that Eve, the purchaser of No 4 (and an original covenantor to Victor) is actually an original covenantee of the covenants made by Polly. As we are told, Polly's covenants are made with her vendor (Victor) but also the 'owners for the time being of the shops in Kings Road'. This description includes Eve, who by then is an owner of a shop in the King's Road, and so under s 56 LPA 1925, Eve is deemed to be a party to the deed of covenant. That section allows a person 'to take the benefit' of any covenant as an original party to it so long as they are in existence at the date of the covenant and the covenant is intended to benefit them, *White v Bijou Mansions*. Thus, Eve may enforce both the positive and negative covenants against Polly in law or in equity, being an original covenantee. Of course, the reverse is not true, as the benefit of Eve's covenant has never been passed to Polly, either by deliberate assignment or under the rules to be discussed below.

We can now turn to the position of successors in title to the original covenantees, in this case of Victor. It is trite law that the benefit of a covenant may be transmitted to a successor either at law or in equity, provided in all cases that the covenant touches and concerns the land. This has already been established. However, each successor needs to be considered in turn.

i) The successors to shop No 1: Albert and Bill

It is clear that Albert and Bill will be able to claim the benefit of these covenants only in equity. Albert's estate in the land is under a four year lease in writing - not by deed - and so it must amount to an equitable lease, *Walsh v Lonsdale*. Albert has only an equitable estate and thus his tenant (the sub-lessee of Victor) can be in no better position. So, both have equitable interests and we need to consider whether the benefit of the covenant has passed in equity.

Clearly, all covenants touch and concern the land and both Albert and Bill have some interest in the land entitling them to sue. We may note here that neither of them need have the same interest in the land as the original covenantee (Victor), so long as they have some interest within s 78 LPA. Moreover, the covenants will be presumed to benefit the land (*Re Earl of Leicester*) and in any event seem to be within the meaning of benefit put forward in *Re Gadd*. However, has the benefit passed under one of the three ways recognised by equity: assignment, a building scheme or annexation? There is no evidence of the first and the second is clearly inappropriate on the facts. However, after *Federated Homes v Mill Lodge Properties*, it is established that the effect of s 78 LPA is to attach the benefit of a covenant automatically to the land, provided it is mentioned in the original conveyance, unless this is explicitly precluded, as in *Roake v Chadha*. There is no such exclusion. Moreover, it is immaterial that the present plaintiffs have an interest in only part of the land originally benefited by these covenants. Under *Federated Homes*, a covenant is attached to each and every part of the land, so long as each and every part is capable of benefitting from it. That is clearly the case here. It should also be noted that *Federated Homes* applies to positive covenants in exactly the same way as negative covenants and so no distinction can be drawn between the covenants made by Eve and those made by Polly. Thus, the benefit of all three covenants has run in principle to Albert and Bill and they can take action to restrain unlawful user of No 4 and No 5 as well as forcing Polly to build a secure fence, subject to the court's right to refuse the discretionary remedies in equity. Of course, the action will be commenced by Bill, the present occupant of No 1 and, indeed, Albert will be permitted to sue in respect of his reversionary interest only if Bill does not take action.

ii) The successor to shop No 2: Claude

The position with Claude is much the same as above, except that Claude has a legal estate in the land. He may sue, therefore, either at law or in equity depending on whether he wishes damages or an injunction and specific performance. To recap: there is no doubt that Claude has an estate in the land, that the covenants touch and concern the land and that the benefit has been annexed to his part of the land under *Federated Homes*. He may enforce all three covenants against Polly and Eve respectively.

iii) The successor/occupier to Shop No 3: Victor and the squatter

We have already noted above that Victor is an original covenantee and may sue on all three covenants as a matter of contract. Moreover, he is still in possession of No 3 so may sue for a legal or equitable remedy at his choosing. Yet, what of the squatter, Desmond, for he may wish to enforce the covenants if his occupation and use of the property is being disrupted? Once again, the covenants touch and concern the land and under *Federated Homes* they are annexed to each and every part of it. However, it does appear that Desmond has no interest in the land which could entitle him to sue. This is not fatal. If we examine s 78 LPA closely, it declares that successors in title may obtain the benefit of covenants and then says that 'in connection with covenants restrictive of the user of land 'successors in title' shall be deemed to include owners and occupiers for the time being of the land'. Clearly, this means that even a squatter, being an occupier, can obtain the benefit of a restrictive covenants if all of the other conditions are met. Thus, Desmond can sue on the covenants restricting the use of premises and so can prevent Eve from selling electrical goods and Polly from breeding rabbits.

Question 39

In 1988, Lucy, an insurance saleswoman from London decided to purchase a country house in the village of Small Steeple. Finding a farm cottage with a paddock in a small private road she offered to buy it from Giles, the owner of the farm of which it was part. The sale was completed by deed and contained covenants by Lucy not to allow the fence adjoining the farmyard to fall into disrepair, to contribute to the cost of the upkeep of the road, to maintain the paddock as an open space, to use the premises for residential occupation only and not to alter the external appearance of the cottage. These covenants are expressed to be made with 'the vendor and the owners for the time being of No 2 and No 3 Flower Lane, being similar properties'.

Three years later, Lucy has been made redundant and finds she can no longer afford the cottage and her house in London. She sells the property to John, a property developer, who announces that he is going to sub-divide the cottage into a flat and a workshop, adding a small studio at the back. He has no use for the field and Paul, a squatter, starts to build himself a small wooden cabin. Farmer Giles has already lost several sheep due to holes in the fence and the residents of Flower Lane wish to resurface the road.

Discuss.

Answer plan

- original covenantees: s 56 LPA
- nature of restrictive covenants
- the running of the burden in equity ✓
- requirements of registration ✓
- mutual benefit and burden ✗

Answer

In this problem, a landowner has entered into various covenants in respect of her land for the benefit of adjoining properties. Unfortunately, when the land subject to those covenants was sold to a third person - that is someone not a party to the covenants - it appears that the covenants may well have been broken. Consequently, the owners of the adjoining land, who have the benefit of those covenants, will wish to enforce them against the successor in title to the original covenantor. The issue thus revolves around the transmission of the burden of covenants in cases where there is no privity of estate.

Before we can deal with the substance of the matter in more detail, two preliminary points must be addressed. Firstly, irrespective of all other matters, only the burden of those covenants which touch and concern the land are capable of being transmitted to purchasers from the original covenantor, *Rogers v Hosegood*. In our case, there are five covenants and it would seem that all satisfy Lord Oliver's test for 'touching and concerning' put forward in *Swift Investments v Combined English Stores*. The only doubt may be over the covenant to pay for the upkeep of the private road, as this seems to be related to property other than land owned by the surrounding occupants. However, in itself this is not fatal, for the benefit is in the use of this road for surrounding properties, rather than the facility of a well made road for its own sake. For that reason this covenant also 'touches and concerns'. Secondly, it is trite law (*Austerberry v Corporation of Oldham*) that it is only the burden of restrictive covenants that may run, and then only in equity. It is necessary, therefore, to determine which covenants are restrictive, and this is done by examining their substance, rather than the form in which they are expressed, *Tulk v Moxhay*. In substance (and one test is whether the covenantor is required to spend money, *Hayward v Brunswick*), the covenant not to allow the fence to fall into disrepair and to contribute to the cost of the road are positive in nature. So, subject to what will be said below about avoidance devices, these covenants cannot be enforced against the purchaser John or the squatter Paul. All the other covenants are restrictive.

In essence, whether the burden of a restrictive covenant will run against a successor in title to the original covenantor will depend on two further factors, as supplemented by the requirements of the Land Registration or Land Charges Act as appropriate. First, at the date of the covenant, the covenantee must have had land capable of benefiting from the covenant. In other words, the burden will run only if the covenant was made for the benefit of other land and that other land is in fact benefitted, *London & South Western Railway v Gomm*. In our problem, there was in existence at the time of the covenant land owned by the covenantee - Farmer Giles - and it is a question of fact whether that land is benefitted by these covenants, with the onus on the defendant to prove that it does not, *Wrotham Park Estate v Parkside Homes*. In any event, even if it was thought that these covenants do not benefit land retained by Farmer Giles because they are 'residence' oriented (which is highly unlikely), it is clear that the covenants are also made with the owners of No 2 and No 3 Flower Lane. Although not parties to the deed, these owners are intended to be benefitted by the covenants and under s 56 LPA they are therefore deemed to be in the position of original covenantees, *White v Bijou Mansions*. Thus, the first criterion is satisfied.

Secondly, the burden of the restrictive covenant must be annexed to the land of the original covenantor. Fortunately, this condition is easily satisfied as s 79 LPA effectively annexes the burden of all restrictive covenants unless a contrary intention is expressed in the deed of creation. There is no contrary intention here and so all four restrictive covenants are annexed.

Presumptively, then, the burden of these covenants are capable of running with the land. However, it is inherent in the *Tulk* rules that such covenants - being equitable - in practice will bind only a purchaser of a legal estate who has notice of them. Notice has, of course, been replaced by registration. Thus, if this is registered land, these covenants need to be registered as minor interests to bind John, as he is a purchaser of a legal estate. If they are not, they are void against him and all future successors. Likewise, in unregistered land, the covenants must be registered as Class D(ii) land charges to bind a purchaser of a legal estate. In short, only if this requirement is satisfied is John bound in practice by these restrictive covenants. The squatter, however, is in a different position. A squatter is not a purchaser of a legal estate in the land and, therefore, it is immaterial whether the covenants are registered or not, *Re Nisbet & Potts Contract*. So long as the restrictive covenants fulfil all other requirements they become proprietary in nature and will bind if the registration rules are satisfied. The squatter cannot plead lack of registration, because he is not a purchaser and he at least will not be able to build on the paddock.

Finally, we should note that there is one way in which John might be forced to pay for the upkeep of the road, even though this is a positive covenant entered into by his predecessor in title. Under *Halsall v Brizell*, if a person wishes to take the benefit of certain rights, he can be compelled to honour his obligation to contribute to the cost of their provision. This is the principle of mutual benefit and burden: for example, he who takes the benefit of a private road must take the burden of the obligation to pay for its upkeep. If John wishes to use the road, he will on this principle have to pay for its repair.

Notes

This question demonstrates that the passing of the 'burden' is reasonably easily achieved although the requirements of registration are vital.

Question 40

The Easy Home Housing Company have just completed the re-development of a large inner-city estate in Liverham. It is their intention to ensure that the entire estate should be for residential occupation only and they propose to impose restrictive covenants on all purchasers to ensure this. They also wish to impose an obligation on all purchasers to keep the properties in good repair, so as to preserve the character of the neighbourhood. Advise them of the various methods by which this can be achieved, if at all.

Answer plan

- original covenantees and original covenantors
- passing the benefit under s 56 LPA and *Federated Homes*
- passing the benefit under a building scheme
- passing the burden: negative covenants and requirements of registration
- mechanisms to pass positive burdens and their effectiveness

Answer

This question invites consideration of the law relating to the transmissibility of covenants between freeholders. Of course, if the Easy Home Co had wished to retain the freehold of this large estate and lease out the properties to tenants on long leases, then the objectives of ensuring only residential occupation and ensuring full repair of the properties could have been achieved with relative ease under the law of leasehold covenants. In those circumstances, privity of estate would have existed between the purchasers and the landlord (the Housing Co) and both positive and negative covenants could have been made to bind successors in title. Of course, it would have meant that Easy Home became responsible for enforcement of the covenants, but at least the objectives could have been achieved. However, that is not to be and we are dealing here with a situation where there is no privity of estate.

Clearly, it is the wish of the development company to ensure two things: firstly, that each purchaser from them is placed under the burden of a covenant against non-residential user and the burden of a positive obligation to repair and, secondly, that each purchaser obtains the right to enforce every other purchaser's covenant. There is, in other words, a need to ensure mutuality of obligation between all the purchasers of properties on the estate. In considering these questions, however, it is wise to deal separately with the benefit of the covenants and then the burden.

a) The benefit

In this problem there is both a positive and a negative covenant, although as regards transmission of the benefit to successors in title from the original covenantee, there is little distinction between the two types of covenant. However, since it is the stated objective to ensure that there is mutuality of obligation amongst the prospective purchasers of the properties, it is clear that we are really concerned with transmission of the benefit in equity. The reason is, quite simply, that the burdens of covenants (at least restrictive ones) can be transmitted in equity only.

Clearly, there is no difficulty with the requirement that the covenants must touch and concern the land, *Rogers v Hosegood* or that the covenants do in fact benefit the land (*Re Earl of Leicester*). Likewise, each intending purchaser will have an estate in the land benefitted and the original covenantee will have land capable of benefitting at the time the covenant was made (although note the problem of the last sale considered below). The difficulty is, however, with the remaining requirement, namely that the benefit must be transmitted by one of the methods recognised by equity. The position is not straightforward for one simple reason. The developer owns all the land prior to any sale. On sale to the first purchaser, that purchaser will make the required covenants for the benefit of the land retained by the developer. In fact, under the *Federated Homes v Mill Lodge Properties* interpretation of s 78 LPA, the benefit of the covenant will be annexed to each and every part of the retained land. So, when the second purchaser comes along, and buys a piece of the retained land, they will clearly obtain the benefit of the first purchaser's covenants. Their own covenants will, of course, then go to benefit the retained land in the same way as those of the first purchaser. The difficulty is however, that on this analysis, it is impossible for the first purchaser to gain the benefit of the second purchaser's covenants and, indeed, for the second purchaser to gain the benefit of the third's and so on. In fact, although later purchasers always get the benefit of earlier purchaser's covenants, previous purchasers never get the benefit of those who buy later because when the subsequent purchasers actually buy the land, the previous purchasers have already bought their plots which are, consequently, no longer part of the developer's retained land. This problem, which is essentially one of timing, can be solved in two ways.

Firstly, when subsequent purchasers purchase their property, they can expressly include all previous purchasers as original covenantees. This will put those previous purchasers in the same position as the developer. Moreover, it is not necessary to list all such persons, or even make them parties to the deed. Section 56 LPA 1925 allows the benefit of a covenant to be passed to a third party provided they were intended to benefit and were in existence and the time the covenant was made, *White v Bijou Mansions*. There may be some difficulty with the last purchaser from the developer, as after that purchase the original covenantee (the developer) will have no interest in the land and this is required for transfer of the benefit in equity. However, the problem can be avoided by ensuring that one of the previous purchasers who does have land capable of benefiting is actually made a party to the deed. Of course, this is a cumbersome method of achieving the desired effect, but it would ensure that the benefit of every purchaser's covenant - negative and positive - was transmitted to every other purchaser.

However, a much simpler way to achieve the same effect is to ensure that the transfer of benefit takes place under a building scheme. This is a rule of limited effect that allows a common vendor (eg Easy Homes) to achieve the mutuality of benefit desired without having to worry about timing, or lack of land for the final sale or even the use of s 56 LPA. Under *Elliston v Reacher*, if there is a common vendor, an allotted plan for the premises wherein the land is laid out in lots, a well defined area and an intention that each purchaser shall be under the same obligation, then the benefit of all covenants can be given to all purchasers without more and irrespective of the time they purchase. Indeed, as later cases show, it may even be possible to omit some of the *Elliston* conditions, as where there is no allotted plan (*Baxter v Four*

Oaks Properties) and where, as in *Re Dolphin's Conveyance*, there is no common vendor. The advice to Easy Homes is, then, to follow this reliable and accepted method of ensuring mutuality of benefit.

b) The burden

This is not inherently difficult, rather it is that the present state of the law allows the burden to flow in only limited circumstances. Thus, it is only the burden of restrictive covenants that can pass to successors in title of the original covenantor (*Austerberry v Corporation of Oldham*). To ensure this, the covenant must touch and concern the land, the covenantees must at the time of the covenant have had land capable of benefiting from the covenant and the burden must be attached to the land. The first two are clearly satisfied, as each purchaser will make a covenant with the developer as they purchase the land. (On sale of the last plot, the developer is treated as having land because of the special rules relating to a building scheme). Moreover, annexation of the covenant will occur automatically under s 79 LPA and there will be no problem of this effect being deliberately excluded. Of course, if the covenants are to bind successors in title from the original purchasers/covenantors, they must be registered as either minor interests in registered land or Class D(ii) land charges in unregistered land. The developer must ensure this takes place as otherwise the covenants will be lost on the first sale.

As to the positive covenant to repair, there is little the developer can do. Of course, as suggested at the outset, he could decide to let the property as a leasehold development and rely on the rules relating to leasehold covenants. In fact, even if the purchasers were later to enfranchise their leaseholds the covenants would still be binding. However, this is not usually the object of a developer who does not wish to become a managing landlord. Neither is there any scope for the doctrine of mutual benefit and burden under *Halsall v Brizell*. That principle applies only in cases where there is some shared utility or service, such as a road or sewer. It would be possible for each original covenantor/purchaser (who of course is under the obligation to repair as matter of contract) to extract a covenant to repair from any purchaser from them, thus creating a chain of covenants. Of course, however, this 'chain of indemnity' is only as strong as its weakest link and depends on the ability and desire of the original covenantor to impose such an obligation on a successor. All other possibilities, of which there are several, are so complicated and remote that Easy Homes should not be advised to pursue them.

In essence then, it is reasonably straightforward for Easy Homes to achieve the desired effect of giving each purchaser a right to sue on these covenants. The burden is, however, more problematical and it is only the burden of the restrictive covenant that could be guaranteed to run.

Question 41

Choco Ltd, a biscuit manufacturer, own large premises on an industrial estate just outside London. Title is unregistered. In 1987, they decide to sell off parts of their property in order to meet mounting company debts. Plot 1 is sold to Martin, who covenants not to carry on any trade or business in confectionary on the site and to require his staff to use the catering facilities established by Choco Ltd on the estate. Later that year, Choco Ltd sells Unit 2 to Norman on a seven year lease in writing. Norman makes identical covenants as to those made by Martin and immediately sub-lets the property to Oswald by a lease in writing on the same terms. Oswald has since inherited a fortune and makes a gift of the premises to his nephew Herod, a major jelly baby manufacturer. Subsequently, Martin sells his property to Penny who begins to make seaside rock and opens a small cafeteria for her staff. Meanwhile, Choco Ltd has sold its remaining property to General Foods Inc. who immediately contemplate litigation. Unfortunately, Norman has disappeared and it transpires that none of these covenants were registered.

How would your answer differ if the covenants had been registered?

Answer plan

- covenants that touch and concern the land
- running of benefit and burden
- lack of privity of estate
- requirements of registration and effect

Answer

It is clear that in this problem there are difficulties concerning both the transfer of the benefit and the transfer of the burden to successors in title of the original parties to covenants affecting freehold land. In order to consider this problem in detail, it is first necessary to determine the nature of these two covenants - the covenant not to carry on any confectionary business and the covenant to ensure that staff working on the burdened land eat at the covenantee's cafeteria. The first point is whether these covenants touch and concern the land. There is no difficultly with the covenant restrictive of user, as this is a type of covenant often employed. On the other hand, however, there is a serious doubt whether the covenant to use the cafeteria of the covenantee does touch and concern the land. It is doubtful whether it affects the value or mode of user of the land (*Swift Investments v Combined English Stores*) and appears to be only personal in nature. If this is the case, then this particular covenant can bind only the original parties, being Martin and Norman. It is a matter of contract. In addition, if, as a matter of construction, Oswald's covenant with Norman in the lease was intended to be made with Choco Ltd (the head landlord) under s 56 LPA, Oswald will be bound in contract also (s 56 applies even to covenants that do not touch and concern). That apart, this covenant binds no successor in title, being personal in nature. So, Penny cannot be sued on this covenant even if it were negative and fulfilled all the other conditions relating to the transmission of the burden. Likewise, its benefit cannot be transferred automatically to General Foods under property law principles when they buy the original covenantee's land. Of course, however, the benefit of it can be expressly assigned as a matter of contract, under the rule that contractual benefits can be assigned to another.

That leaves us, then, with the restrictive covenant against certain types of user. Firstly, does the benefit of this run in equity to General Foods. (NB the position at law is not relevant as the burden of the covenant can only be transmitted in equity and thus the plaintiff must sue in equity.) For the benefit to run in equity, the plaintiff must have some estate in the land within s 78 LPA and the covenant must have benefitted land of the original covenantee. The fact of benefit will be presumed (*Re Earl of Leicester*) unless the contrary is shown. In any event, there is clear benefit within the definition of *Re Gadd* because the covenant affects the mode of user of the land. There is no difficulty with either of these conditions. In addition, however, the benefit of the covenant must have been transmitted in a method accepted by equity. In this case, there is clearly no building scheme and no evidence of an express assignment of the benefit. We must, therefore, rely on annexation. Clearly, there has been no express annexation but this is much less important after the decision of *Federated Homes v Mill Lodge Properties* which makes it clear that this covenant will be statutorily annexed under s 78 LPA unless the covenant contains a contrary intention, which it does not. In fact, the covenant is attached to each and every part of the land so it is not only General Foods that can enforce the covenant, but also Norman and Herod, the first of which purchased an estate in the benefited land before Martin's covenant and the second is an occupier of that land entitled to the benefit of a restrictive covenant within s 78. However, it is likely that only General Foods will wish to enforce this covenant and Norman (if he could be found) will be prevented from doing so unless Herod refuses to act.

Secondly, what of the burden of this covenant, for it appears that it has been broken in respect of both Unit 1 and Unit 2. Turning first to Unit 1, can this restrictive covenant bind Penny? It seems clear that the conditions required to give the burden of this covenant a proprietary nature have been satisfied. On the one hand, at the time of the covenant, there was land owned by the covenantee (Choco Ltd) which was capable of benefiting from the covenant, as required by *London & South Western Railway v Gomm*. Similarly, the burden of the covenant appears to have been annexed to the land under s 79 LPA: there is no contrary intention expressed. So, the covenant is proprietary within the rules of *Tulk v Moxhay*. However, this means only that the covenant is *capable* of binding a successor in title to the original covenantor, not that it actually does so. In order for it to bind a purchaser of a *legal* estate in the land - which presumably Penny is - it must be registered as a Class D(ii) land charge in unregistered land. We are told that it is not and so even this covenant is not binding on her, nor can it be binding on any subsequent purchasers having been statutorily voided by the Land Charges Act. Obviously, however, if the covenant had been registered, the position would have been the reverse.

Thirdly, what of the successors in title to Unit 2, being Norman and now Herod (via a transfer of Oswald's lease). The position on whether the covenant is proprietary is, not surprisingly, the same as with Unit 1: the covenant was made for the benefit of land of the covenantee and it is annexed to that land. However, it also is unregistered. Yet, in this case the position is not the same. Under s 4 Land charges Act 1972, a Class D(ii) land charge is void for lack of registration against a purchaser for money or money's worth of a legal estate in the land. When Norman acquires the land, he acquires it by virtue of a lease in writing - not by deed - so he purchases only an equitable estate. Moreover, Herod does not even purchase the land, for he obtains the land by gift. He also is bound. Of course, had registration occurred, this would make the covenant safe against any future purchaser of a legal estate but it is not necessary on these facts.

Finally, for the sake of completeness, it should be noted that Norman could enforce all covenants against Oswald, his tenant under privity of contract. Likewise, Choco Ltd and then General Foods, can proceed to forfeit Norman's lease for breach of covenant if the lease contained a right of re-entry. Subject to the normal safeguards surrounding forfeiture, this would terminate Henry's occupation also and would de facto enforce the covenant against user.

Notes

This shows that questions can mix both the benefit and burden. It also makes it clear that lack of registration is not *always* fatal to a claim - it depends on the status of the purchaser.

The Law of Mortgages

Introduction

There is no doubt that, for the ordinary person, the purchase of a house is their most direct contact with the law of real property. For this event, most people require a mortgage and the subsequent repayment of the mortgage becomes one of their most pressing economic concerns. However, the use of the mortgage as a device to *acquire* property is a relatively modern development, at least on today's scale. In fact, for so long as people have been capable of owning land (or more precisely, an interest in it), the mortgage has been a way of converting a fixed economic asset (the land) into a flexible economic asset (its monetary value). The mortgage is, in essence, a way of realising and releasing the capital value of the land. Fundamentally, therefore, a mortgage is a security for a loan. This rather bland statement does, however, hide a multitude of consequences, not least the idea that a mortgage - being a proprietary right - is subject to controls not otherwise found in 'ordinary' loan contracts. Indeed, one of the most frequent examination questions asks the student to assess the extent to which a mortgage really is a right in property or just another species of contract.

Checklist

In order to deal with mortgage issues, three reasonably distinct issues have to be addressed. Firstly, how are mortgages, both legal and equitable created and are there any specific reasons for these particular forms. Secondly, what are the rights of a mortgagor (the borrower) under a mortgage and in particular what is the nature and extent of the 'equity of redemption'. Thirdly, what are the rights of the mortgagee (the lender) under a mortgage and what remedies may be suitably employed in the event of a defaulting mortgagor. These questions largely depend on the application of traditional equitable principles as supplemented by statute where appropriate. A good knowledge of case law is invaluable.

Question 42

Analyse the methods by which legal and equitable mortgages may be created after 1925. What was the purpose of any reforms?

Answer plan

- definition of a mortgage: *Santley v Wilde*
- the use of the charge
- LPA 1925 ss 85, 86
- LPA 1925 s 53(1)(c)
- *Walsh v Lonsdale*, s 2 Law of Property (Miscellaneous Provisions Act) 1989
- proprietary estoppel
- purposes of reform: protection of the borrower, the mortgage as a charge
- ease of creation

Answer

All land has an economic value and a mortgage is one of the most effective ways by which the owner of that land may realise that value, although in the world of today, the mortgage is most commonly used in order to enable a person to purchase land in the first place. Historically, however, the true nature of a mortgage is that it is a lender's security for money lent to the borrower. Of course, the mortgage is much more than a simple contract of loan, for the mortgagee will acquire an interest in the land over which the mortgage operates. In technical terms, a mortgage is a conveyance of an estate in the land to the mortgagee, with a provision that the mortgagee's interest shall lapse upon repayment of the loan plus interest and costs and it is one of the most important aspects of the mortgage that the lender obtains not only a right to have the money repaid but also a proprietary interest in the land charged as security for that loan. However, as well as being a powerful form of security for a lender, a mortgage also has advantages for the borrower or mortgagor. It is a general principle of the law of property that 'once a mortgage always a mortgage' which effectively means that the borrower has a right of full access to his property once the loan secured on it has been repaid. In other words, that the proprietary nature of the mortgage lasts only for so long as the debt remains outstanding. Thus, the mortgagee's remedies (which can be proprietary or contractual in nature) only endure so long as the borrower owes money.

Before 1925, if an owner of a legal or equitable interest in land sought to raise money on security of that land, the borrower's interest in the property was usually conveyed in full to the lender. If a fee simple was mortgaged, a fee simple was transferred and so on. In his turn, the mortgagee promised to re-convey the interest on repayment of principal, interest and costs. Moreover, originally, not only did the mortgagee have the actual interest of the borrower vested in them, but the contract made provision for the lender to retain that interest if the borrower failed to repay the loan on the date stipulated in the contract. This date, known as the legal date of redemption, became crucial and the consequences for the borrower of missing payment on that date were severe. Equity, however, was soon to intervene. Adopting the policy position of 'once a mortgage always a mortgage' equity developed the equity of redemption and its counterpart the equitable right to redeem. Essentially, this meant that the borrower was entitled to a re-conveyance of their property should they pay the full charges due under the mortgage, even though the legal date for payment had passed. In fact, this was equity's way of ensuring that a mortgage really was security over the land and not an easy method by which a creditor could obtain the property of someone in debt. Likewise, equity took the view that if a mortgagee went into possession of the property in pursuance of the right they had been granted (which of course they were perfectly entitled to do), they should be called to account strictly for any rent and profits that could have been earned by the land. These rents and profits were held for the borrower and could then reduce the mortgage debt. This effectively meant the end of possession as a remedy except in cases of last resort. This then, was the background to the changes made in the method of granting mortgages in 1925 by the Law of Property Act.

The general principle underlying the 1925 property reforms is that, as far as possible, the owner of land should retain the fullest interest possible in their own property even when seeking a mortgage of it. Hence, since 1926, freeholds can no longer be mortgaged by a conveyance of the fee simple to the mortgagee and the mortgagee is limited to receiving some lesser right in the land. With obvious and necessary modifications, this principle also applies to mortgages of leaseholds.

Firstly, the position of legal mortgages of freeholds. Under s 85(1) of the LPA 1925 there are two methods only of creating a legal mortgage of a freehold. First, the borrower may demise a term of years absolute to the lender and no mortgage may take effect by absolute conveyance of the legal estate, s 85(2). In effect, this is the granting of a long lease to the mortgagee with a provision for cesser on redemption (ie that the term of years shall cease when the loan is repaid). In the typical case, the term granted is usually long, such as three thousand years. The demised term will also fix a contractual date for redemption, being the legal right to redeem and that is usually six months after the date of the mortgage. However, as was the case before 1926, the mortgagor has an equitable right to redeem on the payment of the loan at any time after this legal date has passed. The clear effect of these provisions is that the mortgagor retains his legal fee simple and the mortgage is more clearly regarded as the security for a loan, although all of the pre-1926 rights of the mortgagee are preserved and, of course, the mortgagee still has *some* proprietary interest in the land by virtue of their term of years. Moreover, this 'new' approach has one major practical advantage. Since 1925, it is now possible for the mortgagor to create further legal mortgages of their land, in order to raise further sums. So, because the mortgagor retains the legal fee simple, it is perfectly possible to grant another mortgage for another term to a second lender, as where the first mortgage was for a relatively small sum. The second term granted will necessarily be longer than the first, so as to give the second mortgagee a notional legal interest in the property distinct from that of the first mortgagee. The net effect of these provisions is that the mortgagor always retains final legal title to their property, irrespective of the number of mortgages created and, of course, that every mortgagee gains some legal estate in the land. This has enhanced the basic principle of 'once a mortgage always a mortgage'.

The second method of creating a mortgage of a legal freehold after 1925 is the charge by deed expressed to be by way of legal mortgage. This is an invention of s 87 Law of Property Act 1925: the legal charge is simply a statutory form of mortgage that is easier and less expensive to execute than a formal demise of a term of years. In fact, the legal charge is the main method of mortgaging legal estates currently in use. Under s 87, this charge must be made by deed and it must be expressed to be by way of legal mortgage but, that done, it is clear that a legal chargee (a lender) gets exactly the same protection, powers and remedies as if they had been given a term of three thousand years in the normal way, s 87 LPA, *Regent Oil Company v Gregory*. For all practical purposes therefore, the legal charge is as effective as a mortgage by way of demise of term of years. It is, however, cheaper, shorter and more efficient.

As far as leaseholds are concerned, the methods of creating a legal mortgage are substantially similar to that of a freehold. Before 1925, the leaseholder (the tenant) would assign his lease to the mortgagee just as the freeholder would transfer their fee simple. Now, however, by virtue of s 86 LPA, a legal mortgage of a leasehold can be created by two methods only. The first is the charge by deed expressed to be by way of legal mortgage. This is effectively the same as in the case of freeholds. The second is by a sub-lease for a term of years to the mortgagee. This sub-lease will necessarily be shorter than the term of years that the leaseholder actually has and, in practice, the mortgagee's term will be ten days shorter than the original leaseholders. This is to ensure that the leaseholder can grant subsequent legal mortgages of his leasehold by creating a term longer than the first mortgagee's but shorter than his own. Once again, any attempt to avoid these provisions by assigning a lease will operate only as a sub-lease for a term shorter than that of the tenant, *Grangeside Securities v Collingwood Securities Ltd*.

Turning now to equitable mortgages, these can be split conveniently into two parts. First, it may well be that the borrower only has an equitable interest and it necessarily follows that any mortgage of that equitable interest will itself be equitable. The Law of Property Act has not affected this matter to any great extent and mortgages of equitable interests (such as a beneficiary's rights under a trust) are still carried into effect by a conveyance of the whole equitable interest to the mortgagee. This will of course be accompanied by a provision for re-transfer when the loan is repaid (*William Brandt v Dunlop Rubber*). As far as formality requirements are concerned, there is no need to use a deed, but because this mortgage will amount to a disposition of a subsisting equitable interest (ie that of the mortgagor) it must comply with s 53(1)(c) of the Law of Property Act. This requires the mortgage of the equitable interest to be in writing, on penalty of voidness.

The second issue is the creation of the informal mortgage or, in other words, a mortgage that does not comply with the formality requirements necessary for the creation of a legal mortgage. As with many other equitable interests in land, an informal mortgage commences life as a contract to create a legal mortgage which, if capable of specific performance, will be treated as an equitable mortgage along the same lines as equitable leases in *Walsh v Lonsdale*. It is vital, however, for this informal mortgage that the contract be in writing under s 2 of the LPA 1989. It must also, of course, be capable of specific performance, although that requirement is usually met in the case of contracts concerning land. If the requirements of a written contract and specific performance are met, the contract to grant the mortgage will be treated in itself as an equitable mortgage, *Parker v Housefield*, although usually the money will have to have been advanced already before equity will intervene. Prior to 1989 Act, it was also possible to create an equitable mortgage by deposit of title deeds with the lender. The deposit of the borrower's deeds was treated as both evidence of the contract and performance of that contract under the then s 40 LPA (*Re Wallis*). This was, of course, a very informal but relatively efficient way of creating a mortgage. After 1989, contracts need to be in writing and this cannot be presumed from the deposit of title deeds. As such, it is unclear whether the method of creating equitable mortgages by deposit is now defunct. One view, and probably the correct one, is that s 2 was not intended to do away with this method of creating mortgages and that this is just an unforeseen consequence. If this is true, it may well be possible to treat the deposit of title deeds as a form of proprietary estoppel. As we know from *Taylor Fashions v Liverpool Victoria Trustees*, if one person promises an interest in land to another and that is relied upon to their detriment, equity will enforce the promise and give effect to the claim of the promisee. Thus, if a lender has actually advanced money on the basis of a promise (represented by the deposit of title deeds) it is likely that the mortgage will be enforced despite the absence of any formality. Of course, equitable mortgages do suffer from the vulnerability of all equitable rights in land, although in the case of deposit of title deeds the lender has the assurance that no other dealings can be made with the land while the deeds are in his possession. Finally, mention must also be made of the equitable charge, a completely informal way of securing a loan over property. This requires no special form of words, only an intention to charge property with a debt, *National Provincial and Union Bank of England v Charnley*. Such a method is extremely precarious and is rarely used in either commercial or residential mortgages.

It is apparent then, that the 1925 legislation introduced a significant change in the way that mortgages could be created. Relying on the principle of 'once a mortgage always a mortgage', legal estates could be mortgaged only by giving the lender some subsidiary right in the land, not a transfer of the borrower's entire interest. Not only does this simplify the process of mortgage creation, it emphasises the nature of mortgage as a security. In addition, it also allows the borrower to create successive legal mortgages which gives protection and security to those successive mortgagees as well as bringing certainty for the mortgagor.

Notes

This is as straightforward a question as it is possible to get on mortgages. Good use of case law will re-enforce knowledge of the statutory provisions.

Question 43

To what extent do the rights of a mortgagor under a legal mortgage provide sufficient protection for the borrower?

Answer plan

- the nature of the mortgagor's rights: the legal right to redeem; the equitable right to redeem and the equity of redemption
- the doctrine of clogs and fetters: options; collateral advantages; oppressive terms; unconscionable conduct

Answer

The mortgage is one of the most versatile and unique of property law concepts. It is, on the one hand, a simple contract of loan between lender and borrower and, on the other, it creates a valuable and powerful proprietary right in the land. It is, in fact, a concept governed by contract law and property law and the different philosophies of each can sometimes cause confusion and difficulties. However, since 1925, the very way in which mortgages can be created is designed to re-enforce the essential nature of a mortgage: that it is a security charged on land for a loan.

In the normal course of events, a legal mortgage will be created either by granting a demise of years (a lease) to the mortgagee or by the execution of a legal charge by way of mortgage. The former does, of course, confer a proprietary interest on the mortgagee and the latter is deemed by statute (s 87 LPA) to have the same effect. This means, however, that the mortgagor retains their interest in the land subject, of course, to the rights of the mortgagee. On the other hand, as the mortgage is also a contract of loan, there are stipulations relating to the repayment of the loan and certain remedies that the mortgagee may pursue in the event of default on the loan. However, the mortgage is always still a loan and this means that the mortgagor does have a considerable degree of protection, both of her interest and her position under the loan contract.

As a matter of contract, the mortgagor has a contractual right to redeem on the date specified in the contract. This is usually six months from the date of the mortgage but may be any date specified by the parties. At one time, if the mortgagor did not redeem on this date, he lost his security even though redemption could have been made at a later date. However, equity soon developed the maxim 'once a mortgage always a mortgage' and allowed redemption of the mortgage after this date, on payment of principal, interests and costs (*Thornborough v Baker*). This became known as the equitable right to redeem and, without doubt, is a valuable part of the mortgagor's protection under a mortgage. In fact, however, the equitable right to redeem is just part of the wider rights that the mortgagor has under the mortgage. In equity, the mortgagor is protected by the equity of redemption. This equity of redemption represents the sum total of the mortgagor's rights in the property: in essence the residual rights of ownership that the mortgagor has, both in virtue of his paramount legal estate in the land and the protection that equity affords him, *Re Sir Thomas Spencer Wells*. The equity of redemption is valuable in itself for it represents the mortgagor's right to the property (or its monetary equivalent) when the mortgage is discharged or the property sold. In fact, on subsequent mortgages, the second and third lenders are able and willing to grant further loans precisely because the mortgagor has this valuable right. Indeed, the equity of redemption is a proprietary right in itself and may be dealt with by the mortgagor in the normal way.

In addition to this, however, equity will intervene to protect the mortgagor and her equity of redemption against encroachment by the mortgagee. As noted above, equity regards the mortgage as a loan, which can be redeemed, and not as an opportunity for the lender to acquire the mortgagor's property. This protection manifests itself in various ways.

Firstly, it is a general principle that a mortgage cannot be made irredeemable: it is a security, not a conveyance, and the right to redeem cannot be limited *pro tanto* to certain people or certain periods of time (*Re Wells*). However, a provision postponing the date of redemption may be valid where the mortgage is not otherwise harsh and unconscionable, so long as the right to redeem is not made illusory, *Knightsbridge Estates v Byrne*, *Fairclough v Swan Breweries*. Again, a provision in a mortgage which provides that the property shall become the mortgagee's or which gives the mortgagee an option to purchase the property is void, *Samuel v Jarrah Timber*. The rationale is, of course, that the mortgagor needs protection when negotiating for a loan, often being in a vulnerable position. Thus, an option to purchase given to the mortgagee in a separate and independent transaction can be valid, as not forming part of the mortgage itself, *Reeve v Lisle*.

Secondly, as a matter of principle, the mortgagor should be able to redeem the mortgage and have the mortgagee's rights extinguished free from any ancillary conditions in the mortgage other than the payment of principal, interests and costs. The basic principle is, again, the mortgage as a security which ends when its reason - the money - is repaid. Thus, on several occasions the courts have struck down 'collateral advantages' made in favour of a mortgagee, as where the mortgage contract stipulates that the mortgagor should fulfil some other obligation as a condition of the mortgage. An example is where the mortgagor promises to buy all his beer or supplies from the mortgagee. At one point, such collateral advantages were uniformly struck down, as being a clog on the equity of redemption (cf *Bradley v Carritt*). However, it is now clear that there is no objection to a collateral advantage which ceases when the mortgage is redeemed, *Santley v Wilde*. This is a matter of contract between the parties and providing the terms are not unconscionable or do not in fact restrict the right to redeem they will be valid, *Biggs v Hoddinot*. Indeed, at least with commercial mortgages made between equal parties at arms length, *Kreglinger v New Patagonia Meat and Cold Storage Company* suggests that a collateral advantage which does continue after redemption (eg a continuing obligation to take supplies from the mortgagee) may be acceptable so long as the mortgagor's property returns to the mortgagor in the same form that it was mortgaged. Clearly, this is a flexible principle that can be used to invalidate harsh, unreasonable terms as the situation demands. On the other hand, courts are aware that the parties' business dealings should be upheld as far as possible in the absence of unconscionable conduct.

Thirdly, the court has the power to strike down any term which, in effect, destroys the equity of redemption. Thus, a high interest rate might render the mortgagor's equity of redemption valueless (*Cityland & Property (Holdings) v Dabrah*) or the terms of the mortgage might be so oppressive as to make it harsh and unconscionable, although it must be more than merely unreasonable or unfair, *Multiservice Bookbinding v Marden*.

Fourthly, the mortgage as a whole may be struck down on the ground that it was obtained by the undue influence of the mortgagee or a third party acting on behalf of the mortgagee, as in *Barclays Bank v O'Brien* where a husband induced his wife to sign a mortgage in favour of the bank in circumstances where undue influence could be established. It is clear, however, that the transaction does have to be to the manifest and unfair disadvantage of the mortgagor before equity will intervene. In *National Westminster Bank v Morgan*, for example, the mortgage was not set aside for undue influence precisely because it was not at the time of its creation disadvantageous to the mortgagor.

Finally, it is also clear that mortgages, being contracts, are subject to normal contractual rules governing credit relationships and related matters. Thus, a mortgage may be set aside as an 'extortionate credit bargain' within s 137-140 Consumer Credit Act 1974 or set aside as being in restraint of trade, *Esso Petroleum v Harpers Garage*.

All in all then, the mortgagor does benefit from a considerable amount of protection, both by virtue of equity protecting the equity of redemption and by statute and general common law principles applicable to contracts *per se*. In addition to these, when the mortgagee seeks to exercise his remedies under the mortgage, statute intervenes to restrain, exclude or modify those remedies, particularly in the case of mortgages of dwelling houses. The mortgage is, after all, only security for a loan.

Notes

This is a good question to answer if you know the doctrine of clogs and fetters. A good answer also considers the nature of a mortage as a contract as well as a security.

Question 44

'Although designed for different purposes, the remedies available to a mortgagee of a legal estate in respect of a mortgagor in default should serve as a powerful warning to all those intending to raise money on the security of their real property'.

Discuss.

Answer plan

- action on the contract
- appointment of a receiver
- sale
- possession
- foreclosure

Answer

It is often forgotten that a mortgage is just as valuable to a mortgagee as it is to a mortgagor. Obviously, the main benefit is that a rate of interest can be charged for the money lent and an income generated on the security of what is, in all but the severest economic conditions, an appreciating asset. Just as the property owner uses the mortgage to turn his proprietary right into money, the lender uses the mortgage to turn his money into a proprietary right. It is, however, trite law that a mortgage is always ultimately to be regarded as security for the money lent and that on repayment of that money, the property returns in full to the mortgagor. That is true. On the other hand, the dual nature of a mortgage as a contract and as a proprietary right (or rather bundle of proprietary rights, eg the term of years demised on creation, the equity of redemption) gives the mortgagee a range of options should the mortgagor default on the loan and be unable to pay either interest or principal. After all, the property is security for the loan and should that not be repaid in accordance with the terms of the agreement, that security must and should be utilised.

The particular remedies employed by the mortgagee will, in the final analysis, depend on the precise nature of the default of the mortgagor and the requirements of the mortgagee. Thus, some are more suitable for recovery of unpaid interest, while others are more suitable for recovery of the entire loan and the ending of the charge.

Firstly, as the mortgage is a contract of loan between the parties, the mortgagee has an action on the express covenant for repayment of monies owed that forms part of every mortgage. By this covenant, the mortgagor will have promised to repay the sum due on a certain date plus interest. As soon as this date has passed, the mortgagee has a personal action on the covenant and can have the judgment satisfied in the normal way, such as execution on the property of the mortgagor, whether comprised in the mortgage or not. This remedy is designed to recover the full amount, although, of course, it is of very little use if the mortgagor is impecunious or bankrupt - the very reason why the principal or interest has not been repaid in the first place.

Secondly, and also as a means of recovering the whole sum and ending the mortgage, the mortgagee may seek to exercise the power of sale. In many cases, a mortgage will contain an express power of sale but, if not, a power of sale is implied into every mortgage made by deed under s 101(1)(i) LPA 1925, unless a contrary intention appears. This power *arises* as soon as the legal (contractual) date for redemption has passed or, in the case of instalment mortgages, when one instalment is in arrears, *Twentieth Century Banking v Wilkinson*. However, the power only becomes *exercisable* (s 103 LPA) when either: a) notice requiring payment of the mortgage money has been served and the mortgagor is in 3 months arrears since the notice was served; or b) interest under the mortgage is 2 months in arrears and unpaid; or c) the mortgagor has breached some covenant in the mortgage (other than the covenant to pay) or some provision of the Law of Property Act. These provisions are somewhat detailed and technical but, in effect, they give the mortgagee an effective power of sale of the property should the mortgagor be in serious default. The consequences of a sale are, of course, that the mortgagee receives his money due on the mortgage, with the balance if any returning to the mortgagor. In fact, the sale extinguishes the mortgagor's equity of redemption and transfers the land to the purchaser from the equity of redemption, the mortgagee's mortgage, all subsequent mortgages (ss 88, 113 LPA) but subject to any previous mortgages. If there are any subsequent mortgages, these are paid off in order, before the mortgagor, as funds permit. However, it is clear that a sale of the mortgaged property is calamitous for the mortgagor and equity steps in to soften the blow, albeit only very slightly. Thus, the selling mortgagee is under a duty of care to the mortgagor to obtain the best price reasonably obtainable (*Standard Chartered Bank v Walker*), although an open sale by auction, even when prices are low satisfies this rule, *Cuckmere Brick Co v Mutual Finance*. Moreover, this duty is not owned to any person other than the mortgagor - such as a person with an equitable interest in the property (*Parker-Tweedale v Dunbar*) - and the mortgagee is not trustee of the power of sale. His motives in choosing to exercise the power of sale are irrelevant. However, if the mortgagee is negligent and thereby obtains a lower price than he

would otherwise have obtained, he is liable to the mortgagor
(*Cuckmere*) and the mortgagee cannot sell to himself or his agent
(*Williams v Wellingborough Council*).

Usually, of course, the mortgagee will wish to sell the
property in order to realise their security. To do this effectively,
the property must be sold with vacant possession. So, in practice,
before sale, a mortgagee may wish to exercise his third right: that
of possession of the mortgaged property. Indeed, although
possession is often a prelude to sale, it can also be used as a
method of securing recovery of the outstanding interest on a loan,
as the mortgagee's possession may well generate income which
can be used for this purpose, as where a mortgagee in possession
sub-lets or runs the business over which the mortgage exists.
Possession then, does not necessarily mean the end of the
mortgage. The mortgagee's right to possession is *exactly* what is it
says. By virtue of the way in which mortgages are created, the
mortgagee will have an estate in the land and, in reality, the
mortgagee has an immediate right to possession the moment the
ink is dry on the mortgage, *Four Maids v Dudley Marshall*.

Of course, in the normal course of events, the mortgagee will
not exercise this right and may, indeed, covenant not to seek
possession unless the mortgagor defaults on the interest
repayments. Moreover, there is a positive disincentive for a
mortgagee to take possession as it is clear that a mortgagee in
possession will be called strictly to account for any income
generated by his possession, *White v City of London Brewery*. This
means that the mortgagee will be taken to have received not only
any actual income - which can go towards interest payments - but
also any income that he should have received had he managed
the property to the high standard expected. Any shortfall will
then have to be made up by the mortgagee who may find that he
actually owes money to the mortgagor (if the income that should
have been received is greater than the interest owed). This is why
most commercial mortgagees desist from seeking possession. In
the domestic, residential context, on the other hand, the position
can be very different as possession is often a prelude to sale. Here,
however, the mortgagor is protected from a zealous mortgagee.
Under s 36 Administration of Justice Act 1970 (as amended by s 8
AJA 1973), an application for possession of a dwelling house may

be suspended, adjourned or postponed by the court, in its discretion, if it appears that the mortgagor would be able to pay within a reasonable period any sums due under the mortgage. Due to s 8 AJA 1973, (reversing *Halifax BS v Clark*) 'any sums due' may be treated only as those instalments missed and not, as most mortgages provide, the whole sum once one mortgage payment is missed. Likewise, the relief is available for endowment mortgages, despite the elliptical wording of the statute, *Bank of Scotland v Grimes*, although there is some doubt whether the statutory discretion is available if the mortgagor is not actually in default under the mortgage, *Western Bank v Schindler*. However, what is clear is that while the 'reasonable period' which the mortgagor is given to repay his arrears might actually be the rest of the mortgage - so as to spread the debt evenly, *Middlesborough Mortgage Corporation v Cunningham* - there is no discretion if there is no prospect of the mortgagor making a reasonable attempt to actually repay the accumulated debt, let alone meet future repayments, *First National Bank v Syed*. Clearly, then, this is a restriction on the right of a mortgagee to realise his security by taking possession, but perhaps it is understandable in view of the social policy of protecting residential occupiers. The same cannot be said, however, of Lord Denning's judgment in *Quennell v Maltby* when it was suggested that equity could restrain a mortgagee from taking possession *whenever* there was no justifiable reason for possession. Obviously, this cuts against the mortgagee's pure right to possess as holder of an estate in the land and it is doubtful whether this decision can be justified.

The fourth remedy is also used by the mortgagee to recover the interest owed. The ability of the mortgagee to appoint a receiver is often expressly included in the mortgage but, in any event, such a power will be implied into every mortgage by deed, s 101 LPA. The implied power does, however, become exercisable only in those circumstances in which the power of sale becomes exercisable and it is often an alternative to that remedy. The great advantage of this remedy is that it avoids the dangers of possession because the receiver is deemed to be the agent of the mortgagor, not the mortgagee (*Chatsworth Properties v Effiom*), with the consequence that any negligence is not attributable to the mortgagee.

Finally, there is the remedy of foreclosure which, if successful, will extinguish the equity of redemption and result in the transfer of the property entirely to the mortgagee, free of any rights of the mortgagor. If the property is freehold, the mortgagee will acquire that freehold and similarly for a leasehold. The right to foreclose arises as soon as the legal date for redemption is passed, although it is common for the mortgagee to promise not to foreclose without notice and only in respect of specified breaches of covenant. Essentially, should the need arise, the mortgagee will begin an action asking for foreclosure unless the mortgagor repays the mortgage within a specified time. If this does not occur, the mortgagee will be given a foreclosure *nisi* which in effect gives the mortgagor a further period (usually six months) in which to raise the money to pay off the loan. Failing that, the order of foreclosure will be made absolute and the mortgagor's interest in the property extinguished. This is the end of the matter save that, in exceptional circumstances, the court may open a foreclosure absolute and allow the mortgagor to redeem at a later date, *Campbell v Holyland*, although this is very unlikely if the mortgagee has since sold the property to a purchaser with no notice of the previous mortgage. In view of the powerful nature of foreclosure, the court has power under s 91(2) LPA to order sale in lieu of a foreclosure and, of course, this may mean that any surplus funds after the mortgage is paid will come to the mortgagor. Obviously, such a solution is desirable where the mortgage debt is far less than the value of the property. As noted above, the effect of a foreclosure is to vest the mortgagor's estate in the mortgagee and to extinguish the mortgage and its terms, s 88 LPA. Of course, any prior mortgages remain unaffected as they are still binding on the land, although subsequent mortgages will be destroyed. In practice, this means that subsequent mortgagees are given an opportunity to redeem any previous mortgages if foreclosure is likely. In effect, they take on the previous mortgage.

Clearly, then, the mortgagee has a wide range of remedies, albeit that statute intervenes to provide some relief to the mortgagor. Likewise, we must not forget that a mortgagee is subject to the general rule that there must be no clog on the equity of redemption and that credit controls (in the form of the Consumer Credit Act 1974) and common law principles of undue influence and restraint of trade are applicable to mortgages as loan contracts. Yet, even with these limitations, the mortgagee who bona fide takes security of land for a loan has much to rely on and is well protected.

Notes

The above two questions concentrate on the different sides of the mortgage coin: the rights of the mortgagor and the remedies of the mortgagee. As ever, there is much to say and case law is invaluable. However, the concepts are not difficult and the challenge is to present them in an interesting and clear manner.

Question 45

Florence is the owner of Roundabout House, a large Victorian freehold property in Toytown. The house is surrounded by a private housing project, Restful Towers, owned by Dilan and Dougal. They have sought for many years to buy Roundabout House as it would be easily converted to many smaller units. In order to secure her future, Florence decides to open as a hotel and seeks a loan from Noddy Bank, a private merchant bank, who finance the project by way of legal charge. The Bank are unsure of the financial viability of the scheme and insist on an interest rate at 8% above current market rates. They also stipulate that 'the borrower promises that the mortgagee shall have first option to purchase the property in the event of a judgment debt made by any court against the borrower'. Last year, Noddy Bank was taken over by Double D Holdings Ltd, a private company wholly owned by Dilan and Dougal. Shortly after, the managing director of Noddy Bank, having examined Florence's accounts, threatens to foreclose on the loan unless Florence renegotiates new terms. Florence reluctantly agrees and a new mortgage is drawn up, on the same terms but with an increase in the interest rate by 12% and a promise that 'the borrower will, for 10 years from the date of this agreement, purchase cleaning and other services from the owners for the time being of Restful Towers'. Six months later, Dilan and Dougal as owners of Restful Towers sue Florence for unpaid bills on the cleaning contracts and obtain a judgment debt against her. The Bank now seeks to purchase Roundabout House.

Advise Florence.

Answer plan

- the nature of a mortgage
- the equity of redemption: options to purchase; collateral advantages; unconscionable terms

Answer

In this question, several issues arise as to the enforceability of the mortgage entered into by Florence, both as a whole and in respect of particular obligations undertaken by her. As a preliminary point, we must note that when Florence enters into the mortgage she is creating a proprietary right in favour of the Noddy Bank but, nevertheless, retains paramount legal title to it. In essence, Florence has an equity of redemption, this being the sum total of her rights under the mortgage as residual legal owner, *Re Sir Thomas Spencer Wells*. Moreover, as equity treats a mortgage as security for a loan, which can be redeemed on payment of all monies owed, this equity of redemption will be protected by the court in a number of ways. This is supplemented by various other common law and statutory provisions that may come to Florence's aid.

The first point is to consider whether Florence can have the first mortgage set aside on the ground that its provisions destroy or make illusory the equity of redemption or amount to such harsh and oppressive terms that equity will intervene. As far as the interest rate is concerned, there is no doubt that the court has a discretion to intervene if the rate is so high as to make the mortgage practically irredeemable or is in itself unconscionable, *Cityland & Property (Holdings) v Dabrah*. On the other hand, it is also clear that the court will not interfere if the mortgage between the parties represents a business agreement between them, even if it is unreasonable, for equity acts on the conscience, not to mend bad bargains, *Multiservice Bookbinding v Marden*. In our case, it is unlikely that the court will intervene as the interest rate is not excessively above the market rate and seems to have been imposed by Noddy Bank after a commercial assessment of the viability of Florence's venture. There is then no assistance for her here. However, she may then wish to challenge the option to purchase which is contained in the mortgage transaction. As a matter of principle, any provision which stipulates that the property shall become that of the mortgagee is void (*Samuel v Jarrah Timber*) and this applies in equal measure to an option to purchase. The rationale is that, even though the mortgagee may well promise to pay the market price, it still represents a compromise of the mortgagor's paramount right to recover their property. Of course, if the option is contained in a separate transaction, it may be permitted (*Fairclough v Swan Brewery*) and in this case Noddy Bank may argue that the option is triggered only when the mortgagor is in trouble, thus amounting to nothing more than an express provision entitling them to do what they would be able to do in any event under the remedy of foreclosure. Yet, Florence may meet this argument quite simply as it is clear that the option to purchase is triggered by *any* judgment debt against her (as appears to be the position in respect of the cleaning services bill), even though it bears no relation to the debt charged on her property. This option will, therefore, be struck out and it will not matter that Florence agreed once again to it on the granting of the new mortgage after the first threat to foreclose.

Turning now to the new mortgage, which Florence executes after the takeover of Noddy Bank by Double D Holdings and after the threat to foreclose. As already noted, the option to purchase contained in this mortgage will be set aside. However, are there any other grounds upon which Florence may rely for relief? First, it may well be possible for Florence to claim that the new mortgage interest rate is a clog on her equity of redemption or is unconscionable. The mortgage rate now becomes 20% above the market rate and this does suggest an attempt to deprive Florence of her property by forcing her out through inability to pay. Likewise, it may well be relevant that the new interest rate was set only after the takeover of Noddy Bank by Double D Holdings, a vehicle (cf *Jones v Lipman*) for the persons who so desire her property. These circumstances may well persuade a court to set a new rate under the principle in *Cityland & Property (Holdings)*. In addition, however, the facts do suggest that the new mortgage itself was designed purely for the purpose of forcing Florence into liquidation. Although a mortgagee does have a right to foreclose if monies are owed, a court of equity will not stand by and let that be used unconscionably. In our case, the takeover of Noddy Bank, effectively by Dougal and Dilan, coupled with the insistence on a

new mortgage may well allow equity to come to Florence's aid
and have the mortgage set aside. In reply, the Bank may well
argue that the decision to call for a re-mortgage with its new
terms was a commercial one, carried out by the managing
director of the bank without reference to the 'needs' of the bank's
new owners. This, of course, will be a question of fact, but even if
established, there are grounds at least to have the high interest
rate varied as a straightforward clog on the equity of redemption.

There is, in addition to these issues, one other point for
consideration. The new mortgage stipulates a collateral advantage
for Dilan and Dougal, namely that Florence must purchase
cleaning services and supplies from them. It is interesting to note
here that the collateral advantage is not actually stipulated in
favour of the mortgagee (the bank) but for a third party. If
anything, this supports the above analysis that the second
mortgage was a device designed wholly to acquire Florence's
property. However, in general terms, equity will allow a collateral
advantage providing that it is neither harsh or oppressive nor
extends beyond the moment of redemption by the mortgagor,
Santley v Wilde, Biggs v Hoddinot. Indeed, in some circumstances,
especially where the mortgage is between commercial
organisations operating at arms length, a collateral advantage will
be allowed even if it does continue after the mortgage has been
redeemed, *Kreglinger v New Patagonia Meat and Cold Storage
Company*. In our case, there is little to suggest that the collateral
advantage is harsh or unconscionable *per se*, although the terms of
the contract for cleaning services etc will be relevant. On the other
hand, the advantage is stipulated to exist for 10 years from the
date of the mortgage and this may well be after the mortgage has
in fact been redeemed; for example if Florence can pay off the
mortgage quite soon. To a large extent, this issue will depend on
the facts of the case, although the court will look carefully at the
arrangement, especially as the incurred debts under the services
contract are then used in an attempt to trigger the (void) option to
purchase the property.

All in all, then, Florence has a number of potential arguments
which may either reduce her obligations under the mortgage or
invalidate it altogether. In addition to these, there is also the
possibility that the agreement may amount to an extortionate

credit bargain under the Consumer Credit Act 1974, as well as all the ways in which the court can soften the blow should the mortgagee actually proceed to exercise one of their remedies under the mortgage.

Notes

This problem puts in to practice the law discussed in the previous two answers, although it does concentrate more on the rights and protection of the mortgagor. In one sense, it is little short of an essay in disguise, but the question does ask you to advise Florence and that must be done. An even fuller answer would have gone on to consider undue influence and Consumer Credit Act protection in more detail.

Question 46

Assess the extent to which a court may interfere with a mortgage on the grounds of undue influence.

Answer plan

- the relevance of undue influence and its consequence if established
- manifest disadvantage
- agency
- notice
- *National Westminster Bank v Morgan*
- *BCCI v Aboody*
- *Barclays Bank v O'Brien*

Answer

In recent years, the law of undue influence has often been called in aid by a mortgagor who seeks to avoid the exercise of remedies by the mortgagee on the occasion of default by the mortgagor. In the typical case, a mortgagor (often a husband) has sought to obtain a mortgage from a bank or other institutional lender but the property over which the mortgage is intended to operate may be jointly owned. In such circumstances, it is necessary for the wife or the partner of the intending mortgagor also to consent to the mortgage. Usually the transaction proceeds smoothly and the bank leaves it to the husband to procure the consent of the wife to the mortgage or charge. The money is then lent and the mortgage executed in the normal way. Difficulties arise, however, should the mortgagors lie in default, for then as the bank seeks to exercise their remedies, the wife may well claim that her consent to the mortgage was procured by undue influence. In other words, that there was no real consent to the mortgage at all and it should be set aside in so far as it binds her. In reality then, undue influence is a plea whereby the mortgagor (or consenting co-owner who may also have signed the mortgage) claims that the mortgage should be set aside and not enforced because of some actions which vitiate their consent to it.

In general terms, the rationale for the doctrine of undue influence is clear: namely, that the mortgagee cannot enforce any security which has been obtained unconscionably. At one time, the law of undue influence was regarded as a panacea, available to mortgagors at the slightest hint of unfairness. Thus, it was perfectly possible for a mortgagor to avoid the consequences of default by pleading simply that the mortgagee was in a dominant position when the mortgage was made. However, this rather liberal approach was rejected by the House of Lords in *National Westminster Bank v Morgan* in 1985. In that case, the House of Lords made it clear that there were two major requirements before undue influence could be established. Firstly, the mortgagor need show some victimisation, or unfair advantage obtained, by the mortgagee. The equitable doctrine was not available simply because the bargain was unfair or unreasonable, but only where it could be established that the circumstances were so inequitable as to give rise to no other explanation but that undue influence was used. Importantly, the House determined that there were no relationships (such as banker and customer or husband and wife) that could lead to a presumption of undue influence and so, in all cases, the fact of undue influence needed to be established from the circumstances surrounding the transaction entered into. This clearly roots the doctrine in the unconscionability of the mortgagee's conduct rather than their ability to extract a commercially advantages bargain. Secondly, and more controversially, the House of Lords indicated that even if undue influence could be established, a mortgage would not be set aside unless the mortgage could be shown to be 'to the manifest disadvantage of the mortgagor'. It was not enough, in their Lordships view, that undue influence had been established, for that in itself was no reason to set aside a transaction. There had to be in addition some material disadvantage to the borrower. Thus, in *Woodstead Finance v Petrou* the transaction could not be set aside for undue influence because the mortgage had actually enabled the mortgagor to achieve their desired result, namely the retention of the property. Likewise in *BCCI v Aboody*, Lord Justice Slade declined to set aside a mortgage made by a wife jointly with her husband in favour of the bank on the ground that the wife had not been prejudiced by the transaction but had, over the last few years, gained benefit from the mortgage because this enabled the husband's business to remain afloat. Clearly, this is a very substantial restriction on the doctrine of undue influence for in many cases the whole purpose of the mortgage will be to enable the mortgagor to escape from some liability or attain some benefit. Does this mean that the law of undue influence can only apply where the mortgagor takes out a mortgage which is clearly not in their interests? It is suggested that this is not the case and that the rule concerning 'manifest disadvantage' should take account of the fact that the mortgagor has been induced to enter into a transaction that they would not otherwise have done without fuller consideration. In other words, in some cases the existence of a legal liability to repay procured by unconscionable conduct should in itself be a manifest disadvantage.

That, however, is not the end of the matter for as noted at the outset, many cases of undue influence involve a husband seeking a mortgage from an institutional lender but where the lender also requires the wife's signature or consent to the mortgage. What happens if the mortgage cannot be repaid and the wife claims that she knew nothing of the true nature of the transaction but acted only on the advice and under the watchful gaze of her husband? In these circumstances can the wife claim to have signed the mortgage under the undue influence of her husband and will the bank be affected by this undue influence? It is true to say that the position here is complicated and some of the cases can only be regarded as mutually inconsistent. Recently, however, in *Barclays Bank v O'Brien* and after a thorough review of the authorities, the Court of Appeal has attempted to bring some clarity to the law. According to Lord Justice Scott in that case, questions concerning undue influence and mortgagees must be placed into two categories. In the first category we have the normal situation of a third party agreeing to be a mortgagor on the insistence of the person actually negotiating with the bank. If in these circumstances, the principal mortgagor (they who negotiate with the bank) uses undue influence to persuade the surety (the second mortgagor) to enter into the transaction, then the question remains whether the mortgagee is affected by that undue influence. The answer seems to be that the mortgagee will not be so affected unless they have either notice of the undue influence or where the principal mortgagor is acting as the bank's agent in securing the consent of the second mortgagor. Clearly, this places the liability of the mortgagee firmly on the basis that they are responsible in some way (either through notice or agency) for the undue influence of the principal debtor. In the absence of such responsibility, it is clear that the mortgage will be effective against the secondary mortgagor (the surety) because they should have taken steps to safeguard their own position (cf *BCCI v Aboody*). Secondly, however, Scott LJ says that special considerations should apply when the principal mortgagor attempts to procure the consent of a third person with whom he stands in the relationship of spouse, as where a husband procures the consent of his wife to the mortgage in favour of the bank. In these cases, there is no need to prove that the husband is the agent of the bank or that the bank has notice of the husband's undue influence. All that is necessary is (i) that the relationship between the principal mortgagor and the secondary mortgagor (ie of husband and wife) and the consequent likelihood of influence is known to the lender; (ii) that the secondary mortgagor's consent to the transaction was procured by undue influence or material misrepresentation by the principal mortgagor (the husband) or that the secondary mortgagor lacked an understanding of the nature of the transaction; and (iii) that the lender, whether by leaving it to the principal mortgagor or otherwise, had failed to take reasonable steps to ensure that the secondary mortgagor (the wife) had obtained independent advice and understanding of the transaction before it was entered into. If those matters can be established, then undue influence will vitiate the mortgage. Scott LJ makes it clear that this more relaxed and lenient approach to undue influence arises solely because of the special protection equity gives to the wife against the actions of her husband. It remains to be seen whether this special protection applies in other cases, as where a son exercises influence over his elderly parents (*Avon Finance v Bridger*) or even where a wife exercises influence over her husband or indeed lover. Furthermore there is no mention in *Barclays Bank v O'Brien* of the requirement of manifest disadvantage and it remains unclear whether this is necessary in this special protected relationship. At the moment, however, the Court of Appeal decision in *O'Brien* makes it clear that mortgages can be set aside for undue influence in a wider range of circumstances where the participating parties are related than when they are not.

Notes

A question on case law, pure and simple, although not particularly difficult. The better student might like to finish off by considering the Law Commission's recent proposals to reformulate in statutory form all the protection currently available to a mortgagor, including undue influence.

Question 47

To what extent is freedom of contract inconsistent with the traditional view of a mortgage as being the grant of a proprietary interest in land merely as a security, albeit one which deserves special protection from a court of equity?

Answer plan

- the nature of a mortgage, but founded in contract
- the ability of the mortgagee to impose contractual terms versus the equity of redemption
- the mortgagee's contractual remedies modified by statute
- mortgages as loan contracts under the Consumer Credit Act 1974

Answer

In one very important sense, this question is misleading. A mortgage is both an interest in land and a contract. It partakes of the attributes of both and in the great majority of situations the dictates of contract and property law are complimentary, not mutually exclusive. In other words, just because a contract is at the heart of the dealings between mortgagor and mortgagee does not mean that the mortgage cannot also operate as a proprietary right. Thus, the mortgagee has remedies on the contract (eg to sue for money due), as well as remedies arising because of his proprietary interest in the land (eg the right to possession). Likewise, the mortgagor has obligations under the contract (eg to repay the loan and observe other covenants) as well as rights founded in his equity of redemption, a proprietary right. However, that said, it is true that in some situations the nature of a mortgage as a security over land, regulated by equity, can come into conflict with the contract negotiated between the parties.

The most obvious example of this potential conflict arises because of the general rule that equity will safeguard the equity of redemption, sometimes in contradiction to the express terms of the bargain agreed between mortgagor and mortgagee. Thus, an option to purchase granted to the mortgagee in the mortgage deed will be void (*Samuel v Jarrah Timber*) and terms which make the mortgage irredeemable will be struck out, *Fairclough v Swan Breweries*, even if agreed by the parties. Of course, the court is astute to give effect to the bargain made between commercial parties who are deemed to be able to take care of themselves, especially if they are financing a commercial enterprise, *Knightsbridge Estates v Byrne*, but that does not allow them to change the essential nature of a mortgage. It is still a security for a loan under which the proprietary interest conveyed to the mortgagee can be recovered on the payment of interest, principal and costs, *Re Sir Thomas Spencer Wells*. In particular, this emphasis on the equity of redemption has led the court to examine any 'collateral advantages' that are stipulated in the mortgage, being benefits extracted by the mortgagee in consideration for the loan. Originally, such advantages were frowned upon, as constituting a clog on the equity of redemption, but in recent times a collateral advantage which is neither harsh or unconscionable nor destructive *in fact* of the equity of redemption will be permitted, *Santley v Wilde*. Indeed, if the advantage represents the true commercial bargain between the parties and is not void on the above grounds, it will be permitted as an exercise of freedom of contract, even where it continues after the mortgage has been redeemed, as in *Kreglinger v New Patagonia Meat and Cold Storage Company*.

In addition, however, it is not only a court of equity that will protect a mortgagor. General contractual principles may also be called in aid. Thus, the general common law doctrine of undue influence may allow a mortgagor to avoid a mortgage contract in much the same way (perhaps even more easily, *Barclays Bank v O'Brien*) as a party may avoid any other contract. Again, the Consumer Credit Act applies to mortgages as with other loan contracts as does the doctrine of restraint of trade, *Esso v Harper's Garage*. All of these, essentially contractual remedies, support the court's intervention when seeking to protect the mortgagor's proprietary right in the equity of redemption.

From the mortgagor's point of view, then, both the contractual and proprietary nature of the mortgage can give protection against a mortgagee. When we look at the mortgagee, however, it seems that both statute and general equitable principles do intervene substantially to control (ie limit) the exercise of remedies under the mortgage contract. In this sense, the contractual nature of the mortgage does take a back seat to its essential nature as a security. Thus, although the mortgagor has a contractual (and proprietary) right to take possession of the mortgagor's property, both statute and equity restrict the full exercise of this right. In the former case, s 36 of the Administration of Justice Act 1970 (as amended by s 8 AJA 1973) gives the court power to set aside the claim for possession in respect of a dwelling house, although only if the mortgagor is likely to be able to meet his commitments under the mortgage and pay off any sums due within a reasonable time, *Bank of Scotland v Grimes, First National Bank v Syed*. In the second case, the equitable rule that a mortgagee in possession must account strictly for any income that is derived or could have been derived from the property during his period of possession (*White v City of London Brewery*) means that most mortgagees of commercial premises will not seek this remedy, although they may rely on the appointment of a receiver instead. Clearly, the court's ability to restrict the right of possession is a firm indication that the nature of a mortgage as a security takes priority over the claims of the mortgagee based on his contract and the proprietary right thereby obtained.

Likewise, the power of sale available to most mortgagees is restricted by the intervention of equity, even though statute (LPA 1925) clearly contemplates this as one of the major remedies of the mortgagee. The duty of care owed to the mortgagee to obtain the best price reasonably obtainable (*Standard Chartered Bank v Walker*) and the trust imposed on any surplus from the sale (after payment of the mortgage) do act as a brake on an eager mortgagee, although in so far as they prevent fraud on the part of a mortgagee these principles cannot be criticised. The same is generally true of the mortgagee's power of foreclosure, although this right - itself stemming from the nature of a mortgage as a proprietary right - is often a weapon of last resort. Technically, such a right arises as soon as the legal date specified in the contract has passed, but in reality the mortgagee often contracts not to exercise the right until some specified breach of covenant has occurred, such as non-payment of interest. This is an example of contract modifying the proprietary nature of a mortgage.

To conclude, however, one must reiterate that which was stated at the start of this answer. The mortgage that springs from contract, is effected by means of the creation of a proprietary right in the mortgagee, and partakes of the rules and principles of both contract and property law. It should not be thought that there is a great deal of tension between the two philosophies and even where the equity of redemption is concerned - the most well guarded of the mortgagor's rights - the commercial nature of the mortgage and its role in releasing the economic value of real property has been recognised. The same is true in such matters as undue influence (*National Westminster Bank v Morgan*, but see now *Barclays Bank v O'Brien*) and with the reluctance of the court to interfere with mortgages on the basis of extortionate credit bargains under the Consumer Credit Act 1974, as exemplified by the refusal in *A Ketley Ltd v Scott*.

Notes

This is perhaps one of the most interesting questions that can be asked on the law of mortgages. The interaction between property and contract law does cause problems in practice, especially in commercial transactions. The question also requires some knowledge of how mortgages are created and, therefore, provide a good test of a student's understanding.

Miscellaneous Problems

Introduction

The issues considered in this chapter bear no obvious relation to each other and no attempt shall be made to find one. However, they do share one important practical characteristic: they are issues that feature occasionally in examinations in land law, rather than being habitual favourites of examiners. Of course, that makes them no less important, for a well answered question on say, adverse possession, is worth just as much as a well answered question on co-ownership. However, that said, this chapter deals with issues such as adverse possession and fixtures and fittings with no particular attempt to treat them as intrinsically connected.

Adverse possession - or squatting - is a doctrine that truly reflects the feudal origins of English land law and the common law systems based upon it. Behind the ability of a trespasser to actually acquire 'ownership' of land which formally belongs to somebody else is the concept that, in fact, owners only own 'estates' or titles in the land, not the land itself. Thus, it is perfectly possible for some other person to gain a better title without any formal transfer of 'ownership'. The very idea of adverse possession is based upon relativity of title, not absolute ownership of land. It is now trite law that in England there is no equivalent of the Civil Law concept of *dominium* and in practice this means that one person's title to land is only as good as the absence of a person with a better title.

Checklist

Today, adverse possession is a mixture of common law rules overlain by statute. The student therefore needs to have an understanding of the doctrine of estates in English land law, a working knowledge of the Limitation Act 1980 and a feeling for the purpose behind the principle of limitation of actions. Likewise, recent decisions such as *Buckinghamshire County Council v Moran* and *Colchester Borough Council v Smith* give considerable guidance on the practical application of these rules.

The rules concerning fixtures and fittings is often more important to practising conveyancers than students of land law. Essentially, the question is what, apart from the house/land itself, does a purchaser of property buy on completion of the contract of sale? Does the greenhouse also pass with the title? How about the garden statues and the wall coverings? The answers to these and related questions are to be found mainly in judicial pronouncements which, while developing a general set of principles, can vary considerably in the confused circumstances of a real case. As with adverse possession, there is no better way to understand the law of fixtures and chattels than a thorough knowledge of case law.

Question 48

To what extent is it possible to define the circumstances in which an occupier of land may make a successful claim of adverse possession against the true owner?

Answer plan

- the general purpose and role of adverse possession
- the concept of limitation: the limitation period
- the mechanics of establishing adverse possession
- special circumstances: licences, future intentions
- stopping the clock
- the compromise of disputes

Answer

Adverse possession, squatting or limitation of actions as it is variously called, embodies one of the most fundamental principles of English land law: namely that a person may only own an estate in the land, not the land itself. It follows from this that any person with a superior estate (better title) may assert that title so as to claim seisin of the land. The principle of limitation gives practical effect to this doctrine of the relativity of title by providing that a person may be barred from bringing any claim to recover possession of the land after the period of limitation has passed. In other words, if an estate owner sleeps on their rights, those rights will be extinguished in the sense that a court will not enforce them against the person actually in possession of the land. In this sense, adverse possession operates negatively: it prevents an estate owner from suing on their rights and operates to extinguish their title. It does not, thereby, vest a title in any other person (see, however, the application to register title by the successful squatter of registered land) but by virtue of the doctrine of relativity of title, the person in actual possession may have the best claim to the land and thereby become effective 'owner' of it.

With this general background in mind, adverse possession can be boiled down to three basic points: firstly, how long is the limitation period or, to put it another way, after what period of time does a paper owner of land lose their right to sue to recover possession of it; secondly, when does that period start to run, or in other words, what actions by the actual occupant of the land can form the actual act of *adverse* possession; and thirdly, what is the effect of expiry of this period, both for the paper owner and the adverse possessor?

As far as the first issue is concerned, the period of limitation - the period after which no action can be brought to recover land - depends on the circumstances of each particular claim. Thus, in the normal course of events, the period will be 12 years from the moment of adverse possession by the squatter, s 15 Limitation Act 1980. There are certain special cases where the period is different, as where Crown lands are involved (30 years, 1st. Schedule, Limitation Act 1980) or where possession is alleged to be adverse to a remainderman, when generally speaking the period is six years from the falling in of the remainder or 12 years from the adverse possession against the life tenant, whichever is the longer, s 15 LA 1980.

However, by far the most difficult problem in relation to adverse possession is deciding when the period shall start. In other words, at what moment in time does the actual occupation of land by another person become adverse to the paper owner so as to give them 12 years to enforce their paramount title. Another way of looking at is to ask what actions of a person in actual possession amount to adverse possession so as to give rise to the possibility that after the limitation period has expired, the paper owner's title will be extinguished. The particular rules concerning this vital question are not to be found in statute. The Limitation Act 1980 does not tell use how to assess whether adverse possession has occurred, only how it works and what its consequences are. The rules are entirely judge-made and thus flexible, open-ended and subject to a variety of applications as the circumstances of each case permits. Recently, the Court of Appeal has sought to codify the principles of adverse possession in an attempt to bring some certainty and clarity to the law. In *Buckingham County Council v Moran*, the court was faced with a claim of adverse possession by a squatter against the council. In deciding in favour of the squatter, the court enunciated the basic principles behind establishing adverse possession. First, the adverse possessor should have an intention to possess the land to the exclusion of the whole world, including the paper-owner. It was stressed that this was an intention to possess adversely, so that any belief that the possession was with the permission of the paper-owner necessarily vitiated this requirement. However, it seems clear from *Moran* that the same act that amounts to the second part of a successful claim (actual adverse possession) may also be enough to establish an intention to possess to the exclusion of the whole world, as where the squatter fixes a padlock to a gate on a fence surrounding the paper-owner's land with the object of excluding everybody. Secondly, as indicated, the squatter must actually take adverse possession of the land as a matter of fact, either in consequence of the dispossession of the paper-owner or following discontinuance by him. Dispossession occurs where the paper-owner is effectively driven out by another (*Rains v Buxton*) and discontinuance where the paper-owner abandons the land, *Smith v Lloyd*. In either case, however, the loss of possession by the paper-owner must be followed by actual adverse possession by the squatter. This will be a question of fact in each case, although it is clear that the degree of physical possession required will vary with the type of land involved. For example, it may well be easier to establish adverse possession over land which is not susceptible to developed use (*Red House Farms v Catchpole*) and there are some indications that adverse possession is easier to prove in cases of discontinuance as opposed to cases of dispossession, *Red House Farms*. Yet, as noted, it is a question of fact in each case (*Powell v McFarlane*) and there is no requirement that the adverse possession must actually inconvenience the paper-owner, *Treloar v Nute*. Certainly, it seems that possession will not be taken from acts equivocal in nature or temporary in purpose, such as growing vegetables or clearing land so as to enable one's children to play, *Wallis's Cayton Holiday Camp v Shell-Mex & BP*, *Techbild v Chamberlain*.

Moreover, it is clear that the possession must be adverse to the paper-owner: it must not be with their consent or permission as that amounts to a licence to occupy and will not start the period of limitation. Prior to the decision in *Moran*, this particular requirement could easily defeat a claim for adverse possession as it was held in a number of cases (*Leigh v Jack, Shell-Mex*), that if the squatter's use of the land was not inconsistent with the paper-owner's future intended use of the land, an implied licence would be presumed in the squatter's favour authorising his use of the land and so ensuring that the possession was not adverse. This seemed to be the case whether or not the squatter knew of this future intention. Clearly, such a rule was extremely favourable to the paper-owner and was subject to much criticism on the ground that it could be used in nearly every circumstance to defeat a squatter's claim. Now, however, *Moran* has made it clear that there is no presumption of a licence in favour of a squatter where possession is not inconsistent with the paper-owner's planned use of the land. That is not to say, of course, that a licence cannot be implied from the actual facts of the case - as where a squatter is aware of the future plans and agrees to occupy pending the instigation of those plans - but it does mean that a claim to adverse possession cannot be defeated merely by the existence of some future plan in the breast of the paper owner.

Assuming, then, that adverse possession is running against the paper-owner, the law of limitation means that she has 12 years from the start date to bring an action to recover possession of the land. Of course, a successful action will stop the adverse possession and any future claim will have to begin afresh. The same is true of other acts which show an intention on the part of the adverse possessor to acknowledge the paper-owner's title, as where the squatter pays rent or by written acknowledgement of title before time has expired, ss 29, 30 Limitation Act. However, apart from actually initiating proceedings, it is not clear what other actions by the paper-owner will be sufficient to 'stop the clock'. In *Moran*, a letter asserting title was not sufficient, although a letter evincing a definite intention to sue may well be, *Shell-Mex*. Once again, it will be a matter of construction of the relevant circumstances. However, what does seem reasonably clear is that once the limitation period has expired, both the paper-owner's right to sue and their title are extinguished by operation of statute, s 17 Limitation Act. After this date, the conventional wisdom is that no acknowledgment, written or otherwise, and no payment, can revive the paper-owner's title, *Nicholson v England*. This should be uncontroversial as it is simply the consequence of the existence of the limitation doctrine. Recently, however, the Court of Appeal has held in *Colchester Borough Council v Smith* that in some circumstances a written acknowledgement of the paper-owner's title, even after the period has ended, can be enough to prevent the squatter relying on adverse possession in the face of a possession suit by that owner. This remarkable decision may yet be reversed, but at present it seems to rest on the principle that a bona fide compromise of a dispute between two persons (ie paper-owner and squatter), both of whom had legal advice, should be upheld on public policy grounds, even if the 12 year period has run. In other words, a man will be bound by his contract. Unfortunately, this seemingly unobjectionable principle does not, in the context of adverse possession, recognise that it is also a policy consideration - recognised and effected by Act of Parliament no less - that sleeping on one's rights deprives a person of those rights which cannot later be revived by threatening protracted litigation with the adverse possessor. In short, the judgment in *Smith* fails to explain why 'act of the parties' can override the express provisions of an Act of Parliament.

This case aside, in recent years the law of adverse possession has taken on more clarity and certainty, mainly due to the clear exposition in *Moran*. Of course, each case will depend on its facts, but at least there is clarity in what those facts are supposed to prove. Indeed, unlike *Smith*, *Moran* was a case favourable to the adverse possessor, both in result and in the substance of the rules it established. That case represents a welcome restatement of the fundamental feudal principle of relativity of title and reminds us of the transient nature of 'ownership' in the law of real property in England and Wales.

Notes

This is a general question on the law of adverse possession, although a good answer will rely heavily on *Moran*, being the most recent thorough exposition of the subject. Further matters that could be considered are the social purpose of a doctrine of limitation and the differences between adverse possession and prescription.

Question 49

In 1965, Paulus purchased an island in the middle of the River Trout and built a bridge from his adjoining land on the shore. He intended to use the island as a country retreat and throughout 1965-9 made regular fishing trips. He even built himself a cabin, cultivated a small vegetable garden and laid the foundations for a more substantial house in the future. Unfortunately, in 1970, Paulus became ill and had to leave for the clean air of Switzerland. Eventually, the vegetable garden became overgrown, the cabin ran to ruin and finally the bridge fell down, leaving the island as isolated as it was before. However, in anticipation of his departure, Paulus had managed to sell the land on the shore to his neighbour Aquinas who was enthusiastic about the prospects of establishing a salmon fishery but had no use for the island. Aquinas soon set about making enquiries of the local authority for planning permission for his fishery buildings and sought finance from several merchant banks. Again, however, things went awry and Aquinas could not raise the necessary capital. He resolved to wait until his resources grew and was content to use the land for walking and the occasional spell of private fishing. In 1975, Reginald, the local poacher, decided that the land bordering the river and the island were going to waste and he decided to move in and use the land for his own purposes. Shortly, he was rowing regularly to the island where he re-established the garden, re-built the cabin and began charging tourists for day fishing permits for fishing from the island's shore. This became so successful that he purchased a luxury caravan and parked it on Aquinas's land where he began to live. There he also planted a vegetable garden, cleared the land to make way for a dirt road and began keeping horses, also to hire to tourists. Eventually he had to build a fence to keep the horses from straying. In 1978, Aquinas became concerned about the extent of Reginald's activities on his land, although he had tolerated them up to now, having no immediate hope of establishing his fishery. He confronted Reginald and the latter agreed to quit as soon as Aquinas demanded possession. However, in 1979, on hearing (falsely as it turned out) that Aquinas had raised the money, Reginald extended the fence and placed a locked gate across the dirt road. In 1992, Aquinas eventually raises enough money for his project and seeks possession of the land. Reginald resists and when Aquinas tells him that Paulus will also issue possession proceedings he asserts title to the island as well.

Advise Reginald. The land is of registered title.

Answer plan

- intention to possess
- discontinuance, dispossession and adverse factual possession
- acts of possession: equivocal acts
- implied or actual licences to use
- acts of possession: unequivocal acts

Answer

This question requires discussion of the law of adverse possession, for this is at the root of any case that Reginald may have to resist the claims of possession of both Paulus and Aquinas. In order to establish adverse possession, it is clear from *Buckingham County Council v Moran* that Reginald must establish a number of facts. Firstly, that he had an intention to possess the land; secondly that he possessed the land following a discontinuance or dispossession of the paper-owner; thirdly that that possession was adverse to the paper-owner; and fourthly, that he has been in adverse possession for the 12 year period of limitation specified by s 15 Limitation Act 1980. If all this can be established, then the paper-owner's title to the land will be extinguished (s 17) and Reginald will have a title based on possession that will, in these circumstances, amount to a fee simple.

a) The island

The position in respect of the island seems relatively straightforward. There is no doubt that from 1965-1970, Paulus was in possession of the island and his activities there clearly demonstrated his ownership, backed as it was by paper-title. However, in 1970, Paulus is forced to leave the country and the following events tend towards the conclusion that he has abandoned or discontinued ownership. This is supported by the implication that Paulus wished to sell all his property but, unlike the land on the shore, was unable to find a buyer. He appears to have no future plans for the island such as would indicate continued interest. Indeed, there seems to be positive proof of abandonment in that the bridge falls down and is not re-built, as in *Red House Farms v Catchpole*. Of course, Paulus may argue that he was unable - as opposed to unwilling - to continue possession of the land as his emigration is forced through ill-health. However, this is unlikely to rebut the presumption of abandonment so clearly indicated by the facts we are given. In such circumstances, it seems that even very slight acts by a trespasser will be sufficient to constitute adverse possession of the property, *Wuta-Ofei v Danquah*, *Red House Farms*. Secondly, does Reginald makes use of the land as if he were owner, combined with an intention to assert ownership? Remembering that this is a case of discontinuance, the re-establishing of the vegetable garden and the re-building of the cabin may well suffice, but even if these are regarded as equivocal (*Powell v McFarlane*) the fact that he charges tourists for fishing rights clearly manifests both an intention to possess and sufficient acts of possession. He is, in fact, treating the land as if it were his own. In such circumstances, assuming that Paulus has done nothing in the intervening period to stop time running, the paper-owner's title will be extinguished some 12 years later, around 1987, s 17 Limitation Act 1980. Finally, as this is registered land, we should note that Reginald will be entitled to be registered as proprietor and thus, in fact, he obtains a *de jure* title by statutory conveyance. Pending such registration he will have an overriding interest under s 70(1)(f) LRA 1925.

b) The riverside property

The position in respect of the property owned by Aquinas is not so easily determined. Clearly, on the facts of the case, Aquinas has not abandoned the property. He has a clear, future use for the property and is actively seeking the money to finance it. There is no discontinuance. It is necessary, therefore, for Reginald to establish that he has dispossessed the paper-owner and followed this by his own adverse possession for 12 years.

i) The position up to 1978

Originally, it is clear that Aquinas had a clear, future intention to use the land and that, as a matter of fact, the acts of the trespasser were not inconsistent with this intention. In other words, up to 1978, Reginald's acts on the land did not preclude the later establishment of a fishery by the paper-owner. Formerly (eg *Leigh v Jack*), these facts would have justified the implication of a licence in favour of Reginald issuing from Aquinas. The effect of this licence - or permission - would have been to remove any possibility that the possession of the occupier was adverse to the paper-owner. However, following *Moran*, it is clear that the existence of future intentions cannot, of itself and without more, justify the court in implying a licence in the actual possessor's favour. So far then, as a result of *Moran*, Reginald's claim is not defeated. However, it is still necessary for him to establish his own possession of the land following dispossession of the paper-owner. In this respect, the acts of Reginald may be too equivocal to count. Thus, the planting of the vegetable garden (*Powell*) and the keeping of animals (*Techbild v Chamberlain*) may not be sufficient. Likewise, the building of the fence seems designed as much to keep the animals in as to keep the world at large out. This is also equivocal, *George Wimpey v Sohn*. On the other hand, the clearing of land for the driveway may amount to an act of ownership, *Williams v Usherwood*, although in *Williams* the road was paved and not left as a dirt track. The establishment of the caravan is also important, but again it does not necessarily evince an intention to exclude the world, merely to occupy the land.

ii) The conversation in 1978

In any event, whether or not the acts of Reginald up to 1978 were such as to amount to factual possession becomes irrelevant in light of the conversation and agreement between Aquinas and Reginald in that year. While it is true that *Moran* stipulated that no licence for the occupier to use the land can be assumed merely from the fact of the paper-owner's future intentions, it did not establish that a licence cannot be expressly created or arise by implication from the actual facts of the case. In our problem, the evidence is clear and overwhelming. Aquinas confronts Reginald some time before the 12 year period has expired and Reginald agrees that he will vacate should Aquinas's plans come to fruition. There is here an implied licence - if not an express one - given to Reginald to occupy and he in turn agrees to this. At this moment, the possession, such as it was, ceases to be adverse and the clock stops. If it is to start again, there must be new acts of adverse possession and it must run for a further 12 years.

iii) Reginald's change of heart

Eventually, we come to the actions on which Reginald may well be able to base a successful claim of adverse possession. Although Reginald knows of Aquinas's future intentions for the land and at one point agreed to respect them, the change of heart in 1979 brings a different perspective. The extension of the fence and the erection of the gate in response to the perceived imminent fulfilment of Aquinas's plan are the clearest evidence of an intention to possess the land to the exclusion of the whole world, including (indeed especially!) the paper-owner. The enclosure of the land in this way is without doubt the firmest evidence of adverse possession to date and is similar to the actions of the successful litigant in *Moran*. Reginald looks likely to succeed on this ground, providing 12 uninterrupted years have passed. It is irrelevant that Aquinas may have believed for all this time that Reginald was occupying under the former licence, for so long as the adverse possession was not secret (and that is unlikely on these facts), the trespasser cannot be defeated by the intentions of the paper-owner alone. *Moran* shows us that it is the intentions and actions of the squatter that are most relevant in adverse possession cases. Assuming, then, that in 1992 12 years have elapsed, Reginald will be entitled to be registered as proprietor and will again have an overriding interest pending application to the Registrar to be registered as proprietor.

Notes

This question asks the student to apply the general principles of limitation and most questions of this type give facts similar to those situations found in previous cases, as does this one. The decision in *Smith* does not feature in this question but being so controversial it is likely to play a part in the future.

Question 50

Hannibal arrived in the country from a long stay overseas in 1980 and sought your help in finding a quiet secluded property for his family as well as an office in town from which to run his optician's business. Unfortunately, Hannibal had difficulty in selling his previous house, but last month he went to view Roman Villas, an old property on the edge of town. After some doubt, he has just completed the purchase of Roman Villas from Vesuvius. Hannibal did not, however, have any difficulty in finding suitable office accommodation and in 1981 he agreed with Pontius, the freeholder, for a 7 year lease of suitable premises in a good location. He soon installed his equipment in the premises, fixing lights to the ceiling and a suitable chair to the floor, and in order to make the place more welcoming for his customers he refitted one room with oak panelling and a large wall mounted fish tank. In 1988, on the expiry of the lease, he and Pontius agreed a further four year term. Now, in 1992, on the purchase of Roman Villas, Hannibal has decided to work from home and has removed all the equipment, including the lights and chair as well as the oak panelling and fish tank. He moves them to Roman Villas, only to find that Vesuvius has removed the greenhouse, the rose bushes, the garden ornaments, the television aerial and some antique bannisters, all of which Hannibal greatly admired when being shown around the property before contracts were exchanged.

Hannibal comes to you for advice as to whether he should sue Vesuvius for the return of these items, only to find that you have been instructed by Pontius to sue him (Hannibal) for the recovery of the equipment removed from the office in town as it seems that Pontius had arranged to let the premises to a new optician.

Discuss.

Answer plan

- fixtures and chattels
- the relevance of the distinction: s 62 LPA
- the way to make the distinction: *Holland v Hodgson*
- tenant's fixtures

Answer

It is a general principle of land law that what becomes attached to the land becomes part of the land (*Minshall v Lloyd*). Thus, any articles attached to the land in such a way as to indicate that they have merged with it are treated as the land itself: they are fixtures. In practice this has important consequences. First, it means that when one person conveys land to another they will also convey all fixtures, save those which have been expressly excluded from the conveyance or can be removed by the vendor by virtue of some exceptional right (see s 62 LPA). Secondly, it means that should one person affix articles to land owned by another, those articles fall into the ownership of the landowner, as where a tenant affixes articles to the land they are leasing so that at the end of the lease they fall into the ownership of the landlord. In our problem, although there are two separate factual situations to consider, the essential points at issue are the same. First, whether the articles that are removed from the land by Hannibal and Vesuvius are fixtures so as to make them presumptively liable for such removal. Secondly, if they are fixtures, whether removal could be justified by exceptional circumstances.

1) Roman Villas

The general rule in relation to Roman Villas is clear enough. All articles which, at the date of the contract, can be regarded as fixtures will belong to the new purchaser (Hannibal) on completion of the contract, s 62 LPA, *Phillips v Lamdin*. If Vesuvius the vendor is to have good title to any of the articles he has in fact removed he must show either: a) that he removed them before the contract was made; b) they are not fixtures at all but chattels personally owned by him or c) that if they are fixtures that his removal was by virtue of some exceptional right.

First, it is clear that a freehold owner may, at any time before they contract to sell, remove any item from their land as this is part of their normal rights of ownership, *Re Whaley*. However, in our case there is nothing to suggest that Vesuvius removed the items before the contract was signed and, indeed, we are told that all such items were present when Hannibal was shown around the property prior to signing the contract. In the absence of any other evidence one can conclude that all the articles were present when the contract was made.

Secondly, are the items fixtures or chattels, for it is only if they are fixtures that any problem arises? Chattels are personal goods, not forming part of the land and therefore not conveyed as such to a purchaser of it. The general test as to whether an item can be regarded as a fixture was summarised by Blackburn J in *Holland v Hodgson*. Consideration must be given to the *degree* of annexation to the land and the purpose of annexation to the land. It is clear, however, that the primary test is the degree of annexation and presumptively any item which rests upon its own weight is only a chattel (*Mather v Fraser*), for a fixture needs to be attached to the land in some substantial way, even though it could be removed quite easily, *Culling v Tufnal*. Yet, there is also no doubt that the answer supplied by this simple practical test can be overridden (or indeed supported) by the *purpose* of annexation. Thus, where affixing is necessary for the proper use of the article and implies nothing about its relation to the land, the item may remain a chattel (*Leigh v Taylor*) and, conversely, items intended to enhance the value of the property may be fixtures even though resting on their own weight (*D'Eyncourt v Gregory*). All in all, whether an article is a fixture or a chattel can only be decided on the facts of each case, bearing in mind the nature of the property, the use of the articles and the physical relation of them to the land itself.

Turning then to the articles removed in this case.

i) The greenhouse

If the greenhouse is fixed to the land it will be a fixture, as with the temporary sheds in *Webb v Frank Bevis*. However, there is clear authority that a free-standing greenhouse is to be regarded as a chattel, (*H E Dibble Ltd v Moore*) and a 'dutch barn' was still a chattel even though it was founded in sockets in the land to give it more support, *Culling v Tufnal*. It is, then, reasonably clear, that Vesuvius was entitled to remove the greenhouse providing that it was not actually affixed to the land in a permanent way or was not part of an ornamental garden designed for the betterment of the land as a whole (see below).

ii) Garden ornaments

Prima facie, the garden ornaments are chattels as they are in all probability free-standing and not attached to the land at all. This was at the root of the decision in *Berkley v Poulett* when a sundial and statue on plinths were held to be fixtures. However, it is clear from *D'Eyncourt v Gregory* that if garden ornaments are part of a general garden design, created to enhance the particular house, they will be regarded as fixtures which pass with the land. This is a clear example of the purpose of annexation overriding the degree of annexation (see also *Hamp v Bygrave*). Once again, then, presumptively these will be chattels unless the ornaments are integral to the property. They can be removed by Vesuvius.

iii) Television aerial

This is a somewhat difficult article to consider as it is clearly designed to facilitate the use of another article (a television) which is so obviously a chattel. However, it is quite common that television aerials are attached to property (eg on the chimney) and if this is the case, the presumption will be that it is a fixture. This is reinforced by the fact that the aerial can be detached from the television and is not an integral part of it. *Jordan v May* could be of assistance here, for there a fixed electric engine was held to be a fixture even though the batteries which powered it were held to be chattels. On the other hand, however, *Credit Valley Cable v Peel Condominium Corp*, held a television cable to be a chattel, being for the better use of a television and not better use of the land. Perhaps the only solution is to revert to the basic *Holland* test: the degree of annexation. If this decrees that the aerial is a fixture, it is no reply that it thereby confers a personal benefit on the new owners of the land; so do ornamental statues, fixed greenhouses and permanent tapestries.

iv) The bannisters

Once again, this will depend on an application of the *Hodgson* test, although there seems little doubt that these will be affixed to the land in what is intended to be a permanent fashion. If fireplaces can be regarded as fixtures (*Buckland v Butterfield*), surely so must bannisters. Vesuvius is not entitled to remove them any more than he would be entitled to remove the floorboards.

v) The roses

Here, the position is clear. Roses, as with other trees, shrubs and flowers growing on the land are part of the legal definition of the land within s 205 LPA. Thus, they belong to the estate owner and were conveyed to Hannibal when he purchased the land. Vesuvius is not entitled to remove them.

Thus, as far as Roman Villas is concerned, it is clear that the roses and bannisters and probably the television aerial are fixtures. This means they are conveyed to Hannibal with the conveyance, s 62 LPA (assuming no express reservation of Vesuvius's title was made). Moreover, there are no grounds by which Vesuvius can claim an exceptional right to remove these fixtures once the purchase is completed.

2) The office

As noted at the outset, a tenant who brings articles on to the land and then fixes them to it, effectively passes title to those articles to the landlord. They cannot, therefore, be removed at the end of the lease unless some special rule provides. In our case, there are the lights, the chair, the oak panels and the fish tank. However, before we consider whether these are fixtures or merely chattels, one important issue must be considered that may well save time.

There is a general rule that a tenant has a right to remove certain types of fixtures from the land at the end of the lease; ie that even though in law they are fixtures and within the title of the landlord, the tenant may re-assert ownership for special reasons. One important category of such fixtures are 'trade fixtures' which may be removed by the tenant during the continuance of the lease or (probably) within a reasonable time after its end, *Poole's* case. Of course, this right is lost if the tenant does not remove trade fixtures during the term (or just after), but it is clear that the tenant does not lose the right to remove fixtures attached during one lease which then ends, if that lease is immediately followed by a new term in continuation of it, *New Zealand Government Property Corp v H & M Ltd*. This is the case here and it seems certain that the lights and the chair can be removed by Hannibal as trade fixtures when he quits. Of course, if they are not fixtures, he can remove them anyway. Indeed, the same may be true of the oak panelling and the fish tank, for we are told they are added to the property for the benefit of Hannibal's customers. However, they are not necessary for trade as such and probably must be considered outside this rule.

However, perhaps they are not fixtures at all and merely personal chattels? This also seems unlikely, at least for the oak panelling, as there is authority that panelling (*Buckland v Butterfield*) and even tapestries (*In Re Whaley*, but contra *Leigh v Taylor*) are fixtures because of the degree of annexation to the property. If this is followed, the oak panelling is a fixture and must remain. The fish tank might be different, as Hannibal could claim that it is fixed to the wall for steadying purposes, not as an attachment per se and indeed, it is a curious item to regard as part of the land. Some help is given by *Viscount Hill v Bullock* where a collection of stuffed animals nailed to the wall were held to be chattels. In any event, however, even if the fish tank is a fixture, Hannibal can claim that he has a right to remove it under another exception, namely the right of a tenant to remove ornamental fixtures during his lease so long as this can be done without damage to the building, *Martin v Roe*. Indeed, one case (*Spyer v Phillipson*) suggests that even panelling (assuming it is a fixture) may be removed under this general heading, although it will be rare that this can be done without damage to the premises.

All in all then, the chair and lights can be removed whether they are fixtures or not (the trade exception); the fish tank may not be a fixture but if it is, could be removed under the 'ornamental/domestic' exception; and the oak panelling is probably a fixture and could be removed under the 'ornamental/domestic' exception only if there is no damage to the premises.

Notes

This is a long question, although really quite straightforward. It
concentrates on the definition of a fixture and asks in what
circumstances even fixtures can be removed from the land. Case
law is important here, although *Holland v Hodgson* (supplemented
by one or two others) is vital.